The Cultural Regions
of East Africa

The Cultural Regions of East Africa

JOHN D. KESBY

Faculty of Social Sciences,
The University, Canterbury, England

1977

ACADEMIC PRESS

LONDON
NEW YORK
SAN FRANCISCO

A Subsidiary of Harcourt Brace Jovanovich, Publishers

ACADEMIC PRESS INC. (LONDON) LTD.
24/28 Oval Road,
London NW1

United States Edition published by
ACADEMIC PRESS INC.
111 Fifth Avenue
New York, New York 10003

Library of Congress Catalog Card Number 77-71828
ISBN: 0-12-405450-1

Text set in 11/13 pt. Intertype Baskerville, printed by letterpress, in Great Britain by
Clarke, Doble & Brendon Ltd.
Plymouth and London

Preface

There is a vast amount of information available in print on the peoples of East Africa. Much rarer are the attempts to put some of the information together, and to draw some general conclusions about the relations between the different peoples of the area. This book is not designed to summarize all that is known about the assumptions and practices of different ethnic groups, nor to compare the divergences between them in detail. What does require attention is that there is a large number of these groups in East Africa, that they vary greatly in size, and that they present considerable problems of comprehension. How do they differ from each other? Are there greater differences between some groups and others? And does their diversity and distribution correspond with other features, of social order or of the physical landscape? Perhaps the question which occurs most readily to most people is: how did these groups, these "tribes" as they are usually called, come into being?

Awkwardly, the answer to this popular question is obscured by the lack of clear information about the events even of the period 1600–1850, let alone earlier than that. The lack of facts, however, has not prevented numerous writers from inferring, or guessing, what happened. As a result there has come into circulation a sort of folk-history of East Africa, which, in its more crystallized and official forms, is taught to pupils in East African schools. In this folk-history, or more correctly these folk-histories, waves of migration, with appropriate arrows on the accompanying maps, play a conspicuous part. Thus the Maasai arrive from the north, and the Gikuyu from the coast. As I attempt to show later, neither the Maasai nor the Gikuyu seem to have arrived from anywhere, but rather to have come into being in the areas where they now live. Indeed much of what is currently taught as history, or prehistory, in East African schools is ethnic myth. Myth may be true or false, and much of this is, I suggest, false.

I would be very pleased to put in the place of the pseudo-history currently taught a complex narrative which reflects more accurately what really happened. Regrettably the shortage of information prevents me from doing so. In Chapter 11, where I have attempted a reconstruction of cultural changes since about 5000 B.C., I emphasize that the whole exercise is tentative and nothing more. What has prompted me to attempt the exercise, however, is that I feel on much surer ground when discussing the processes of change among East African peoples, and one purpose of the reconstruction is to emphasize that the same processes which have operated in modern changes have been effective at earlier periods also.

Three themes run through everything I discuss in this book. The first is that the physical resources, and especially their effective productivity, must always be considered in examining the differences between the ethnic groups. The second theme is that East Africa can be divided into a limited number of cultural regions, into the pattern of which the numerous ethnic groups can be fitted. And the third of the themes is that no group of people live in isolation from others, and I devote some attention therefore to the admiration, fear, contempt, tolerance and indifference which enter into the attitudes of members of one group to those of another.

Although the book covers the period from c. 1890 to the present time, much of what is being discussed is especially relevant to the period 1900–1950. Before 1900 recorded facts were still relatively sparse, and by 1950 some idiosyncratic features of the local cultures, such as age-sets in some areas, were only memories. Since 1950 the cultures of most East African peoples have been "stripped-down" versions of what they formerly were, and future changes, which would shed some light on what is now happening, are necessarily known only to God and not to people. Despite the difficulties of discussing the generation from 1950 onward, I have tried to refer where necessary to events of this modern period.

One feature of the book which is likely to strike some readers is the absence of detailed population-figures for each of the ethnic groups of East Africa. The rough areas occupied by most members of each ethnic group can be shown on a map (Maps 9–13), and so can a rough estimate of population-densities in different parts of East Africa (Map 6), but detailed ethnic figures are difficult to give, and questionable when once given. Between 1900 and 1960, census-returns in all the territories were certainly inaccurate, and usually too low. By 1960 the administrative conditions were developed to the point where more accurate census results could be expected; but soon afterwards the countries become formally independent; and the governments of Kenya, Uganda and Tanzania have decided not to include ethnic affinity in census-returns, because of the divisive effects the process, and the published figures, might have on relations between ethnic groups in these polyglot countries. It is still possible, however, to recognize on the ground that some whole ethnic groups are densely settled, and that others are spread very thinly; and such differences are of great importance for the interpretation of present ethnic distributions.

One fact is worth bearing in mind about populations. There are eight ethnic groups which are the largest in all East Africa, and which each include a million people or more. Together these eight peoples are nearly a half of the population of East Africa. They are distributed in a rough crescent astride Lake Victoria, and they are: the Rundi, with over 2·5 million people; the Rwanda, with over 3 million; the Ganda, with over a million; the Luo of the lake-shore, with between one and 2 million; the Luhya, with over a million; the Gikuyu, with approaching 2 million; the Kamba, with about a million; and the Sukuma, with over a million. It is tempting in a book about East African peoples to spend much of the available space on these eight "giants". I have tried to avoid such an emphasis, and, without ignoring the importance of the very large peoples, to pay some attention to other groups, many of them not widely known.

When I went to live in East Africa in 1963 I certainly was not able to write this book, and I suspected then that it would never be possible to discover how the present distribution of ethnic groups came about. After over three years of living in the hills of Langi country, where they rise above the Maasai Plains, the importance of different habitats had impressed itself upon me, and what I had learnt about the peoples of the Kondoa and Mbulu districts had even convinced me that some historical reconstruction might indeed be possible.

A book of this kind, however, must depend on much more than the personal experience of the writer, and the bibliography gives the sources of much of the information here reproduced, as well as of much more which has coloured my judgement but been excluded for the sake of space and clarity. With such a wealth of sources, I could have filled many pages with footnotes, but for the sake of space again I have confined notes to especially pertinent or contentious issues, notably the classification of languages.

My debt to the authors of numerous books is clear enough, but the bibliography does not show my debt to various people with whom I have talked about East Africa over a period of twenty-two years. I would like to thank them all, and to single out for mention by name Mrs Pam Forrest, who typed and retyped a manuscript full of totally unfamiliar names. My biggest debt, however, must be to the peoples of the Kondoa and Mbulu districts of Tanzania who, without realizing what the consequence would be, convinced me that this book was possible.

August 1977   JOHN KESBY

Contents

A Note on Names and Spelling

The names of ethnic groups which are used in this book are those by which the peoples in question refer to themselves. For example, the people who are usually known in Europe by the Amharic term Galla are here called Oromo, their own name for themselves. This leads in some cases to the dropping of familiar terms, like Nuer, Dinka – or Galla, and the adoption of unfamiliar terms in their place. At the risk of being pedantic, I prefer to be consistent, and to use names which are unexceptionable in the eyes of the particular peoples concerned. This practice does, however, lead to difficulties in cases where the name by which a group call themselves has not yet been recorded in writing, or else where the accounts of them are so scanty as to leave some doubt as to whether the recorded name of the group is that by which they call themselves. Where this situation occurs, I have placed the recorded name in inverted commas, as in "Tepes" and "Gidole".

In the spelling of ethnic names I have again adopted a procedure which, while consistent, may antagonize more people than it pleases. First of all, I have tried to spell these names in a way which gives a strong indication, to someone whose native language is English, of how that name is pronounced. Here again, however, there are difficulties, because of the idiosyncracies of English spelling. Thus the word Soomaali is liable to be pronounced Sumeali by an Englishman, although an Italian, Hungarian or Japanese would probably get it right. The rule with pronunciation therefore is that the consonants have roughly the same value as in English, the vowels much as in Italian. To render a precise transcription of the ethnic names would require symbols which are unfamiliar to most readers, and sometimes the use of diacritical marks, a procedure which most people find daunting. However, I must stress that my spellings are approximate, and that anyone who wants to know more about the linguistic details should consult Tucker and Bryan (1956, 1966) and Guthrie (1971). In the process of trying to make the names pronounceable yet close to the original I have ignored the issue of phonemic values, that is whether a sound is significantly different from another to the point of changing the meaning of any word which contains that sound. Phonemically the two peoples whom I call Ogiek and Sambur should be spelt Okiek and Sampur, but to an English-speaker the names sound like Ogiek and Sambur.*

Another difficulty is presented by the complex inflection of many African languages. More than half of the ethnic names used in this book contain prefixes, which in most cases change according to the role of the word in the sentence. Among Bantu languages this feature is very marked. An example ought to make the point. The Sukuma, as they are named here, call themselves *Basukuma* and their country *Busukuma*. An individual member of the group is called *Musukuma* and their language *Kisukuma*. In these circumstances, most writers prefer to use only the stem, Sukuma, and to leave off the relevant prefixes, since to retain these requires that they be used consistently as if it were *Kisukuma* which were being written, with probable confusion to the English reader. Hence, in this account I write of the Gikuyu, and not Agikuyu, of the Zande, and not Azande, and of the Luo, and not Joluo. At the same time, some East African peoples, for instance the Maasai and Hadza, use no prefix with their names for themselves. For the sake of simplicity I have not indicated where a prefix has been omitted, but it is a safe generalization that all the groups who speak Bantu languages use a prefix before the stem of their name.

There is one final point. Since 1960, African governments have shown a, for many people bewildering, tendency to change the names of states and towns. In this book such changes are followed up to the time that the text was revised for printing. The parallel tendency to change the names of lakes, rivers and other physical features has, however, not been followed, since no stable pattern of new names has yet appeared. I refer to Lakes Tanganyika and Nyasa, and I call the large river which flows through the centre of Africa the Congo.

---

* There is one special orthographic point. Where ng is printed without an apostrophe the sound represented is as in the English word anger, but where there is an apostrophe, ng', the sound is that in the word sing.

1

East Africa in its Context

The Establishment of the Modern Boundaries

The East African Plateau is a broad oval, its long axis aligned north-to-south, and its rims formed by highlands associated with the rift valleys. It is these highlands indeed which underlie much of the distinctiveness of East Africa, and without them the lower parts of the plateau would merge undramatically into the rest of the rolling plateau surface of the interior of Africa.

On the west, however, the plateau is marked off clearly by the steepness of the gradient down to the Congo Basin, and this gradient marks, for much of its length, a frontier between two cultural regions, as will become clearer shortly. In the north, the hills on the margin of the plateau drop away to the lowlands of the southern Sudan and of the Lake Rudolf area; and these lowlands are continuous with those of the east coast, extending from the Eastern Rift Highlands to the Indian Ocean. Finally, in the south, the highland rims of the plateau, namely the Eastern and the Western Rift Highlands, converge, and then join to form the highlands bordering Lake Nyasa.

East Africa owes its distinctive relief to the two rift valleys, and their associated features, but in most respects the countries which are now conventionally grouped as East Africa lack characteristics which, on the one hand, group them together, and, on the other, set them apart from other African countries. The use of a single term to cover this area arises from a common history which began only around 1800.

At the present time, the term East Africa covers only the republics of Kenya, Tanzania and Uganda, but, until the partition of German East Africa in 1919, Rwanda and Burundi were also included under this heading. The East African Plateau, and its neighbouring coast, were set apart as a distinct political zone in the period 1880–1900 by British and German diplomats engaged, somewhat reluctantly, in determining the areas for which their respective countries had to take responsibility. Behind their activities, however, there was another historical development, centring on the town and island of Zanzibar.

In 1840 Sultan Sayyid Said of the Arabian state of Oman moved his capital from Muscat to Zanzibar town, in order to pay closer attention to the trade of his state and family on the East African coast.[1] His decision to move was prompted, it seems, by the increasing volume of trade in the Indian Ocean, itself linked to the increased activities of British and other European merchants in the area. The establishment of the court on Zanzibar island itself increased the commercial activities of that part of the coast, and the overall effect of increasing commerce on the coast was the involvement of coastal merchants in the interior, from c. 1830 onward. Although merchants from Arabia had been trading on the coast in the twelfth century, and probably for centuries before that, the Indian Ocean trade penetrated the interior only in the nineteenth century. The coastal traders, most of them Swahili-speaking, made most of their profits from the interior by gathering, and exporting, ivory and slaves.

European knowledge of the interior began even later, from 1848 onward, the European travellers following routes already known to the coastal traders. It was along one of these traders' routes, the grand trunk-road of its day, from the coast near Zanzibar to Lake Tanganyika, that Burton, Speke, Livingstone and Stanley all travelled on their way inland, in the period 1858–71. This recent knowledge of the interior, still skimpy at that time, formed the geographical basis of the detailed agreements between the British and German governments, in 1885 and 1890, to divide the area into a northern, British, and a southern, German, sphere of influence.

Essentially, the British and German negotiators were partitioning the hinterland of Zanzibar, its trade-web in the interior, which had grown up in the nineteenth century from coastal bases. The western edge of the two spheres of influence was agreed in 1911, and corresponded roughly with the western slope where the East African Plateau falls away to the Congo Basin. It also coincided roughly with the frontier zone between the Interlacustrine cultural region and that of the Congo wet forest. Swahili and Nyamwezi traders from the plateau had penetrated the Congo wet forest before 1880, but the boundary was drawn along the western edge of the plateau because here the German and British administrators encountered another sphere of influence, spreading from the west coast, that of the International Association of the Congo, founded by King Leopold of the Belgians, in 1876.

European administrative intervention in East Africa had been prompted by the affairs of Europe, and events in Europe soon overtook the frontiers agreed in 1911 between Belgians, British and Germans. The outbreak of war in 1914 involved East Africa, although at first only on a small scale. In 1916, however, German East Africa was invaded by the allied British and Belgians, and, in 1919, by the Versailles Peace Treaty the Germans lost their East African territory, along with all their other overseas territories. Rwanda and Burundi were to be administered by the Belgians and most of the rest of former German territory[2] by the British, who called it Tanganyika. The new British and Belgian dependencies were to be administered as mandates under the League of Nations.

The frontiers of 1919 are those of the present day, except for a change of part of the boundary between Kenya and Uganda in 1926. Hence, when the period of European administration ended, after 1960, the newly independent countries were defined by frontier lines drawn only in the recent past. Tanganyika was granted independence in 1961, Burundi, Rwanda and Uganda in 1962, and Kenya and Zanzibar in 1963. In the course of 1964 Tanganyika and Zanzibar merged to form a single country, called, before the end of the year, Tanzania.

The western boundaries of Burundi, Rwanda and Uganda do roughly coincide with a cultural divide, as has been noted already; and Burundi and Rwanda do represent states each of which has a long history as a united country with common traditions. However, most of the modern boundaries coincide neither with cultural divides nor with old-established traditions of local loyalty. With the exceptions of Rwanda and Burundi, the traditional centres of local loyalty were much smaller than the, comparatively vast, areas of the newly delineated states.

East Africa, then, makes sense as a unit in the context of the recent history of European diplomacy and administration, but it has no cultural unity, nor a cultural identity of its own. Furthermore, the area has no separate identity in terms of the non-human animals and the plants found here, which, in most cases, also occur further afield in Africa. It is, however, an important area both florally and faunally in that the East African Plateau has provided a corridor dividing the wet forests of the Congo Basin from the dry coastal area. Through this corridor plants and animals have, at some times at least, been able to move between the northern and southern savannas, through country which, vegetationally, resembles them both. As we shall see, in Chapter 11, when we consider the prehistory of East Africa, there is strong evidence that the plateau has played the same part in the movements of people in Africa, most of whom have avoided the wet forest of the equatorial lowlands, between the Atlantic and the Western Rift Highlands.

Although East Africa's identity has only been defined separately from the main mass of tropical Africa by relatively recent events, the area is now widely regarded as a unit. For the sake of clarity, throughout this book East Africa is taken to be the area covered by Kenya, Tanzania and Uganda, together with Rwanda and Burundi, which belong culturally in the Interlacustrine region. However, in order to place the area in the wider context of sub-Saharan Africa, it will be necessary repeatedly to draw attention to areas beyond the boundaries of these republics, for example, to the Congo Basin and the southern Sudan.

In addition to defining the area to be covered, it is essential to make quite clear the period of time which is involved. The peoples of East Africa are here considered during the decades of European administration and in the period since then, from c. 1890 to the present. Before c. 1890, documentation for most areas is thin, or absent altogether, and there are still areas, for instance parts of southern Tanzania, where documentation is still very sparse. During the more than eighty years from the beginnings of European administration, there have been striking changes, affecting some areas more than others. For example, the three largest kingdoms of East Africa in 1890 have all, since 1960, had their monarchies abolished, Rwanda in 1961, Buganda and Burundi in 1966.

Major factors in the changes of the modern period have been administrative centralization, of increasing complexity, and the increasing volume of production and trade. New jobs for East Africans have been generated in great numbers, farmers have earned money in some quantity, and have been able to afford goods, such as cloth, which in 1890 were either luxuries or altogether unknown. The better watered areas, and the densely populated areas, usually the same, have changed more dramatically than the drier, and the more thinly populated areas. Ganda, Gikuyu and Chaga country have all changed more markedly than the areas of the Sambur or the Gogo, and the same applies to the social order in these different places. It is thus essential throughout this comparison of different cultural regions to state exactly when a certain feature or practice that is mentioned was present, if indeed it no longer is. Broadly too, it is possible to divide the period into two phases, the first from *c.* 1890 to *c.* 1930, and the second from *c.* 1930 to *c.* 1975. The first phase is marked by rather slow changes, as East Africans became used to the presence of European administrators and missionaries, and of Indian traders. The phase from *c.* 1930 is marked by more rapid discernible changes, including a notable increase in overall production and trade.

Throughout the period, the cultural regions and sub-regions have retained their identity, despite the veneer of transistor radios, national propaganda, bottled beer and lorries. As will be clearer from the sections on different regions, modern changes have not left the local people unmoved, and I shall make no effort to predict whether these cultural regions will still be discernible in five hundred or a thousand years' time. Perhaps they will not, but they are still clearly recognizable in the 1970s.

Classification into Major Regions and Regions

In order to focus properly on the numerous ethnic groups of East Africa, they must be seen as members of cultural areas of differing size and generality. Each people is very similar in general culture to each of its neighbours, although sometimes nearer to some than to others. For example, the Gikuyu, Meru and Embu speak different, although very similar, languages, or else dialects of one language, depending on definition, and they resemble each other very closely in culture, as they did when first described by European writers in the period 1880–1900. They are recognisably different from their common neighbours, the Maasai, but they still resemble these more than they do, say, the Ganda. Again, Gikuyu, Maasai and Ganda resemble each other culturally more than any of them resemble the Amharic-speaking peoples of Shoa in the Ethiopian Highlands.

These varying degrees of cultural similarity and difference make it possible, and valuable, to classify African peoples into regions and sub-regions, using criteria of distinction in much the same way as do taxonomists when dealing with animals and plants. Biological taxonomists, however, are implying that behind the units which they recognize is a history of organic evolution, resulting in genetic segregation so that often closely related animals or plants are unable to interbreed. Cultural classification has no such cosmic intensity. It is true that, by classifying peoples together, one is implying a common history, a shared tradition of cultural background. At the same time, however, cultural regions and sub-regions merge into each other on the ground, in a way that most animal and plant species do not.

An example from outside Africa may help here. Most people in Europe regard Europe as a major distinctive cultural area, different from, say, the Near East or the Far East—or Africa. Even so, they are convinced that there are differences within Europe : that Spanish and Portuguese are different from people round the North Sea, say, English and Scandinavians; that Russians are different from Balkan peoples; and that these again are different from Italians. Outside observers agree with the Europeans' assessment of themselves : that Europe is a major cultural unit, but internally culturally divided, and then sub-divided. Not only is north-west Europe distinct from south-west Europe, but, within northwest Europe, people from the British Isles are culturally distinct from Scandinavians.

The units which I propose to use in this account of East African peoples are based on three stages of grouping into progressively larger clusters. Individual ethnic groups, with a distinctive name for themselves or a distinctive language, and often both, are grouped together into cultural sub-regions, each with a high degree of internal cultural homogeneity. Gikuyu, Meru and Embu, for example, belong to a single subregion, but the Maasai, their neighbours, belong to another sub-region. However, all four peoples belong to the same region, into which these two sub-regions are grouped, with some others. The Ganda, on the other hand, belong to a different region altogether. This region also includes the Rwanda and Rundi, who belong to the same sub-region as each other, but to a different sub-region from the Ganda. At the third stage of clustering, all African peoples south of the Sahara belong to a single major cultural region, the largest cultural unit apart from the whole human species.

It is not necessary to detail all the major regions in the modern world, but, to set East Africa in perspective, it is useful to mention those which neighbour the major regions of the African continent. South of the Sahara, but excluding the Ethiopian Highlands and the Horn of Africa, is the Sub-Saharan African Major Region. In this account, for the sake of brevity, I will call it simply the African Major Region. It is bounded on the north by the North-African-Near-Eastern Major Region (NANE in this account). To the north of that again is the Western Eurasian Major Region, including most of Europe; and to the south-east of NANE is the Indian (or some would prefer South Asian) Major Region, with the South-East Asian Major Region beyond that. The island of Madagascar probably has to be recognized as a separate major region, despite its relatively small size, since it seems to be too distinctive to fit into any other major region.

The classification which I use here is my own, and it is likely to be challenged in detail by other writers. Anyone, however, who tries to systematize human cultural areas will produce a scheme very like this one. Indeed, the major regions are assumed in many discussions, so that I am making no claim to originality.

The Characteristics of the Two Major Regions

Turning to a more detailed examination of East Africa, we need only to consider parts of two major regions. Most of the area is included in the African Major Region, but in the extreme north-east the peoples of the Horn of Africa are represented by some groups of Oromo and Soomaali. It is, therefore, necessary to look carefully at the NANE Major Region, even though it is only its extreme southern edge which touches East Africa.

The boundary between the two major regions follows the vegetational transition between the deserts of the Sahara and the Horn, to the north, and the dry woodlands and the grasslands, to the south. The desert peoples belong to the NANE, the savanna and woodland peoples to the African Major Region. This divide crosses the continent from the Senegal River valley, in the west, to the Ethiopian Highlands, and then southeast to the Tana River. Only the Ethiopian Highlands break the even flow of the divide. They are high enough to be well watered, and climatically similar to the much smaller areas of East African highlands, further south, but culturally they belong with the Horn, and the Near East.

Between the two major regions the overall cultural differences are dramatic. The NANE is vast, stretching from Mauritania to Afghanistan, and at its centre, both culturally and historically, is the Fertile Crescent, cradle of civilization in the Old World. The NANE Major Region has been the arena for vast empires, some of them very durable, for instance, the Persian, Roman, Arabic and Turkish Empires. Even for people not involved in these major empires, the scale of social organization has usually been large, during the last two thousand years at least, and the degree of social differentiation and specialization correspondingly high.

By contrast, over much of the African Major Region, to this day, the largest social unit is an autonomous village of perhaps three hundred people. There have been large states, it is true, but the largest, in or near the sub-Saharan Sahel zone, such as Mali, have been ephemeral, and not impressive to someone who knew, say, the Turkish Empire. For the desert peoples of the NANE, however, such as Soomaali, Oromo, Badawin and "Tuareg",[3] their own scale of organization has always been small, because of the demands of desert conditions, but their cultural ties have been with areas to the north of them.

A second overall difference between the two major regions is that writing has been used in the NANE, by the *élites* and not the majority, for hundreds of years at least, and for five thousand years in the Fertile Crescent. In the African Major Region, outside some limited border areas, writing is an introduction of the last hundred years. Even in the literate border areas, the Sahel, the West Coast and the Swahili Coast, it is known by the local people to be an introduction from the NANE, or from Europe. Along with the lack of writing, there is in the African Major Region a lack of detailed history from the distant past. There are memorized king-lists in many states, and traditions of migrations and famines, but little to compare with the Fertile Crescent, or even the Ethiopian Highlands. Associated with the lack of literacy and with the absence of vast durable empires, is the small extent in the African Major Region of even the most widespread languages. Swahili spread into the interior only after 1830, with the growing trade-hinterland of Zanzibar; Mande (Dyula) is more ancient in its spread in West Africa, but is restricted to the markets. There are no languages comparable to the imperial languages Persian and Arabic, or to the former lingua franca of the first Persian Empire, Aramaic.

While touching on languages, it is worth commenting that the language families of the one major region hardly overlap with those of the other. The families of the NANE are: Afro–Asiatic; Altaic (which includes Turkish); Indo–European; and two or more small language families in the Caucasus. The Afro–Asiatic family reaches into the Sahel zone, already mentioned as a cultural borderland. Hausaawaa (Hausa), and a few smaller related languages, belong to this family, but the rest of the languages of the African Major Region are members of families unrepresented outside it: the Niger–Congo family; the Shari–Nile groups; the Khoisan family; and a number of families scattered in different areas.[4]

There is a third important difference between the two major regions which is connected to some extent with the previous two. For the last two thousand years, the NANE has been affected by two of the major missionary religions of the world. After six hundred years of growing influence from Christians, of various sects, from the seventh century onward there was the growing influence of Islam. As with literacy, so it is with missionary religions. Islam is older established in the Sahel and on the Swahili Coast than elsewhere, and Christian missions are older on the Guinea Coast than anywhere in the interior. On the whole, missionary religions are new to most of the African Major Region, arriving in the last hundred years.

A fourth distinction between the two major regions lies in their material culture. Iron smelting, although not as old in the African Major Region as in the NANE, and doubtless spreading to the African from the NANE, was nonetheless widespread by the last hundred years, and the working of gold and copper was elaborate in some areas, for example, the gold working of the Akan-speaking peoples, in West Africa.

More of a contrast appears in textiles and dress. Cotton weaving was widespread on the northern and southern savannas a hundred years ago, and persists in many areas of West Africa today; but large numbers of people, even in cotton-weaving areas, frequently wore little clothing. In some large areas, for instance much of the southern Sudan, most of the men have gone naked up to the present time. In the NANE, by contrast, clothes are ancient, usually voluminous, and obligatory, but in the African Major Region extensive clothing was, before the twentieth century, and largely up to 1930, a prerogative of the royal and the noble. Between the northern and southern savannas, in the wet forest and the Interlacustrine states, cotton-cloth was replaced by bark-cloth, which is still made in some areas, but is not important now as clothing. Again, however, the African rule held : abundant clothing was for the *élite* only.

In the material culture of Africans there was another feature which has distinguished them from the NANE : the lack of durable architecture of great finesse. There is no African Taj Mahal or Palace of Knossos; and not even the sedulously preserved wooden temples of Japan, rebuilt on the existing plans when the present building shows signs of decay. There are mosques in dried mud in the Sahel belt, and mosques of stone on the Swahili Coast, again those two doorways into Africa. There are Zimbabwe and masses of other stone ruins on the Rhodesian Plateau, but they are hardly elegant. In architecture, as in the lack of literature, we could say that the major region was comparable with the Pacific Islands and the Amazon Basin, but not with India or China.

The African Major Region, however, is in no sense culturally simple. By far the most sensitive indicators to the identity of a cultural region, of whatever scale, is provided by certain features to which the terms "art" or "culture" are applied in the narrowest senses. When one walks round a museum, many of the objects on display strike familiar chords, the number which do so varying according to the individual's knowledge of material culture from different parts of the world. Many people can recognize a painting as Chinese, or at least Far Eastern. Not so many would be able to identify a certain mask as from the north-west coast of North America, although the style is as distinctive as the Far Eastern style in painting. These stylistic idiosyncrasies are readily recognized, given the necessary experience of objects from that culture, but they are painfully difficult, and indeed impossible, to describe or define.[5] Hence, there are essential restraints on any discussion of the fifth distinction between the two major regions, namely the differences in style between the painting, sculpture, music and dancing of each of them.

To some extent, the attempt is made easier by the absence of statuary in the NANE, and by the extreme poverty of representational painting west of Iran. However, the highly distinctive abstract painting of the Arabic-speaking areas (the original "arabesque") takes the place of representational painting. South of the Sahara, moreover, there is a concentration of statuary on or near the west coast, and a marked lack of any statuary in the east and south of the continent. The sole exception, prior to the arrival of "airport art" wood carvings, was the sculpture, in wood again, of the Makonde of the lower Ruvuma area. Painting south of the Sahara was, prior to contact with Europeans, largely an adjunct of sculpture. The important theme to emphasize is that African sculpture does have an idiosyncratic style, which cannot adequately be described, but which can be discerned by looking at examples.

To say that the clearest distinction between cultural regions lies in their styles may sound like an evasion, but observation will show it to be realistic. Music is as idiosyncratic as painting or sculpture, and probably more so. Whereas most people find other cultures' plastic art comprehensible to some degree, most find the music of other cultures a cacophony. This is true of Chinese listening to Indian music, or of Africans listening to Beethoven. The systematic study of African music is still in its early stages, but on the available evidence it is possible to say that there is a unity of style throughout the major region, setting it apart from all other areas of the world. At the same time the NANE has a unity of style also, setting it apart. As with African music, so dancing, in Africa as elsewhere, is, so far, thinly studied systematically. Again, however, there is a perceptible African style. Just as it is a commonplace of knowledge that African music is marked by abundant complex drum rhythms, so it is widely known that Africans dance readily and often, with a staccato style, to those rhythms.

In emphasizing the cultural distinctions between the African and NANE Major Regions, five different aspects have been noted: the scale of organization; the history of literacy; the role of the missionary religions; craft industries; and artistic style. Nothing, however, has been said about one of the most visible and striking features which separates the two areas: the people are different in bodily appearance. French writers distinguish "l'Afrique Noire", the area here called the African Major Region, and "l'Afrique Blanche", the African area of NANE. With the exception of European immigrants and some Berbers in the Atlas, Africans are all some shade of brown in their skin colour. In NANE Africa they are mostly pale to dark brown rather than looking black. South of the Sahara most people are dark enough to look black.

The difference in skin colour, however, is accompanied by other features. South of the Sahara, most people are of negroid physical type. They have broad, fairly flat noses and tightly curled, "frizzy" hair. Many have everted lips and prognathism (forward projection of the jaws). Away from the head, they have little hair.

In the NANE, by contrast, noses are prominent, often very prominent like eagles' beaks. Hair is wavy, and body hair relatively abundant. Everted lips and prognathism are rare. This physical type most in evidence is called caucasoid, and these northern Africans are varieties within a large group which includes the peoples of Europe.

There are some people of negroid type in northern Africa, probably all of them descended from slaves brought ultimately from south of the Sahara. There are also caucasoids of a North African type in East Africa, well south of the Horn, but they are few in number and concentrated in the Mbulu and Kondoa Districts of Tanzania.

There is also in Africa a third physical type, the bushmanoid, represented by most of the, few, people of the Kalahari and Namib Deserts in south-western Africa, and by some, formerly all, of the people of the Namaland Highlands, in the same area. This type is also represented by a minority of the Sandawe in the Kondoa District of Tanzania. The skin colour of bushmanoids is yellow-brown, they have sparse body hair, and the hair on the head is tightly curled, in a form called "pepper-corn", on account of its appearance. Their faces have a distinctive tri-angular shape, with the chin as the apex, and some of them have the epicanthic fold over the inner corner of the eye, as do many Chinese, for example. Some of them also have peculiarities of the genitals. Many of the men have a permanently semi-erect penis, and many of the women greatly elongated labia minora, sometimes called "the Hottentot apron". Some women also show an enormous backward projection of the buttocks called steatopygia. These pecularities of the bushmanoids indicate pro-longed relative isolation of their breeding-population in southern Africa.[6]

Mention of the bushmanoids prompts a necessary digression. Although today the people of bushmanoid physical type, namely the Bushmen and Hottentots, occupy only an arid area of south-western Africa, in the seventeenth century they covered about half of the area of Africa south of the Limpopo, and at one stage, perhaps two thousand years ago, they occupied the whole area south of the wet forest and the Interlacustrine plateau. At that time Khoisan languages, such as those of modern Hottentots and Bushmen, probably also covered this large area, and the whole of southern Africa was probably a cultural region distinct from the area to the north. In the last three hundred years, however, the Bushmen and Hottentots are not sufficiently distinctive culturally to give them their own major cultural region, and to exclude them from the African Major Region.

There remains still one theme, and a contentious one, to examine. Many people who have lived in the NANE and in Africa south of the Sahara assert that there is a difference of temperament between the peoples of the two areas. They say that the people of the NANE are intensely aware of their personal honour, constantly suspicious that they are being insulted, and consequently fiercely sexually jealous. Shake-speare's Othello and Shylock are both characters who illustrate different aspects of this type. These NANE people are also devious, both in personal and political pursuits, and prone to tempestuous outbursts of feeling. In the literature describing the peoples of North Africa, the Sahara and the Horn the words "fierce" and "proud" are used repeatedly to describe them; and in the fourteenth century the Arabic writer Ibn Khaldun, himself a North African, said that every Arab deemed himself fit to command.

Africans further south, by contrast, are repeatedly described as cheerful, spontaneous and sociable, subordinating personal feelings to communal harmony. Outbursts of feeling are bad form, and good humour must be maintained, it is said. The Africans south of the Sahara are characterized as: tolerant, within their community, but not of enemies; straightforward; and their motives transparent.

Whether these characterizations are broadly true, given individual differences within the general type, is certainly disputed. Even if they were true, we lack the knowledge to say whether temperament is an aspect of culture, not genetically transmitted, whether it has a genetic basis, or whether it results from a combination of both sets of factors.

Before moving from the major regions to consider the regions into which they are divided, it is important to notice that these cultural units show some close correlations with major territorial units in the distribution of non-human animals and of plants. The Ethiopian Sub-region, in animal distribution, tallies closely with the African Major Region, although its transition zone to the north runs well into the Sahara, the Horn, the Ethiopian Highlands and the Yemen Highlands, unlike its cultural parallel. In the distribution of plants, the African Sub-kingdom occupies much the same area as the Ethiopian Sub-region, if one excludes its arid northern margins, which are transitional. The NANE Major Region is not so closely paralleled by floral and faunal zones although having some correlations (Maps 1–3).

On a smaller scale, the East African fauna has strong links with both the northern and the southern savannas, all three areas forming a horseshoe-shaped band around the very different fauna of the wet forest in the equatorial lowlands. There is a close parallel in the floral provinces, the Eastern African Province comprising the southern savanna and East Africa, which itself adjoins the Savanna Province of the northern savanna. Hence East Africa plays for flora, and for fauna as a whole, the part of bridge between the two savannas which has also probably been its role in human activities in Africa. By way of a contrast, there is no cultural parallel, nor any clear faunal parallel, for the very distinctive floral Cape Kingdom, occupying the "Mediterranean-climate" area on and near the Cape of Good Hope.[7]

Behind these correlations of cultural, faunal and floral areas are common factors of vegetation regions, themselves dependent on climatic factors. These will be considered in some detail in Chapter 2. The correlations are the more remarkable when it is realized that they reflect floral and faunal changes, with accompanying climatic fluctuations, over one hundred million years, but much "edited" by the events of the last one million. The cultural regions must be no more than three thousand years old, in their agricultural forms at least. With such differences in time scale, notable exceptions like the Cape Kingdom become comprehensible, but the correlations remain strikingly neat. Furthermore, differences between vegetation regions are an important, if indirect, factor in the differentiation of cultural regions, as will be discussed in Chapter 10.

Cultural Regions and Vegetation Regions

As we have noted already, the major cultural regions are divided into regions, and these into sub-regions. Detailed discussion, down to the scale of the sub-regions, must wait until the chapters which deal with specific regions of East Africa. At this stage, it is only necessary to refine the cultural pattern of the area to the scale of the regions. There are eight regions either on or near the East African Plateau. Two of these, both off the Plateau, are in the NANE Major Region, and these are:

1. the Horn of Africa;
2. the Ethiopian Highlands.

The remaining six regions are in the African Major Region:

1. the Savanna Stateless Peoples;
2. the Forest-edge States;
3. the Interlacustrine States;
4. the Wet Forest;
5. the Eastern Rift Coast;
6. the Southern Savanna States.

Of these, only two, numbers 3 and 5, are wholly within East Africa, as defined already, while the Ethiopian Highlands and the Forest-edge States are entirely outside. The remaining four regions are largely outside East Africa, the Wet Forest only just crossing the boundaries on the west (Map 8).

From the discussion of the two major regions, it is possible to gauge the kinds of criteria being used in the identification of regions. At this scale, however, it is useful to state explicitly what the criteria are. For the sake of clarity they can be listed:

1. the staple crops and livestock;
2. the scale of organization and the specialization of social function;
3. the form of rituals and of symbols;
4. crafts, e.g. weaving;
5. distinctive material objects.

In the fifth category, houses are very important, being both prominent and also regionally variable. There is no need at this stage to comment on these criteria, but it is worth stressing that language families, or their sub-divisions, have not been used. There will be further discussion of languages in Chapters 4, 10 and 11, and all that needs to be said here is that often people who are close neighbours, and share a common culture, speak languages which are unrelated to each other. Examples are the Gikuyu and Maasai. A map of language groups differs substantially from a map of regions based on cultural criteria other than language (Maps 7, 14).

Before giving a brief sketch of each of the regions, they need to be set in the context of the vegetation types of the area. In later chapters it will be necessary to detail the connections between vegetational and cultural regions. The Oromo and Soomaali groups of the north-east of Kenya are the most southerly of the peoples of the Horn of Africa. Vegetationally, the area is desert or very dry woodland, the result of low and unreliable rainfall. The most conspicuous plants are thorn-trees, of the family Mimosaceae, and various shrubs, again often thorny. There is no complete plant cover except by ephemeral herbs springing up briefly after rain. This type of vegetation extends beyond the Horn region into the country of Turkana, Sambur and other peoples near Lake Rudolf; and there are strong indications that the whole of East Africa is getting drier, and that the desert is expanding.

In sharp contrast to the Horn are the Ethiopian Highlands on its north-western edge. Whereas the landscapes of the Horn are predominantly brown, except after the sparse rains, some parts of the Highlands are green through the year, others through a high proportion of it. At the present time, much of the area is used for growing crops or for grazing, but stands of trees, and more extensive areas of forest, indicate that the area could support highland subtropical forest, green through the year, if it were not for the human interference. Rainfall is high and reliable, compared with the regions to east and west of it, and population dense by comparison with them.

To the west of the Ethiopian Highlands, the northern savanna stretches yet further westwards in a huge belt as far as the Senegal River and the Futa Jalon. Throughout this vast extent the rainfall is lower, and less reliable, in the north, increasing southward in both total amount and reliability, until, along much of the southern margin, the vegetation shades into wet lowland forest. The longitudinal patterns of human organisation are also strikingly similar throughout this savanna belt. In and near the Sahel zone, at the northern margin of the savanna, is a line of states, stretching from those of the Wolof in the west to the area of the, now defunct, Funj kingdom, in the Nile valley. To the south of this belt of states is an attenuated belt of peoples who lack state organizations, apart from the recently superimposed European versions. This belt forms a cultural region, the Savanna Stateless Peoples, and it occupies the zone of middle-range rainfall, where tree growth is better than in the Sahel zone. South again from the stateless peoples is another belt of states, reaching the Guinea Coast in and near the relatively dry Dahomey Gap. These states occupy the best watered part of the savanna and spill over into the wet lowland forest, in Benin for example.

We are not concerned here with the details of most of the northern savanna, but it is necessary to look at the eastern extremity, where a small part of it enters East Africa. The states of the easternmost Sahel zone, Funj, Kordofan, and Darfur, are too far away to enter into the East African patterns, but the Stateless Peoples occupy most of northern Uganda, as well as extending through the southern Sudan and then westward. Their country, for instance that of the Acholi, supports enormous areas of grass, as well as scattered trees, and areas of dry woodland. Without burning and grazing it would presumably support woodland throughout, with gallery forest along the rivers.

Southward from the Acholi the country becomes better watered and greener as the Interlacustrine region is reached, and, to the north-west, the Stateless region gives way southward to the states along the Nile–Congo watershed, part of the southern belt of states mentioned already. Lying astride the frontiers of the Sudan, Zaire and the Central African Republic, the Forest-edge States nearest East Africa are mostly Zande, although these are not a homogeneous group. The region is also astride the savanna wet forest boundary zone, with some of the peoples living in clearings of the wet forest, and some on the best watered areas of the northern savanna.

Immediately to the south of these states, and stretching far to the west, is the Wet Forest region, whose vegetational habitat is explicit. The region coincides so largely with the equatorial lowland forest of the northern Congo Basin, and westward, that the name is appropriate. Vegetation here is characterized by tall trees, with leaves at all times of the year, forming continuous forest, except for the small clearings made for human settlement, and rainfall is more reliable than in any other region of Africa.

The Interlacustrine States are perched on the East African Plateau well above, and to the east of, the Wet Forest region. Population is in places dense, even very dense, and much of the spontaneous vegetation has been cleared. Large areas are cultivated, grazed or under rough grass, but it is probable that, without human intervention, the area would be covered with wet permanently green forest on the plateau, for example in Ganda, rather like the forest of the equatorial lowlands. In the south-western, highland, areas, such as Rwanda, much of the country would be covered, presumably, as some now is, with wet permanently green forest of a subtropical highland type, rather like that of the Ethiopian Highlands. Positionally, the Interlacustrine region is like an eastward extension of the Wet Forest region, but at a greater altitude. Socially, however, the two regions are strikingly different.

On the north-eastern shore of Lake Victoria, the Interlacustrine States merge eastward into another markedly different region, the Eastern Rift Coast. This region is physically complex, with highland masses rising above the general plateau surface, and this itself rises gradually from the coastal lowlands. Lowlands and plateau are covered with dry woodland, but the highlands, where they have not been cleared, carry subtropical highland forest, somewhat like that of the Western Rift Highlands and the Ethiopian Highlands. The nearness of wet country to dry has some important consequences for human settlement and organization.

Finally, the south of the East African Plateau, and the adjoining coast, are occupied by the peoples of the Southern Savanna region, which stretches far beyond East Africa. Extending from the Indian Ocean to the Atlantic, the Southern Savanna peoples reach southward from the edge of the wet forest to the Zambezi valley. In vegetation, and in climate, the region is the southern analogue of the northern savanna, but it lacks the extensive areas of grassland so important in the north, and is largely covered with dry woodland, much of it of the well known *miombo* type. Another difference is that the southern savanna is culturally fairly homogeneous, lacking the conspicuous belts of its northern analogue.

This brief survey has shown that each of the cultural regions has a distinctive vegetation, but that there are more cultural regions than main types of vegetation.[8] The significance of this partial correlation will be examined more carefully in Chapter 10.

The Characteristics of the Different Regions

Having placed the regions in relation to each other, on the ground, it is necessary to run through them briefly again in order to emphasize the assemblage of characteristics which makes each of them distinctive. Reversing the order, the Southern Savanna peoples grow the crops which are widespread in tropical Africa outside the wet forests. The staples are cereals, sorghum and bulrush-millet, with maize important in many areas. Although cattle occur in some areas, and are even locally abundant, as in Sukuma country, most of the region is marked by their absence, although goats are widespread. Throughout this region there is a critical link between population density, vegetation cover, cattle and tsetse flies. Large concentrations of people result in intensive clearance of woodland, tsetse are eliminated by the loss of suitable breeding conditions, and cattle may flourish. This is the situation among the Sukuma. With small populations, and low density, cattle are largely or entirely eliminated by the presence of the flies. In the Southern Savanna, it is the tsetse which flourish in most areas, and not the cattle.

The tradition of kingly states is found throughout the region, although a few ethnic groups lack royal families and state organization. An example are the Tonga. Associated with the kings, there are, as usual, rituals special to the kings, and also insignia of kingship, such as the shell pendant, *kibangwa*, worn on the chest by the Nyamwezi rulers. Apart from the royal families and, in the larger states, families of nobles, social specialization was not accentuated, although there were craft specialists in the recent past (certainly in *c*. 1900). These were rarely full-time. It is important to add that some of the "kings" ruled over states which were, and are, tiny, perhaps two or three villages, of a few hundred people in all. Some states, however, were large, involving thousands of people, like the hegemony of the Mwaant Yaav in *c*. 1880.

Population density was low in the nineteenth century, except in a few areas, and this is still true. Most settlement is in the form of villages, scattered through the woodland, and dispersed settlement is rare. In *c*. 1880, most houses were round, with conical roofs, although a few other types are now frequent (Fig. 1 and Map 16). Also, in the last century, cotton-weaving was widespread in this region, in striking contrast to the three regions immediately to the north. Circumcision was not old-established in the region, and in *c.* 1900 was practised only by the converts to Islam, for instance among the Yao.

Although it is the aggregate of features which provides most of the distinctiveness of each cultural region, the Southern Savanna is very distinctive since the majority of the ethnic groups there show matrilineal descent. This is the largest area of matrilineal descent in Africa, and indeed the world, and even groups in this region now showing patrilineal descent were probably matrilineal in descent and inheritance in the recent past.[9] Elsewhere in East Africa, patrilineal descent is universal except for a few groups in central Tanzania, near to the Southern Savanna region.

Some of these groups, for example, the Mbowe, belong to the Eastern Rift Coast region in most of their cultural features. The crops of this region are similar to those of the Southern Savanna, but there are large numbers of cattle, as well as goats and sheep.

Except for peoples on the edge of the region, who are culturally transitional to other regions,[10] there are no states or kings, the largest social unit until recent decades being an autonomous settlement of, at most, a few hundred people. The men were organized into a graded series of age-sets, and these are still important in some areas, for instance, among the Maasai. Everywhere, leaders were either hereditary priests, or else individuals excelling at conciliation or fighting. In most communities, both hereditary and individually talented leaders occurred, side by side. Beyond this point, however, there was little or no social specialization, except for the universal differences based on sex and age.[11]

Although the present situation is complex, in *c.* 1900, over a large part of the region, a position of unchallenged supremacy in prestige was occupied by the Maasai. Their pastoral way of life was the envy of their neighbours, and they were imitated widely in details of dress and weaponry. However, they had no tributaries and established no administrative empire. In this respect, their position of prestige differed widely from that of peoples in the Southern Savanna, where states were general. Different peoples occupied the summit of the prestige-pyramid in different parts of the savanna. Examples are the northern Lunda, whose ruler was the Mwaant Yaav, and, further east, the Hehe. Both these groups annexed tributary-peoples, and extended the scale of their organization,

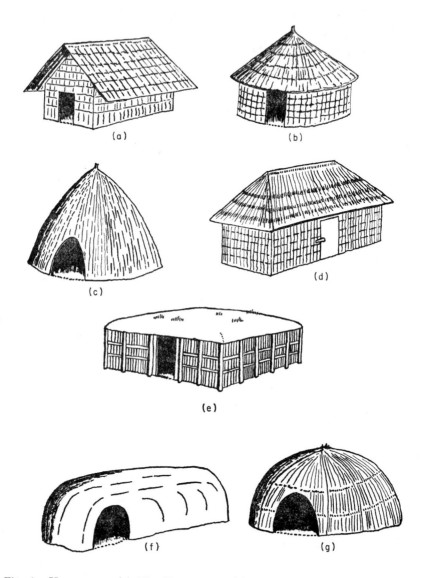

Fig. 1. House-types. (a) Wet Forest type. (b) Savanna type. (c) Interlacustrine type. (d) Coast type. (e) *Tembe* type. (f) Maasai type. (g) Horn type.

as well as enjoying local prestige. It will be necessary, in later chapters, to return to the "league-tables" of local prestige, and to examine them in greater detail.

Density of population differs markedly within the Eastern Rift Coast region, with "islands" of high density in some wet areas, set in the midst of huge expanses with very low density. Most settlement is dispersed; and, in addition to recent types, there are three kinds of houses: the round-conical form; the flat-roofed *tembe*; and the Maasai form (Fig. 1 and Map 16). Material culture is sparse. Throughout the region, men are circumcized and women have the clitoris cut out.

To the west, the Interlacustrine region provides a number of contrasts. Although sorghum, bulrush-millet and maize occur, finger-millet is more important than in the previous two regions, and so are bananas, which are a staple in Ganda. Cattle, sheep and goats are abundant in some areas, but they have to compete with intensive crop-farming over much of the region.

Away from its border-zones, all the peoples of the Interlacustrine region were organized into states by *c.* 1880. Among these states, three, Rundi, Rwanda, and Ganda, were, by that date, very large, according to African standards of the time. Along with the large scale of organization went a high degree of social specialization, with nobility and specialist craftsmen, some of them full-time. The smaller states were socially less complex than the largest, but still showed diluted features of their great neighbours. In *c.* 1880, Rwanda and Ganda were each at the summit of their respective prestige-pyramids, and were the two most powerful kingdoms of the region.

By African standards, population density is high, becoming very high in and around Rwanda and Rundi. Settlement is dispersed, without many nucleated villages, and these mostly recent. There are also new styles of house, arrived in recent decades, but a specialized form of the round-conical type is old, and reached great size in the palaces of the most powerful kings (Fig. 1). Very distinctive of the region were the great drums associated with the kings, and themselves symbols of each state.

The trend towards the greater importance of bananas, begun in the Interlacustrine States, continues in the Wet Forest region, where bananas and yams are the staples, in contrast to the cereal-staples in the regions to north, east and south. There are some goats in the Wet Forest, but sheep and cattle are very rare.

Social organization is on a very restricted scale, the autonomous unit being a village in a clearing in the forest. Local prestige-pyramids are on a small scale also, competition for superiority being between villages, so that it is not possible to speak of whole ethnic groups having high prestige, as with, say, Maasai or Rwanda. Apart from hereditary priests and leaders emerging by individual ability, there is no social specialization beyond the minimum. There are, however, important men's organizations, the "secret societies", not usually secret but sometimes frightening, as were the "leopard-men" of the eastern area, suppressed by the Belgian authorities in the period 1920–40. Circumcision is old-established.

It is already clear that population-density is low, but that settlement is nucleated, in villages. Houses are of a rectangular form, with roofs sloping away either side of a longitudinal ridge-pole (Fig. 1). This form of house is highly characteristic of the wet forest areas, not only here, but on the Guinea Coast as well. One other local feature was the making of bark-cloth, in the Wet Forest, and also in the Interlacustrine States, but in both regions it is now only rarely used, its place taken by imported cloth.

Bark-cloth was used also, *c.* 1900, in the states of the Nile–Congo watershed, occupying a transition area from wet forest to savanna. Their staple crops are similarly transitional, the usual savanna cereals, but with finger-millet very important, and with bananas and yams. Livestock, above the size of chickens, are mostly goats.

Organizationally, as already indicated, the region is marked by states, each with a royal family, many of these families being inter-related. The states, however, are small, and social specialization slight, without numerous full-time craftsmen. Population is sparse, and settlements are nucleated villages. Houses are of the rectangular, wet forest, type or of the round-conical, savanna, type. Culturally, the region is simply transitional from Wet Forest to the Savanna Stateless Peoples, except for the presence of states and kings. In terms of prestige, much of the Watershed States area is dominated by the Zande, a broad category, with considerable internal heterogeneity because so many small local groups have endeavoured to join this high-status category. The Watershed States and the Wet Forest peoples are set apart from the other regions near them in East Africa by their practice, now largely suppressed by governments, of eating enemies they had killed in raids.

To the north of the states lies a very long belt of peoples on the northern savanna who show some considerable cultural similarities to each other, despite the local diversities occurring in the great extent of territory between the Volta tributaries, in the west, and the Ethiopian foothills. Their crops are the classic savanna cereals, as well as other plants widespread in the areas of tropical Africa outside the wet forest. Goats are numerous, there are some sheep, and cattle occur in patches, for instance, and famously, in the Jieng'–Naath area[12] to the north of East Africa.

Kings and states are lacking except on the transitional fringes of the region, and hence the name used here of Savanna Stateless Peoples. With the exception of hereditary priests, and spontaneous leaders, social specialization hardly goes beyond the minimum, and the largest social units are local settlements, rarely above three hundred people. Density of population is low in the eastern part of the belt, but high in some areas, for instance in the Volta tributaries area, in and beyond the north of Ghana. Settlement is either dispersed, as in the East African part of the belt, or nucleated, in villages, as in Jieng'–Naath country, but, prior to the last few decades, houses were overwhelmingly round-conical in most of the area.[13] In such a huge region, there were large numbers of local prestige-pyramids. The Naath were at the apex of one of them in c. 1930, if not still, and, in East Africa, the Acholi were then at the summit of another.

When one moves, however, from the northern savanna through the western foothills of the Ethiopian Highlands, one enters a very different cultural world, part of another major region, the NANE. The savanna cereal-staples are still sown, but in these wetter conditions finger-millet is very important. Cattle, sheep and goats are abundant, but are affected, as in parts of the Interlacustrine States, by pressure of people on the land resources.

The scale of organization since c. 1880 has been vast, with the whole Highlands area united into a single, if loose-knit, empire under the supreme ruler in Addis Ababa. There is an elaborate administrative hierarchy linking districts into provinces, and provinces to the capital. The pattern is similar to that of territories further west and south under European administrators, but with the difference that the Ethiopian pattern has its roots in the history of the central part of the Highlands, and is not an importation from another continent, as the European patterns have been. In such a large-scale state, social specialization is very marked, with full-time specialist craftsmen, and a long history of slavery.

From *c.* 1890 to the present the people at the apex of the prestige-pyramid have been the Amharic-speaking inhabitants of Shoa.

Population density is high by African standards, and is very high indeed in some favoured areas. Much of the settlement is nucleated, in the form of both villages and towns, and many of the houses in the central areas are flat roofed, a Near Eastern feature. Furthermore, the difference from the African Major Region is emphasized by the frequent use of stone, and by the presence of numerous old churches and monasteries, also built in stone. Pitched roofs on rectangular houses also occur, as well as the round-conical form. The principal implement of cultivation is the plough, as in the Near East, but in striking contrast to the dominant hoe-cultivation of the African Major Region. In contrast also is the long history of literacy and written records which go back to the sixth century, at least. Circumcision and excising the clitoris are widespread.

Although the Horn of Africa peoples also belong to the NANE, they give the impression of being the poor relations of the Ethiopian Highlanders, although they would be very offended to be told so. Both in terms of habitat and social order, they bear the same relation to the Highlanders as do the Arabian Badawin to the peoples of the Fertile Crescent. The overwhelming fact of their habitat is aridity, with cultivation, by hoe and not plough, largely confined to river valleys, notably those of the Shebeli and Juba. Their staple crops are the same cereals as on the savanna, but livestock assume far greater importance than in any of the other regions outlined. Camels, sheep and goats are the most important animals, and their grazing needs dominate the activities of most peoples of the Horn.

Social units are not large, usually only a few hundred people in number, but temporary alliances on a larger scale are frequent, depending on the political pressures of the moment. There are no kings, but both spontaneous war-leaders and Muslim notables[14] are important, and there is some degree of social specialization, with slaves. Hunters and smiths form endogamous castes, parallel to similar castes in the Ethiopian Highlands. The composition of alliances is constantly shifting, and positions of high prestige are rapidly gained and lost by different groups.

Population density is, predictably, very low outside the river-valleys, where the house forms are either round-conical or pitched-roofed-rectangular. Over most of the area the nomadic pastoralists use temporary "bee-hives" of matting on a frame, clustered into camps (Fig. 1). Literacy is a thousand years old in some groups, especially in the coastal city states, but has not yet extended right through the Horn to the non-Muslim Boorana. Circumcision and the excision of the clitoris are practised throughout the region.

Factors in the Differentiation of the Regions

Moving back from the NANE Major Region to tropical Africa, examination of Map 8 shows that there is a horseshoe-shaped band of states round the edge of the Wet Forest region, which is itself lacking in states. This pattern, together with the distributions of various other features, such as the divide between the major regions, prompts a number of questions about the factors underlying the pattern of regions which has just been described. Could it be, for example, that the wetter savanna, on the edge of the wet forest, has been a corridor along which state-organization has spread at some time? Has the East African Plateau played the part of a bridge between northern and southern savannas which it has done in the history of plants and of non-human animals? And are the Interlacustrine States critically important in this process? We shall return to this theme in Chapter 11.

At this stage it is only necessary to review, in more general terms, the major factors which can be discerned in the differentiation of cultural regions. These factors can be grouped into five complexes:

1. social specialization within a society;
2. prestige gradients inducing imitation between societies, and, conversely, avoidance of imitation to retain ethnic identity;
3. pressure on resources, leading to migration;
4. cultural features spreading to fill the habitat area;
5. accumulation of factors, to cross critical thresholds.

The period since c. 1890 has seen in East Africa the establishment of new territories much larger than the earlier units. At the same time the total production of wealth, through farming, mining and trade, has increased enormously. By these processes new jobs in government, and to a lesser extent in commerce, have become available, and all of the East African republics are marked by new elites. The processes involved in this social specialization, although on a larger scale than ever before in the area, are very similar to the processes which elaborated the great states of the Interlacustrine region, and, on an even smaller scale, the other states mentioned in the survey of the regions. Social stratification,

which involves an elite, who do not dirty their hands, implies the production of enough food to feed both them and the food producers themselves.

It is clear, however, again from the survey of the regions, that over
large parts of eastern Africa social stratification of this kind has not
occurred at all, while in many areas, for instance the Southern Savanna,
it is very slight. As will be demonstrated in later chapters, no single
factor can account for these regional differences in stratification, but a
combination of rainfall reliability, population density and historical contacts seems to offer a key to the problem.

Mention of historical contacts introduces the second complex of factors,
those governing imitation by one group of another, or the avoidance
of such imitation. Prestige gradients have been emphasized during the
survey of the regions, and one form of imitation which is widespread is
for an ethnic group relatively low on the local pyramid to imitate
features of the group at the apex. Maasai, as has been noted already,
were widely imitated by their neighbours, for instance by the Gogo, in
dress and weapons. Most Maasai, however, have not imitated the Europeans who have so impressed some other East African groups, the Chaga
for instance, and have been imitated by them accordingly. This failure
of the Maasai to imitate Europeans is an example of a group retaining
its classic identify by refusing, albeit implicitly, to adopt something from
others. By this refusal the Maasai are tacitly asserting that they need
nothing from the Europeans and that Maasai are at least the Europeans'
moral equals.

Although, through the action of various factors, the cultural regions
have shown considerable stability over several, probably many, generations, there has been much movement of individuals between regions.
People settling in new regions become absorbed culturally, their children
usually being indistinguishable from those of long-settled neighbour-
families. These migrations by individuals have kept continual contact
between areas, and are generated partly by the tendency of some, always
well watered, areas to generate a larger population than the land can
support. Rwanda and Gikuyu country are such areas. In addition, all
areas, even the best-watered, suffer from recurrent droughts, and the
resulting famines force some people to emigrate. This process, which
could be called famine-swirl, has continually mixed together people from
different areas, and probably over a period of millennia. Migration, and
its causes, constitute the third complex of factors.

The fourth complex is also connected to the habitat. Already, in review-ing the cultural regions, it has been emphasized that they show a remark-able coincidence with vegetation regions. Cultural features are certainly able to cross from the people of one vegetation region to those of another, but, in a high proportion of cases, they spread to the edge of the habitat, and then stop. It is remarkable how the rectangular form of house which is general in the wet forest hardly spreads beyond it. This process some-times also involves languages. The Afro–Asiatic languages reach to the Sahel zone on the southern edge of the Sahara, but only cross it in one section. They also cross the deserts of the Horn to reach nearly to the rim of the East African Plateau. In order to demonstrate that they are not confined to desert, or areas with summer drought, it should be noticed that they occur all over the Ethiopian Highlands; but they have not penetrated the tropical woodlands and parklands except for a limited incursion near Lake Chad. Cultural regions thus, over time, come to coincide with vegetation regions, but the indirect links between the two must wait for elaboration at a later stage.

In discussing the fifth complex of factors, it is essential to note that they involve the operation of all the factors grouped in the previous four com-plexes. The brief examination of social differentiation in East Africa, prior to European administration, has already made it necessary to mention the cumulative effect of several factors in bringing about strati-fication in a society. This is one example of changes brought about by the total effect of more than one factor, when any one factor alone would not have sufficed to induce a change. In the same way, some events in the ethno-history of East Africa appear to be the result of more than one of the four complexes working together, and thus able to cross a threshold which would otherwise have remained inaccessible to change.

We have now seen East Africa in the context of the African and NANE major regions, and we have also seen the regions which occupy or touch the East African area. Much of what has been outlined requires expan-sion. The regions need to be examined in greater detail, and their rela-tions one to another brought into focus. At the same time, the processes which have brought them into being, and maintained them to the present, will have to be discussed more fully, and with reference to specific areas and peoples. Before these considerations of the regions and the processes, however, it is essential to review the vegetation regions which are their physical setting.

1. Notes

1. For a detailed account of the role of Zanzibar and of the diplomatic activities of the British and the Germans : R. Oliver and G. Mathew (Eds) (1963). "History of East Africa", Vol. 1, Chapters V, VI, X, XI, XII.
2. The Portuguese acquired territory which they claimed south of the Ruvuma River.
3. "Tawariq" is the Arabic name for them, not their own term.
4. For the language families of the African continent : J. Greenberg (1963). "Languages of Africa" (Distribution map at end).
   Greenberg has here attempted to reduce all the small language families to membership of one of the large ones. His Shari–Nile family is plausible but not certain, and even his Niger–Congo has to be regarded with caution. It is very unlikely that all languages south of the Sahara can be reduced to just four families. Even Europe has one isolated relict-language, Basque. Map 15 shows the main language groups of Africa.
5. Anyone who reads F. Boas' (1900) book "Primitive Art" can readily check for themselves the truth of this statement by comparing the vivid illustrations with the ponderous, and unilluminating, text.
6. For a detailed comparison of the physical types : J. R. Baker (1974). "Race", pp. 204–231, 333–335. He uses the terms Negrid, Europid and Sanid for negroid, caucasoid and bushmanoid respectively.
7. Readily accessible maps of the major faunal and floral regions are in : W. T. Neill (1969). "The Geography of Life", pp. 98, 99, 103, 104. Neill shows the boundaries of the Ethiopian Sub-region and the African Sub-kingdom very far north, in their transition-zones.
   The role of East Africa for the mammal-fauna of Africa is discussed by J. Kingdon (1971). "East African Mammals", Vol. 1, pp. 51–82. Academic Press, London and New York.
   For the bird-fauna see J. P. Chapin (1932). "The Birds of the Belgian Congo", Vol. 1, pp. 204–264. Other animal groups are affected by similar factors to those affecting mammals and birds.
8. A detailed examination of the links between vegetational and cultural regions, for North America, has been carried out by A. L. Kroeber (1939). "Cultural and Natural Areas of Native North America".
9. This applies especially to Tanzania, where "islands" of matrilineal descent persist : Ilamba–Iambi–Isanzu; Mbowe; Kaguru.
10. Historically very important are the city-states of the coast, including Lamu, Mombasa, Zanzibar and Kilwa, all of which have strong cultural

links with Arabia. Their culture, and their role in the cultural regions, will be detailed in Chapter 4.

While Lamu and Mombasa are in the Horn and Eastern Rift Coast regions respectively, others, for instance Kilwa, are on the coast of the Southern Savanna.

11. For a survey of types of leaders and of political organization in East Africa c. 1900 : Lucy Mair (1962). "Primitive Government".

12. The Jieng' are usually called "Dinka" by Europeans and the Naath "Nuer".

13. The Volta tributaries area has a special flat-roofed form of house.

14. The Boorana and Bararetta are not Muslims, and have their own hereditary priests.

2

The Human Habitats of East Africa

The Vegetation and Soils of East Africa

The whole of East Africa is well within the tropics, and the main plateau-surface, as well as the coastal lowlands, experience temperatures which are characteristically tropical. Frost and snow are unknown, and there is a relatively slight variation of mean temperatures throughout the year, and also of actual temperatures during the course of any day. However, the normal lowering of temperature which occurs with increasing altitude results in the highland areas being marked by temperature patterns which are not strictly tropical. Daily and yearly variations of temperature between 1700 and 3000 metres are markedly greater than are those below this height; and frost does sometimes occur at the upper levels of this higher zone. Higher still, above what may be called the subtropical zone, is the non-tropical zone. Very little of the land surface of East Africa is actually occupied by this zone, but it is sufficiently distinctive to require separate comment. Means of temperature throughout the year are still lower than in the subtropical zone, and variations are extreme, especially those between day and night temperatures. Thus the saddle between the twin peaks of Kilimanjaro is subjected on some days to intense insolation during the hours of daylight, while after dark the temperature drops well below freezing point.

Apart from these very high altitudes, however, temperature differences do not provide very marked contrasts in the climates of East Africa. Much more dramatic are the divergences from one area to another in the amounts and reliability of rainfall, and other precipitation. In broad terms, the areas nearest to the Equator go through two wet seasons every year while areas further away, both northward and southward, experience only one wet season. Thus Ganda and Gikuyu country both have two wet seasons, while the areas of the Otuho and Nyamwezi have only one. In the north-west quarter of East Africa this means that areas astride the Equator usually receive more rain in a year than do areas further away. However, in north-eastern East Africa, including Maasai country, the Lake Rudolf area and the Horn, the situation is complicated by the air-mass patterns of the Near East and northern Indian Ocean, with the result that most areas, whether on the Equator or three degrees from it, receive little rain in most years.

On the whole again, precipitation increases with altitude up to 3000 metres, although it falls away again above that height. The highland areas are thus relatively wet; while the only lower areas with similarly high rainfall are the western, northern and eastern shores of Lake Victoria. Here the presence of the huge evaporating-surface of the lake, as well as the equatorial position, presumably affects the rainfall amounts.

Totals of precipitation, however, reckoned as annual means, are little comfort to East African farmers during a drought year. Over large areas of the tropics rainfall reliability is notoriously low, with wide fluctuations from year to year in the quantity of rain which actually falls. Usually reliability varies with mean amounts, so that, to use examples mentioned earlier, Ganda and Gikuyu enjoy fairly reliable falls, while Otuho and Nyamwezi can rarely predict accurately how much rain will occur in the coming wet season. Even more extreme is the position of Maasai or Soomaali, living in areas with even lower annual mean values, and even lower reliability.

Rainfall, and to a less marked extent temperature, are critical factors in the vegetation cover of East Africa; and their distribution controls that of the four major complexes of vegetation, which themselves are the habitats for the different human groups of the area.[1] These four complexes of vegetation are:

1. lowland wet forest, scrub and grassland;
2. highland wet forest, scrub and grassland;
3. dry woodland, scrub and grassland;
4. dryer woodland, scrub and grassland.

Each complex, as is clear from their names, is made up of various types of vegetation, these being linked together in all probability by successional sequences, as well as by differing factors in their present habitat. For instance, it is just about certain that most of East Africa would support closed forest or dense woodland communities were it not for human activities, and that most of East Africa was in the past covered with such communities. Most of the scrub and grassland, therefore, which now covers in aggregate vast areas of East Africa, would give way to forest or woodland if left alone by people and by their domestic animals.

As the names indicate also, the first two complexes are marked by higher mean precipitation than the next two. At the same time the fourth complex is overall dryer than the third. Indeed the fourth includes some extensive areas of true desert, where there is never, at any season of the year, a complete cover of the ground by vegetation. However, the principal habitat factor separating the lowland wet forest complex from the highland appears to be temperature. This lowland complex is truly tropical, while the highland complex is strictly subtropical. It will be necessary shortly to outline the distribution of these four main complexes, but at this stage only examples of each are needed. The country of the Ganda is a typical sample of the lowland wet forest complex, while Gikuyu country is typical of the highland complex. Both the Otuho and the Nyamwezi live in habitats belonging to the dry woodland complex; and the Maasai Plains are a classic example of the fourth, dryer woodland, forms. Finally, many Oromo and Soomaali groups live in extreme versions of this complex, that is in true desert.

All the evidence that there is indicates that there have been great changes in the vegetation over the last three thousand years. In about 1000 B.C., at a time when most, or even all, the peoples of East Africa were hunters-and-gatherers, the areas of scrub and grassland must have been much less extensive than at present, although firing of the cover by hunters had probably begun already to roll back the forest and woodland. The basic outline of the vegetation pattern of that period is indicated on Map 5, although such a reconstruction is unavoidably tentative. The highlands were then still forest covered, with few clearings, and forest extended over most of the Interlacustrine plateau, as well as between Lake Victoria and the Eastern Rift Highlands. In the south the earlier dry woodland had not yet been replaced by *miombo*; while in the north the savanna was largely made up of woodland, with few areas of grassland or scrub. Even the dry north-east was better wooded, with more trees, and the trees often larger, than at present. The vegetation there had not yet been eaten down by sheep, goats and camels.

However tentative such a reconstruction of earlier conditions has to be, there is not much room for doubt that the modern vegetation cover has been heavily affected by human activities. Burning, grazing by domestic stock, and the clearing of tree-covered areas for cultivation has greatly reduced the numbers of trees in the northern half of East Africa. In the southern half, the well-wooded *miombo* areas apparently represent a fire-climax, generated by human agency. All around Lake Victoria, the large areas of grassland and scrub presumably represent areas of former cultivation which are now fallow, although most of them are re-used before a complete tree cover is again established.

The four major vegetation complexes provide the habitats for most of the human groups in East Africa (Map 4). Even so, there are some other complexes which occupy much less area and are less used by people. The tops of the highest mountains, above the subtropical zone, have already been mentioned. They have a number of very distinctive vegetation types. Also very distinctive are the types occurring in swamps, and those of the sea coast. In addition, therefore, to the four major complexes, it is necessary to recognize three minor ones :

1. high mountain complex;
2. swamp complex;
3. sea-coast complex.

These will be considered briefly later.

Intimately connected with the vegetation are the soils which underlie and partially nourish it. From a human point of view the outstanding feature of most East African soils is their poverty. There are exceptions, notably in places where the soils contain the breakdown products of recently disintegrated volcanic rocks or where alluvial deposits are renewed frequently by river or lake-flooding. Such areas support the only extensive areas of dense population in East Africa.

Most soils, however, are rich in iron and aluminium, and in little else. Under the tropical and subtropical conditions bacteria are active much of the time, and the breakdown of plant debris is rapid. In addition repeated heavy rain rapidly carries off any soluble products of bacterial action. Even the dry north-eastern quarter of East Africa does not escape these twin effects of bacterial liveliness and of leaching. Most of the soils in East Africa appear pale and white-grey, or else some shade of red, the effect of large quantities of oxidized iron compounds. The outstanding exceptions are the black soils occurring in areas which are seasonally swampy, and known in Swahili as *mbuga*. Widespread and often small in extent, these *mbuga* are an example of the fertility of alluvial soils, albeit on a small scale. They provide good grazing at some seasons, and can be used for highly productive crop cultivation. Even so, it is important to stress again that the soils which form the basis of most East African farming are poor.

Lowland Wet Forest, Scrub and Grassland

Turning again to the major vegetation complexes, lowland wet forest, scrub and grassland occupy a high proportion of the north-western quarter of East Africa. Even further west, beyond the Western Rift Highlands, is the greatest extent of vegetation of this complex in the whole of Africa. There, in the Wet Forest region, clearings in the forest are relatively few and small, and the forest is far more abundant than areas of cultivation, scrub and grass. On the plateau of the Interlacustrine region, however, and on the neighbouring eastern shore of Lake Victoria, forest is only preserved in a few places, such as the Bukoba forest in Ziba, the Mabira forest in Ganda, and the Kakamega forest, on the eastern shore of the lake.

The climate of this area would probably support forest in all places which are not swampy, and even in some of these; and it is probable too that the area was covered with wet forest at the time when the first knowledge of farming reached there, probably in the first millennium B.C. Since then clearing, cultivation, and the regeneration of local plants have produced the present mosaic, largely of scrub, grass and of woodland, with the trees scattered rather than forming a closed canopy. The wet climate, however, permits the cultivation of large quantities of bananas, sugar-cane and coffee (species *"robusta"*), which cannot thrive over a large proportion of East Africa. Also, it is likely that clearance and cultivation have obscured the vegetational transition which, in the period before farming, occurred between the north and the south of the area which is now Uganda. At that time, probably the south was wet forest and the north dry woodland, although with patches of wet forest in places; and there was a mosaic of the two types in the central transition zone. At the present time, by contrast, the vegetation of northern and southern Uganda are somewhat similar, although the greater dryness of the north is reflected in some differences of species between north and south.

The sparse woodland and grassland with scattered trees, usually called parkland, which have replaced wet forest in the south, and on the eastern lake-shore, is dominated by species of *Combretum* and *Terminalia*, both of them genera which are important locally in the vegetation of other parts of East Africa. Although the species of grass which have flourished as a result of forest clearance are numerous, one is strikingly conspicuous. *Pennisetum purpureum*, elephant grass, grows to heights of about five metres and forms pure stands in some places on the more fertile soils.

It is difficult to form a clear picture of the earlier, continuous, wet forest from the remnants of it which are still standing. In some of these, one or a few species of tree are locally dominant, but it is probable that at the former period, as now in the wet forest of the Congo Basin, there were no overall dominant species, and few, if any, locally dominant. Lowland wet forest is very rich in tree species, while shrubs and herbaceous plants flourish best in the temporary clearings formed where a tree has fallen and brought others down with it. There is no season when the trees are leafless, and the forest is therefore green all the year round. Furthermore, this type of forest has an elaborate social structure, with three tiers, or more, of tree-crowns, one below the other, forming the total canopy (Fig. 2).

In the present landscapes of the Interlacustrine plateau the special features of the Dry Zone are not as prominent as they were when the forest cover was almost complete. Nevertheless, they are still conspicuous

Fig. 2.   Lowland wet forest.

enough to an observer of the vegetation. The Dry Zone is a series of pockets of dryer climate spread through the central band of the region, and the vegetation of these pockets is distinctive, with species of *Acacia* usually dominant. It will be necessary to return to these features of the Dry Zone when discussing the northern savanna.

Although the Interlactustrine region and the eastern lake-shore are the largest area covered by vegetation types of this complex in East Africa, it is represented on a smaller scale elsewhere. Towards the coast, on the southern and eastern slopes of the Usambara, Unguru and Uluguru mountains, are areas of wet forest of this type, which merge upwards into highland wet forest. On these coastal highlands the subtropical wet forest begins lower down the slopes than it does in the interior. Despite the floristic distinction between the highland and lowland types, however, their differences have no effect on the human groups of this area. The Shambaa, Nguru and Ruguru peoples each inhabit highland and lowland forest alike, and the areas of wet forest on the coastal slopes are each effectively a single habitat rather than each being sub-divided into a highland and a lowland component, with a different people in each of the altitudinal divisions.[2]

Highland Wet Forest, Scrub and Grassland

The vegetation of the highland wet forest complex on the hills of Shambaa, Nguru and Ruguru covers in all a rather limited area. Vegetation of these types is more extensively represented in the interior. They cover the highest parts of the highlands which form a Y-shape in : the Southern Highlands of Tanzania, the area around the northern end of Lake Nyasa, and the hills which extend north-west from there to the southern end of Lake Tanganyika. The second major area is the Western Rift Highlands from Rundi northwards to the Ruwenzori Mountains; while the third major area is the Eastern Rift Highlands. There are also considerable zones of this complex on the massive isolated volcanoes of Elgon, Kenya, Meru and Kilimanjaro. Beyond East Africa, vegetation types of this complex occur on a much vaster scale in the volcanic Ethiopian Highlands.

Although examples of forest still stand, this complex has been greatly affected by human activities, but it seems likely that in *c.* 1000 B.C. most of the terrain between 1700 and 2200 metres in altitude was covered with this type of forest.

The hills are more attractive to farmers than the plateau surface wherever there is a marked difference in rainfall between the two; and where there are volcanic soils these highland areas support some of the highest population-densities in East Africa, as in Gikuyu, Chaga and Nyakyusa areas. The Y-shaped highland area of the Southern Savanna region does not support any very great concentrations of people except for that of the Nyakyusa. Even so, amidst the sparse populations and recurrent drought of the *miombo* woodland these highlands provide relatively reliable rainfall and sustain densities of settlement above the mean for the region. More strikingly to the observer, they are green when the *miombo* woodland below them is brown during the dry season, and the contrast is most apparent where stands of forest still occur, the mass of leaves appearing so dark as to be black.

In the Eastern Rift Coast region the dense populations on the volcanic soils of Kilimanjaro, Meru, Kenya and Elgon are an important element in the total distribution of people over the area. On all these mountains there are considerable stands of forest still, and there are more extensive areas of it on the Eastern Rift Highlands.

The contrast between wet green highlands and dry, often grey or brown, lowlands, which is very marked in the Eastern Rift Coast region, and conspicuous enough to be noticed in the Southern Savanna, does not appear in the Interlacustrine region because here the lowlands are wet and green also. Indeed the highlands, including Rundi, Rwanda and Chiga, now carry very little forest, which has presumably been cleared over many centuries by the dense populations, again on volcanic soils, which set these highlands apart from the lower-density areas of the plateau, such as the interiors of Ziba and Ganda. Grassland and scrub are the vegetation-types of almost all the highland areas, as they are on the plateau.

The highlands support some productive areas for the growing of coffee (species *arabica*), for example in Rundi, Rwanda, Gikuyu, Chaga and Nyakyusa, but sugar-cane is not successful at these altitudes, since the lower temperatures reduce sugar formation. Some varieties of banana, however, flourish, and bananas are the staple crop of the Chaga and Nyakyusa, as they are of the Ganda and Soga on the wet plateau. Another crop which produces well in areas where wet highland forest has been cleared is finger-millet, but this is also grown lower down.

Areas under cultivation are extensive in the Interlacustrine highlands, and in the more densely peopled parts of the other highlands. The huge areas under grass and scrub are presumably the sites of former cultivation, reverting towards forest. In most areas, however, the stage of forest cover is not reached, either because cattle, sheep and goats graze too intensively to allow it, or else because the land is taken back into cultivation.

The forest itself is less complex than the lowland wet forest, the canopy consisting of only one or two tiers instead of three or more (Fig. 3). At

Fig. 3.   Highland wet forest.

the same time there is not the same extreme diversity of tree species as in the lowland type, and one or two species are dominant over consider- able expanses of the forest. Lind and Morrison (1974) recognize eight communities which together constitute a high proportion of the highland wet forest type in East Africa. These communities, named after their dominant species, and arranged roughly in order from wettest to dryest, are :

1. *Ocotea usambarensis, Podocarpus milanjianus*;
2. *Aningeria adolfi-friedericii*;
3. *Ficalhoa laurifolia, Afrocrania volkensii*;
4. *Cassipourea malosana*;
5. *Chrysophyllum gorungosanum*;
6. *Juniperus procera*;
7. *Podocarpus gracilior*;
8. *Brachylaena hutchinsii, Croton megalocarpus*.

The eighth community, abundant in and near Nairobi and on the Ngong Hills, is marginal to the wet forest and transitional to dryer types, such as *miombo* woodland, and the woodlands of the northern savanna. In the Nairobi and Ngong areas, moreover, it is succeeded rapidly downhill by the dryer woodland of Maasai country.

As has been noted already, rainfall reliability and amount increases upslope from dry woodland to highland wet forest, while at the same time the drop in temperatures to subtropical conditions lowers evapo-transpiration, so that the rain that falls is more effective for plant growth. Another significant feature of these highland forests is the large amount of time during the year when they are swathed in mist, with the result that total precipitation is increased through condensation on the vegetation, and that water loss through evaporation and transpiration is further reduced because of the moisture-saturated air.

Miombo Woodland, Scrub and Grassland

At lower altitudes where there is dry woodland, climatic conditions are markedly different. The dry woodland complex is divided into two great blocks, the northern and the southern savannas.[3] Of these the second corresponds very precisely in area with the Southern Savanna cultural region, which is named after the vegetation types which form the habitats of the peoples there. Areas of vegetation within this cultural region which are not of the dry woodland complex have already been noted, since large numbers of ethnic groups live higher up, in the wet forest complex of the hills. However, the shape of the cultural region on the map is traced out by the dry woodland, most of which is of the type usually called *miombo*.

Unlike the areas of the wet forest complexes, where grass and scrub predominate in total area over the remaining patches of forest, the country of the *miombo* woodland types is largely covered by trees. Although grass, scrub and areas of cultivation occur, they are relatively small in extent, and also inconspicuous. Population is sparse, and, as noted already, there are vast numbers of tstetse flies. The crops which are grown are those typical of East African cultivation, but the low reliability of the rain, and its relatively low mean totals, account for the unimportance of the crops with high water-needs, notably bananas, coffee and sugar-cane. Although there are plantations of sugar-cane in the Kilombero Valley in Tanzania, these are grown with irrigation, and as a government-sponsored scheme, not a local initiative.

Miombo woodland, unlike the two wet forest types, does not retain its canopy of leaves all the year, and there is a dramatic contrast between the green colours of the wet season and the greys and browns of the dry, when almost all the tree species are leafless. Impressive too are the coppery-reds of the young leaves at the beginning of the rains. There is a simple canopy, of one tier only, and even during the leafy season the canopy is not dense, so that shrubby and herbaceous species flourish beneath the trees (Fig. 4). Another contrast with both the wet forest types,

Fig. 4.   Dry woodland complex: *miombo* woodland.

although most markedly with the lowland form, is the number of tree species, which are relatively few, although numerous compared with the wet forests of Europe. Most of the trees belong to the family Caesalpiniaceae, and two genera, *Brachystegia* and *Julbernardia*, are very important. Indeed the term *miombo* woodland was coined by European foresters from the Nyamwezi name for *Brachystegia boehmii*, which is *muyombo* (plural: *miyombo*), precisely because this species, and its close relatives, form such a high proportion of the woodland in southern and western Tanzania. In some area, *Pterocarpus angolensis*, with its pale yellow flowers and distinctive spikey fruits, is one of the dominant trees, but it is not as regular a feature of these woodlands as the *Brachystegia* species. *Miombo* country is alive with wild animals and provides visiting naturalists with vast amounts of information on animals and plants with much less effort than is needed in lowland wet forest. However, to most Europeans who are not passionately interested in the animals, plants or the local peoples, *miombo* woodland seems monotonous and even depressing.

Despite its being a homogeneous plant community over a vast extent of south central Africa, and its appearance therefore of being the spontaneous climax for its region, *miombo* woodland, like the forests of modern Europe, results from human activities. All the evidence indicates that it is in fact a sub-climax, more specifically a climax generated and maintained by repeated firing, the end-product of both deliberate and accidental burning by the local peoples, presumably over a period of centuries. This conclusion is the more remarkable because the density of population is low, less than three to the square kilometre in many areas, and indeed, at any one period, large areas are totally uninhabited except for occasional hunting parties. However, shifting cultivation involves even very small numbers of people in the burning of large areas of woodland over a period of sixty or seventy years, so that a thousand years of such farming alters the vegetation drastically. What the spontaneous climax-community would be, if human intervention were to cease or change, is difficult or impossible to predict or reconstruct. Around 2000 B.C. the northern part, at least, of the *miombo* woodland belt was covered with wet forest of the lowland type, a southward extension of the Congo Basin and Interlacustrine forest mass. However, the overall decrease in rainfall since then would have eroded this type in some, if not most, areas. Presumably there would be a form of dry woodland, but with a different set of dominant tree species, presumably again species less resistant to fire than the forms of *Brachystegia, Julbernardia* and *Pterocarpus.*[4]

Already in this chapter it has been necessary to refer to *mbuga,* areas of seasonal swamp. These are very abundant throughout the *miombo* country, and their vegetation is distinct from that of the surrounding dryland communities. Particularly prominent are the gall acacias, *Acacia drepanolobium,* sometimes called whistling-thorn because the wind whistles through their distinctive hollow excrescences, the so-called "galls". Ground-water also affects vegetation in conditions other than those of seasonal swamp. *Acacia xanthophloea,* the fever tree, forms stands of woodland in river valleys and marshes. Marshy areas also support conspicuous stands of certain palms, such as *Borassus aethiopum* and *Hyphaene coriacea,* which grows in numbers on the river plains near the Southern Highlands of Tanzania, such as those of Sango country. The river valleys even support tree species which occur in lowland wet forest, with the result that in the Rufiji and Ruvuma valleys there are some stands of gallery wet forest, which lack, however, the complexity of the canopy found in classic lowland wet forest. Similar local variations in the plant cover, generated by the conditions of the ground-water, occur in the northern savanna and in the dry north-eastern quarter of East Africa.

Northern Savanna Dry Woodland, Scrub and Grassland

Although the northern savanna is vegetationally the equivalent of the southern savanna, so that there is some purpose in using the two parallel names, the human history of the two belts has been very different. In East Africa the northern savanna reaches only into the north of Uganda, but from there it extends northwards and for a great distance westwards, as far as Senegal and Guinée. Much of its area is occupied by Savanna Stateless peoples, such as the Acholi and Otuho, but the wetter southern border-zone, near to the Wet Forest region, is occupied in the east by the Forest-edge states of the Zande, while, in West Africa, the states of the Guinea Coast region occupy this zone. Over a period of centuries these border-zone states have been incorporating more and more of the stateless groups into their population, and a parallel encroachment has taken place on the northern, dry, margin of the savanna, where the states of the Sahel zone have extended their aggregate area.

The northern savanna differs from the southern in the balance between woodland, scrub and grassland. Although there are extensive areas of dry woodland, this type does not dominate the landscape for hundreds of miles, as it does in the *miombo* belt. Parkland is very extensive, as well as grassland and scrub. The vegetation as a whole, and the lesser numbers of large mammals over much of this belt, compared to its southern counterpart, indicate more intensive use by people over a long period. However, the eastern end of the savanna, in and near East Africa, has been much less affected by human activity than has the western half of the belt. As in the southern savanna, the water-needs of bananas, coffee and sugar-cane prevent these from being important crops, and the cereals and legumes which are the local staples are themselves subject to recurrent droughts.

Much of northern Uganda is parkland, with species of *Combretum* and *Terminalia* as the dominant trees (Fig. 5), sometimes forming woodland. This landscape is not strikingly different from that further south in Uganda, where lowland wet forest has been cleared. More drought-resistant species, however, become increasingly important the further north the area is situated, a prominent form with a more northerly

Fig. 5. Dry woodland complex: parkland of the northern savanna.

distribution being *Butyrospermum paradoxum*, widespread in *Combretum*-dominated woodland and parkland in the north of Uganda. Further north-west, on the Nile–Congo watershed, Zande country is covered with woodland and parkland in which prominent trees are *Isoberlinia doka, Daniellia oliveri* and *Afzelia africana.*

As has been stressed already, the clearance of the lowland wet forest on the Interlacustrine plateau has effectively extended the northern savanna southward so that this vegetation region now joins the southern savanna in the country of the Ziba, Dzindza and Shumbwa. However, the pockets of dryer conditions which collectively form the Dry Zone of the Interlacustrine plateau are marked by vegetation reminiscent in appearance of much of the Eastern Rift Coast region, a parkland of *Acacia* trees among grasses. In these Dry Zone pockets the grass usually dominant is *Themeda triandra*, also frequently dominant in the herb layer in and near the Eastern Rift Highlands. As will be discussed later, in Chapter 6, the Dry Zone has played an important part in the establishment and maintenance of specialized cattle-rearing in the Interlacustrine region; and this zone may even have provided the corridor of entry into the wet forest of the plateau for the first farming settlers to reach what was to become the Interlacustrine region (Chapter 11).

Dryer Woodland, Scrub and Grassland

As we have seen already, most of the north-eastern quarter of East Africa is dry, even dryer than the southern savanna. This predominantly dry quarter is occupied by the plateau and coast sub-regions of the Eastern

Fig. 6. Dryer woodland complex: *Acacia* woodland. There is an individual of a candelabra-shaped species of *Euphorbia* on the small rocky outcrop in the left middle distance.

Rift Coast region and by the Horn of Africa. In addition the Lake Rudolf depression and the neighbouring plateau-edge of the Karimojong' belong climatically and vegetationally to this dry area. Climatic conditions change on the whole northwards and eastwards, total rainfall and reliability both decreasing in these directions, until the mass of the Ethiopian Highlands reverses the tendency in the north. Vegetation changes also from the south and west, the tree cover thinning out as the rainfall totals decrease. Indeed the country of the Turkana, pastoral Oromo and Soomaali is mostly desert, without a complete vegetation cover, not even of herbaceous plants in the wet season (Fig. 7). In many ways it is better to treat the dry quarter as belonging to two vegetation-complexes rather than one, since there is a visible distinction between the dryer woodland complex (Fig. 6) and a desert complex which replaces it in the north and north-east. The dividing zone between them largely coincides with

Fig. 7. Dryer woodland complex: desert.

the transition from the dry parts of the Eastern Rift Coast region to the Horn region. The Lake Rudolf area, however, does not fit neatly into the correspondence between vegetational and cultural regions, because Turkana country is very similar to that of the pastoral Oromo, but the Turkana belong to a transition area between the Eastern Rift Coast and Savanna Stateless regions, rather than to the Horn, although their camels link them to the Soomaali.

Despite the increasing dryness of the country to the north and northeast, the dry quarter is unified by the prevalence of species of *Acacia*, usually flat-topped, and very distinctive features of the dryer landscapes of East Africa. In and near Maasai country they frequently form true woodland, a closed cover of trees, but in the Horn such woodlands are usually found only along water courses, most of which have surface water for only weeks or days in any year. The landscapes of the Horn are of scattered *Acacia* and *Commiphora* trees or shrubs, while even the grasses and other herbs fail to cover the ground, whereas in the dry parts of the Eastern Rift Coast there is a complete ground cover of herbaceous plants, mostly grasses, as well as numerous shrubs. Thickets of shrubs also are frequent in the Eastern Rift Coast areas, the genus *Capparis* providing a number of thicket-dominants; and the huge and striking candelabra *Euphorbia* species are abundant, usually on tors (*kopjes* in Afrikaans) of shattered rock. Prominent too are the massive baobabs (*Adansonia digitata*). On the whole different species of *Acacia* are found in the south and west from those in the Horn. *Acacia tortilis*, for example, is very abundant in Maasai country, while *Acacia senegal* is a plant of dryer areas. In these dryer places *Acacia mellifera* is spreading where overgrazing has destroyed the earlier vegetation cover.

The present vegetation of the Horn indeed reflects heavy human intervention, or, more precisely, it reflects the grazing of domestic livestock. Landscapes which are now desert were probably once more thickly treed and carried a complete herbaceous cover between the trees and shrubs. Probably here, as in other parts of East Africa, rainfall totals have fallen since 1000 B.C., but the increase in livestock over the last few centuries has made the decrease in precipitation more serious. Vegetation can hardly have been lush in this, the dryest, area of East Africa at any time during human occupation, but heavy grazing by sheep, goats and camels has generated a sub-climax more desertic than the spontaneous climax, were it allowed to develop. In the wetter areas beyond the Horn, the country of the Maasai and their neighbours, grazing and burning have also greatly affected the plant cover, so that the area carries a mosaic of woodland, parkland, scrub and grassland; but there is no desert.

Human use of the dry quarter has been heavily weighted towards livestock husbandry for centuries and even for as much as two millennia (Chapter 11). Grazing, and over-grazing, are not only features of the vegetation, but also of the ambitions and resentments of the peoples who live here. Success and power are demonstrated, for both individuals and groups, by cattle in the wetter areas, and by camels in the dryer. Sheep and goats have less prestige attached to them, but are still very valuable assets. Over most of the quarter, raids for cattle or camels, or both, are part of the everyday affairs of adult men, despite the official disapproval of the governments of Ethiopia, Somalia, Kenya and Uganda.

In terms of the options open to people in the dry quarter, there has not been much room for choice, nor is there now. Hunting-and-gathering is practicable, but only for much smaller populations than those which have been generated since livestock husbandry reached the area two thousand years ago, or perhaps earlier in the Horn. Only a drastic reduction in the population could allow hunting-and-gathering to re-emerge as the dominant mode of subsistence. On the other hand, the cultivation of crops is hazardous without irrigation, and water sources for irrigation are not readily accessible away from the very few permanent rivers. Camels, cattle, sheep and goats, however, can be moved to water when their present supplies fail, provided, that is, that the people whose flocks and herds are already at the new supplies can be persuaded, or forced, to let them in. On the borders of the dry quarter there are peoples, such as the Baraguyu, Gogo and Kamba, who combine some not-too-energetic cultivation with their animal husbandry, but for them, as for the exclusive pastoralists, the main investment, and the best insurance against famine, is livestock.

Five major rivers cross the dry quarter and empty into the Indian Ocean: the Shebeli, Juba, Tana, Galana and Pangani. Their valleys provide ground-water for cultivation under climatic conditions which are only marginally suitable for crops, if at all. Although human use of the valleys has removed much of the tree cover, species which occur in the lowland wet forest are found there, and more extensive wet forest probably existed in the past (Map 5). As in the southern savanna, there are also places where seasonal swamp has formed, and where *Acacia xanthophloea* and stands of palms reveal a high watertable. An example are the *Borassus aethiopum* groves near Lake Manyara.

High Mountains, Swamps and the Sea-Coast

From many parts of Maasai country, in the right weather conditions, it is possible to see the great mountain masses of Kilimanjaro, Meru and Kenya, but even the peoples who live on their slopes rarely, or never, go to their summits. The upper slopes of the high mountains, above the highland wet forest, are not of great importance in peoples' activity. In the first place they occupy a small fraction of East Africa's surface. Although there are extensive areas of highland, only a small proportion of them rises above 2200 metres, that is above the generalized upper limits of the highland wet forest. In the second place, they involve considerable effort to reach them, and, in the third place, there is no great return to be had on the effort.

Above the highland wet forest there is usually bamboo thicket, dominated by *Arundinaria alpina*, and above that usually dwarf woodland, the most frequent dominants being *Hagenia abyssinica* and *Rapanea rhododendroides*. Higher up still is the vegetation which is unique in its forms to the East African high mountains, but very few areas are high enough to carry these forms. Whereas bamboo thickets and dwarf woodland occur widely in the Western and Eastern Rift Highlands, only the Ruwenzori Mountains, Elgon, Kenya, Meru and Kilimanjaro, with small areas of the Virunga and Aberdare highlands, carry the higher-altitude forms of vegetation. These include tussock-grassland, bogs and scrub, as well as a little bare desert, all of which are undramatic enough, but also, and famously, woodland and parkland dominated by species of *Lobelia*, *Dendrosenecio* and *Philippia*.

However exciting, and puzzling, these areas are for botanists, however, they offer little to most East Africans. The bamboo offers some good house-building material for peoples of highland wet forest, and the climb up is not too hard, but above that there is even less to reward any effort. On Elgon, Sabiny and Gony graze the dwarf woodland, a practice which they perhaps adopted when Nandi raids were severe in the later nineteenth century; while, on Kilimanjaro, Chaga men will go up to the highest vegetation types to collect wild honey. They are also ready to act as porters to the European visitors who actually want to get to the top, where there is no vegetation at all.

Swamps, on the other hand, are less arduous to reach, and more rewarding, even if few people live there permanently. Although not a major vegetation complex, swamps cover a large area in East Africa, especially in Uganda, where a maze of swamp valleys leads down to Lake Kyoga, in the centre of the country. There are even more extensive areas of swamp further down the Nile, beyond the East African Plateau, including the well known Sudd, bordering the country of Jieng' and Naath. Kenya does not have any extensive areas of swamp, but in Tanzania there are the levels along the Malagarasi River. Seasonal, as distinct from permanent, swamp has been mentioned already, since it forms an extension of grazing and cultivated land during part of the year. In some parts of Tanzania, notably in the Wembere Valley, it covers vast areas.

There are some stretches of shallow swamp which support wet forest of species which thrive in these conditions. Such swamp forests occur on the lakeshore of the Interlacustrine region, and also in the valleys of the highlands in the same region. More extensive, however, are the swamps with herbaceous plant communities, consisting especially of monocotyledonous species. These swamp communities look very similar to parallel types in Europe, and some of the species are actually identical. An example is *Phragmites australis*, the common reed, while *Typha latifolia*, the reed-mace, also occurs. However, the most famous swamp plant of the area, dominant over considerable areas of Uganda, and further down the Nile valley, is *Cyperus papyrus*, the papyrus-sedge, after which paper is named.

The main value of swamps to East Africans is as sources of fish, although most of the catch in many areas comes from the open water of the lakes, beyond their swamp fringe. Locally, swamp forest provides wood, for fuel and construction; and some groups of Ganda especially value the insect-resistant wood of *Podocarpus usambarensis* (variety *dawei*) from the Lake Victoria swamps.[5] No East African people is entirely confined to a swamp-habitat, but there are some Vinza, in the Malagarasi Swamps, who spend most of their lives in canoes, and rely on fishing for a livelihood.

Fishing is important also for most of the peoples along the coast, but the narrow belt of strictly sea-coast vegetation, between the low-tide line and the land communities, provides rather little compared to fishing and farming. Coral rock provides building stone and lime; salt is obtained by evaporating sea-water; but the only major product from the vegetation is the wood of the mangrove trees. There are three distinct types of sea-coast vegetation : of sea cliffs; of dunes; and of salt-marsh. The salt-marsh communities are dominated by species of the highly specialized and distinctive mangroves, such as the genera *Avicennia*, *Rhizophora*, and *Sonneratia*.

As has been stressed already, these communities of coast, swamp and high mountains have relatively little significance in the distribution of ethnic groups. On the other hand, it is clear that the four major complexes correspond remarkably closely, although not absolutely, with the distribution of the regions and sub-regions. The dryest areas are almost all in the Horn region, and the next dryest in the Eastern Rift Coast region. *Miombo* woodland coincides with the lowland areas of the Southern Savanna; and lowland wet forest used to cover the plateau sub-regions of the Interlacustrine region, except for the Dry Zone. Highland wet forest occurs in four regions within East Africa, and is an important factor in the internal differentiation of the regions into sub-regions. At the same time, it needs to be stressed that the eastern shore of Lake Victoria belongs vegetationally with the Interlacustrine region but culturally with the Eastern Rift Coast; while the Turkana belong vegetationally with the Horn but culturally to the Savanna and Eastern Rift Coast regions. There are more factors at work than the response of people to their physical habitats.

2. Notes

1. A detailed account of the vegetation and soils of East Africa can be found in E. M. Lind and M. E. S. Morrison (1974). "East African Vegetation".
   To their account I owe the identification of important species mentioned in this summary of the vegetation.
2. Before farming spread into the coastal zone, lowland wet forest probably covered an extensive area there, and relict-patches of it persist on the coast of Kenya (Map 4) as well as on the lower slopes of the Usambara, Unguru and Uluguru mountains. An estimation of the extent of this coastal wet forest in *c.* 1000 B.C. is given in Map 5. At the present time dry woodland covers most of this area.
3. The term savanna has been used to mean variously grassland, parkland, dry woodland and thicket, all within the tropics. It is used here to refer

to the two blocks, northern and southern, of the tropical dry woodland complex in Africa. Grassland, parkland, dry woodland and thicket are all types belonging to the complex.

4. Lind and Morrison (1974), op. cit., pp. 201, 205, and quoting Lawton (1963, 1972).

Although relicts of lowland wet forest survive in the *miombo* woodland of northern Zambia, it is very doubtful if either there or in Tanzania the *miombo* areas would be under wet forest even if there had been no shifting cultivation and burning, since climatic conditions are now much too dry for the maintenance of this type except where ground-water is unusually abundant.

5. Lind and Morrison (1974), op. cit., p. 53, quoting Dawe (1906).

3

The Horn of Africa Peoples

Distinctive Features of the Region

To the north-east of the plateau of East Africa the region of the Horn stretches away towards the Gulf of Aden and Arabia. Most of the area and population of this region lie well outside East Africa, but all the north-east, and most of the east, of Kenya are inhabited by Oromo[1] and Soomaali groups who constitute the most south-westerly peoples of the Horn region (Maps 8, 9). As has been described in the preceding chapter, the landscapes of the Horn are dominated by desert vegetation, with the trees and bushes well scattered, or else by very dry woodland. Flat-topped *Acacia* species are abundant and conspicuous in both desert and dry woodland plant communities.

The cover of trees and shrubs is denser along the courses of the streams, most of which are dry for most or all of the year, although there is water underground in their beds. Broadly the amount, and reliability, of the rainfall decrease from south to north; and it is only in the south that there are rivers which flow for all of the year. The three major water courses with a perennial flow are the Shebeli, Juba and Tana, and the abundance of ground-water in their valleys, derived from the highlands of the interior, allows the growth of a distinctive vegetation. Trees and other plant species typical of the wetter parts of East Africa, for instance river valleys of the Southern Savanna, grow well in these valleys of the Horn; and at one time, before intensive human occupation of the valleys, they must have supported dense woodland of a type where most of the trees shed their leaves in the dry season. At the present time, however, only small patches, or isolated plants, of the spontaneous vegetation survive. Most of the valleys' area is either cultivated, or is reverting to

c

scrub or woodland after cultivation. In the twentieth century, as in the period when the woodland cover was still complete, these areas are vegetationally outliers of the less dry vegetation types of East Africa, and the same applies to some of the area between the lower Juba and the lower Shebeli, including the plateau of Isha Baidoa and the country called, by Soomaali, the Doi.

Not surprisingly, over most of the region population is sparse, but there is a conspicuous concentration of people in the lower reaches of the three main river valleys, and in the country between the lower Juba and the lower Shebeli. Over most of the region the people are nomadic pastoralists, who either grow no crops at all, or else snatch a quick crop from a favourable site after rain. In the more densely peopled areas, however, most individuals cultivate; although in the Juba–Shebeli area there is an intricate intermixture, and interdependence, of cultivators and pastoralists.

The key to the survival and activities of the pastoral groups are their camels, without which most of them could not live as they do. Pastoralists also keep goats, sheep and donkeys. Both pastoralists and cultivators highly prize horses, as do all the desert peoples of the Near East and North Africa, but horses are difficult to keep, scarce, and concentrated in the cultivated areas. In these areas too are many of the herds of cattle of the region, and the cultivators also keep chickens, as well as sheep and goats.

The main cultivated crops are :

Maize (*Zea mays*)
Sorghum   (*Sorghum bicolor*)
Bulrush-millet (*Pennisetum typhoides*)
Finger-millet   (*Eleusine coracana*)
Common beans   (*Phaseolus vulgaris*)
Hyacinth-beans   (*Lablab niger*)
Ground-nuts   (*Arachis hypogaea*)
Cassava   (*Manihot esculenta*)
Sweet potatoes   (*Ipomoea batatas*)
Onions   (*Allium cepa*)
Tomatoes (*Lycopersicon esculentum*)
Pumpkins (*Cucurbita* spp.)
Bananas (*Musa* cvs)[2]
Pawpaws   (*Carica papaya*)
Sugar-cane   (*Saccharum officinarum*)

Cotton   (*Gossypium herbaceum*)
Sesame   (*Sesamum indicum*)

In addition to these crops, the northern coast of the region, like southern
Arabia nearby, has been for more than three millennia a main source of
incense for the Near East. Myrrh and frankincense are still gathered from
the wild trees and shrubs of this coast, and so is gum arabic.

Over most of the area, where the vast majority of people are pastoralists, the rights to land tenure are concentrated on the possession of
reliable water-holes and upon access to areas of especially fine grazing.
The areas occupied by different groups are large, ill defined, shifting,
and frequently fiercely contested. Rights to land for cultivation are here
of no importance. When crops are planted, it is only where conditions
are temporarily suitable, and the individuals who sowed the crops, if
they are not disturbed beforehand, reap them, and then move on. By
contrast, in the cultivation areas, rights to land for cultivation are
important, and clearly defined, and land tenure is more complex than
for the pastoralists of the dry areas. Some cultivating groups are independent, owning their land, but others are dependents, their land belonging to neighbouring groups, to whom they are attached as tenants and
share croppers.

The pattern of societies in the Juba–Shebeli area is thus intricate, since
there are independent cultivating groups, independent pastoralist groups
and also interconnected cultivator groups and pastoralist groups, where
the cultivators are dependent upon the pastoralists, and vice versa. In
the lower Tana valley, however, the Pokomo cultivators are at present
independent of their Bararetta and Soomaali pastoralist neighbours.

Social patterns are complicated still further by the presence in some
areas of endogamous castes, each with a specialized occupation. Some
are castes of smiths, others of hunters. These castes are not autonomous
but clients of either pastoralist or cultivator groups. The one people of
the region with a strong claim to being an autonomous hunter-gatherer
group are the "Sanye", but these, whatever their earlier status, are now
clients of the Bararetta. It is important to stress that these societies with
castes are not caste systems like those of India or, more simply, of
Rwanda, since most of the people involved do not belong to castes at all.
There is, however, a very close analogy between some of these Juba–
Shebeli societies and Hasaniya, "Tuareg" and Tuda–Daza societies in
the Sahara, where pastoralists own the land, cultivators work it as their

clients, and there are specialized caste groups, including smiths and hunters. The Saharan societies are, however, more aristocratic in outlook than those of the Horn, with the subordination of cultivators to pastoralists less ambiguously asserted than it is in the Juba–Shebeli area.

Away from the few city-states, the units of loyalty of the Horn are small, usually no more than two or three hundred people at the most. In the settled areas, before European administration, raiding and counter-raiding were on a local scale, except when pastoralists swept in from the desert, which was rather often. Pastoralists' conflicts were, and frequently still are, on a much more ambitious scale, the speed of movement provided by their camels enabling war-leaders to build up widespread alliances against their enemies, alliances, however, which disintegrated soon after they were formed.

Throughout the region people use an elaborate genealogical idiom, relating one local group to another by way of remembered ancestors, who themselves share common ancestors. All the pastoralist Soomaali indeed claim to be descended from a single ancestor, Soomaal. Although there is no justification for assuming that these genealogies are complete or historically accurate, they do contain some historical records, and they are a conspicuous and idiosyncratic feature of the region's culture. The genealogical idiom, indeed, is uncommon in the other regions of East Africa, but it links the peoples of the Horn to other desert camel-nomads of the NANE Major Region. Arabian Badawin and the peoples of the Sahara also relate one local group to another by way of the genealogies of their respective ancestors. In the Horn, as in Arabia and the Sahara, assumed kinship does not preclude violent raids and reprisals. The pastoralist Soomaali, for example, are notorious for their vengeful quarrels.

In the cultivated areas settlement is dispersed, the houses scattered among the fields, but the pastoralists live in nucleated settlements, albeit temporary and frequently moved. Larger, and much more permanent, are the city-states of the coast, such as Mogadishu, and of the Juba Valley, such as Lugh. Their elaborate centralized government is in striking contrast to the rural peoples who live near them, and to the pastoralists of the dry country; and they represent the penetration of the large societies of the Near East into the Horn.

Castes have been mentioned already. A further feature of social organization among the peoples of the Horn are age-sets. These will be mentioned again in the context of the Eastern Rift Coast region. Age-sets are established when all the men of an area who are initiated together form a group who recognize their common membership in one community or club throughout their lives. Some other men belong to age-sets formed earlier, and these are senior to them, while yet other men belong to later formed, and junior, age-sets. All adult men belong to an age-set even if they have to wait until middle age to fully join theirs. Age-sets are confined to the more southerly peoples of the Horn, the Oromo and the Soomaali groups who live near them. Most, or all, of these southern Soomaali are descended in part from Oromo ancestors, and derive their age-sets from their Oromo past. The original Soomaali, in the northern highlands of the Horn, probably had age-sets, which were subsequently lost.

Associated with age-sets is the circumcizing of men, the central act of initiation into an age-set being circumcision. All men, however, throughout the Horn, are circumcized, even where there are no age-sets, and they were probably circumcized long before any of them professed to be Muslims, although the first Muslims on the northern coast may date from as early as the seventh century A.D., i.e. the first century A.H.[3]

Throughout the region too, women have the clitoris cut out. This practice, clitoridectomy, is probably a deliberate analogue to the circumcision of men, a way of showing the equivalence, and symmetry, of the two sexes. It probably also serves as an initiation aimed to make the women more completely female, by eliminating the part of their genitals which looks like, and is, a small penis. Clitoridectomy is an old practice in areas near to the Red Sea, and has spread from there widely with the propagation of Islam. Apart from its distribution in the dry quarter of East Africa, clitoridectomy is also widespread in West Africa, predating Islam in both areas.

Outside Africa and the Muslim world, the practice crops up again among the Conibo, and neighbouring peoples of the Ucayali valley, in Amazonian Peru. Like circumcision, clitoridectomy seems to have more than one centre of origin.

A more localized and unusual feature than clitoridectomy is the practice called infibulation, normal among the Soomaali, and among their northern neighbours the Afar and Saho. When girls are at about the age of puberty not only is the clitoris cut out but the lips of the vulva are sewed together by an older woman, leaving a hole large enough only for the escape of urine and of the menstrual discharge. This opening is enlarged when the girl is married, and enlarged further just before the birth of her first child. Presumably, infibulation was originally designed to prevent premarital copulation, and would thus be an extreme expression of that high valuation of virginity, and of female chastity in general, which is characteristic of the peoples of the Near East and of the Mediterranean Basin.

Another feature of the Horn region also occurs again further southwest in the dry quarter of East Africa, and this is a widespread aversion to eating fish. People in the coastal city-states, and in areas very near to them, are exceptions to this rule, but this only emphasizes the alien nature of the city-states, with their elaborate administrations and immigrant languages. In many ways they have been, at least until the twentieth century, outposts of the urban Near East.

In the more southerly cities some of these alien elements are Bantu languages: Tikuu, close to Swahili, in Mogadishu, Merca, Brava and Kismayu; and Amu, a dialect of Swahili, in the Lamu archipelago. Since this group of Bantu languages pretty certainly arose in the east of what is now Tanzania,[4] the presence of some of its members on the coast of the Horn implies strong trade links coast-wise in earlier centuries, presumably between the eleventh and the sixteenth, possibly earlier. Another Bantu language is spoken by the Pokomo in the lower Tana valley, but these can be treated as part of the Eastern Rift Coast region. The vast majority of the people of the Horn speak languages of the Cushitic sub-family of the Afro-Asiatic family, which links them culturally with the peoples of the Near East and North Africa. In the south-west of the Horn, Oromo is spoken. North of this, and in most of the region, the language is Soomaali; and in the north are Afar and Saho.

The region can be divided into three sub-regions:

1. the Afar–Saho;
2. the Soomaali;
3. the Oromo–Soomaali.

The first occupies the extremely dry and hot plains and foothills between the Ethiopian Highlands and the Red Sea. By comparison with this barren habitat the Soomaali sub-region is moderately productive, at least according to the standards of Horn pastoralists. It stretches from the hills bordering the Gulf of Aden southwards to the valley of the Shebeli. From this valley to the country of the Sambur and Kamba, in the Eastern Rift Coast region, is the third sub-region, where Soomaali are

in the process of absorbing Oromo, who thus eventually themselves become Soomaali. The central and southern sub-regions of the Horn are
distinguished from each other partly by the transformation of Oromo
into Soomaali in the southern area, and also by the large area of cultivated land in this sub-region, between the lower Juba and the lower
Shebeli.

In the course of the last four hundred years one of the major processes
in the Horn has been the expansion of the Soomaali at the expense of the
Oromo; and there is every indication that this process is continuing. It
has not, however, affected Oromo groups in the wet Ethiopian Highlands, a habitat to which Soomaali have not spread.

Although the Oromo of the south-western Horn would not admit any
inferiority to the Soomaali, the speed at which one group after another
have become Soomaali betrays an implicit recognition, at least among
some of them, of Soomaali precedence. In the north the Afar are not
similarly impressed, and there has been no corresponding advance of the
Soomaali language, and identity, into the Red Sea lowlands. West of
the Afar, the Saho include some groups at least which have been impressed by the Tigrinya-speaking Ethiopians. For example, the Irob
group of Saho profess to be Christians. In day-to-day events, however,
more important than the prestige-relations between language groups are
those between small local loyalty groups. Pastoral communities, as has
been noted, can move swiftly, and achieve dramatic military successes.
However, even though such expanding and successful groups may increase
rapidly in numbers, by absorbing clients from their less successful neighbours and rivals, very soon both the demands of widespread distribution,
for the sake of grazing, and the rancour of internecine feuds, often
focussed on grazing rights, splinter the new agglomeration into two or
more sub-groups. Soon also, if not at the time, the new sub-groups
describe themselves in the genealogical idiom : each sub-group are the
descendants of a different son of one father, founder of the original
group, which sub-divided. Significantly, it is precisely in the least pastoral
area of Soomaali territory, the Juba–Shebeli cultivated area, that one
group of Soomaali, the Rahanwiin, have retained a reputation as "top
people" over a period of several generations. In an area with so many
sedentary cultivators the division of groups has not been so bewilderingly
rapid.

The Oromo–Soomaali Sub-region

It is only this southerly sub-region, with its large numbers of sedentary Soomaali, which needs to be considered in more detail. Most of its area is dry country, with desert or dry woodland cover, but it includes the relatively well-watered Juba–Shebeli cultivated area, and also the lower Tana valley. The Pokomo and their neighbours here are very close culturally to the Giryama and other peoples of the Nyika, and are best treated as belonging to the Coast sub-region of the Eastern Rift Coast region. Nevertheless, they are in very intimate contact with the Bararetta group of Oromo, mostly now in the dry country west of the river-valley, and with the pastoralist Soomaali in the dry country to the east. In the lower Tana area the NANE and African Major Cultural Regions meet and interdigitate closely.

Between the lower Tana valley and the cultivated areas of the coast peoples, and of the Kamba, is the dry territory of the Bararetta pastoralists. These also occur in smaller numbers east of the Tana, but here their country was invaded during the nineteenth century by pastoral Soomaali from the north and north-east, and most of the descendants of the former Bararetta inhabitants now speak Soomaali and have lost their Oromo identity. Near the Bararetta east of the Tana live the "Sanye", hunting-and-gathering people of the dry country, but effectively clients of the Bararetta and absorbed into their societies. They speak Oromo as a second language, and seem to be in process of losing both their language and identity to the Oromo, who are losing theirs to the Soomaali.

North of the Tana valley, and stretching northwards to the foothills of the Ethiopian Highlands, are another group of pastoral Oromo, the Boorana. As with the eastern Bararetta, there is no clear distinction in habitat between themselves and the pastoral Soomaali who are their eastern neighbours, and it is likely that they are in process of being absorbed by the Soomaali, who may well expand to fill all the dry country as far as Lake Rudolf and the Sambur. They may even spread further, into Turkana and Sambur territory. Such an extension of the Soomaali area would involve the camel-herding Rendile, who speak a Cushitic language and occupy the dry country between the Boorana and the Sambur.

Although camels occur in this south-western borderland of the Horn, the most valued herds of the Bararetta and Boorana consist of cattle, and this applies equally to their neighbours the Sambur and Turkana. Although the only sharp breaks in the landscapes of the dry country are Lake Rudolf and the lower Tana valley, the rainfall steadily decreases northwards and eastwards, with the result that Maasai country, although dry, is better watered than Soomaali country, which is marked, away from the rivers, by herds of camels. The cattle herds of the Boorana, Turkana and Sambur are thus living at the margin of their habitat, a situation which becomes more severe with increasing desiccation of the climate and the deterioration of the grazing. Even so, Boorana cattle are well known for their quality to many East Africans. Up to the first decade of this century, Maasai were repeatedly raiding northwards into Boorana country in order to obtain breeding stock with which to improve their own herds; and European farmers in Kenya have crossbred European strains with Boorana animals. The survival of these Boorana herds under the conditions of their habitat, for many generations, has made them peculiarly well adapted to withstanding extreme heat and drought.

In the long run, however, their present pastures may become the grazing of the camel herds of pastoral Soomaali, who occupy the country from the Boorana and Bararetta to the Juba valley. Most of these pastoral groups claim descent from Darod, also claimed as an ancestor by large numbers of groups north of the Shebeli. Such apparent kinship, however, does not imply an absence of raiding for camels, nor a refusal to press rival claims to water-holes and grazing. At the same time there is no one group of these Darod Soomaali acknowledged to be superior in any way to the others, nor to have authority over them.

At the Juba valley there is a change of landscape and of social order. From here to the valley of the Shebeli, in the lower country away from the foothills, cultivating groups are interspersed with pastoral groups, all of them, however, speaking Soomaali. Pastoral groups occupy the dry foothills of the Ethiopian Highlands; and to the north and north-east of the Shebeli is more dry country, reminiscent in its appearance, and in the social organization of its people, of the area west and south of the Juba. Indeed a high proportion of the groups claim descent from Darod, as they do beyond the Juba. With these people north-east of the Shebeli begins the Soomaali sub-region, as here defined.

In the south-west of the Horn, the major distinction is between areas of permanent water in relatively large quantities, and those where water is scarce. The lower Tana valley and the Juba–Shebeli area are very distinct in terms of their scenery and also of their populations. Quite apart from cultural distinctions, the Pokomo cluster of the Tana valley are negroid, unlike the predominantly caucasoid Oromo and Soomaali. In the Juba–Shebeli area also a high proportion of the people show negroid features, although here there are many people with markedly caucasoid features, unlike the Tana valley. It will be necessary later to discuss the significance of these physical differences.

Above the pastoral Soomaali of the dry foothills live the Arsi, a major group of Oromo, their habitat grassland and scrub in the higher areas, where the country would presumably support highland forest, were it not for human clearance. Most of them cultivators, they belong in the Ethiopian Highland region, but some of them are pastoralists and live in dry woodland areas below the wet hills, and similar to the habitat of the nearby pastoral Soomaali. To the south-west of the Arsi, and where the rift valley comes out of the Highlands, are a number of small groups of cultivators, "Bambala", Konso, "Gowaze", "Gardulla" and "Gidole". They speak Cushitic languages, and live on the hills just above the dry country of the Boorana. With the Arsi, they belong in the Ethiopian Highlands region.

It has been necessary already to mention the old-established city-states of the coast. Those of the north, for instance Berbera, have considerable numbers of Arabians in their population, while those of the south, along with their Soomaali inhabitants, have large groups of people speaking Bantu languages. Along the coast called by Europeans in the eighteenth and nineteenth centuries the Benadir Coast, the city-states of Mogadishu, Merca, Brava and Kismayu are the homes of Tikuu, while, further south, the people of Lamu speak a dialect of Swahili. All these city-states are evidence of the trade between the Horn and various parts of the Near East. There are other cities, with similar backgrounds, further south in the Eastern Rift Coast and Southern Savanna regions; and all of them will be considered together in the next chapter.

Before the involvement of the various peoples of the Horn in European administration, the city-states were the most elaborately ordered societies of the region. Most of the people, however, belonged either to autonomous sedentary settlements, if they were cultivators, or else to autonomous pastoral bands, their settlements shifting with their flocks and herds. Despite the elaboration of administration in modern Somalia, Ethiopia and Kenya, these small local groups are still largely autonomous. As has been indicated already, one local group would ally with another, or others, for purposes of defence and attack. Furthermore, one group would become the client of another, and such links of clientage persist at the present time. In addition, there are slaves, attached to both sedentary and nomadic groups; and these slaves still retain their social status despite the refusal of the governments of the area to officially recognize slavery.

A further important social distinction is the status of people who belong to endogamous castes, most of them associated with either hunting or iron working. The Midgan and Yibir are widespread castes among the Soomaali, attached as clients to both cultivating and pastoral groups. They combine hunting with leather working. Similar to them are the Ribi attached to Rahanwiin groups in the Juba–Shebeli area; and the Rahanwiin groups also have as clients the Musa Deryo caste, who specialize in making baskets. Another caste attached to a restricted number of Soomaali groups are the Ga'ansibir, iron-workers found among those Marehan communities who live west of the Juba. (Marehan are classic camel-pastoralists, who claim descent from Darod, and are represented both west of the Juba and north-east of the Shebeli.) More widespread among the Soomaali are the Tumal, also smiths, and found as clients of various groups.[5]

The pattern just outlined of pastoral and cultivating communities, of slaves and castes, and of city-states, refers at present to the Soomaali. The Bararetta and the Boorana consist of localized, although often widely dispersed, communities of pastoralists, with recognized castes of hunters and smiths, and also with some slaves.

These Oromo peoples, the Boorana and Bararetta, however, are the remnants of a once extensive area of dry country Oromo pastoralists, progressively absorbed by the Soomaali. Most of the Soomaali of the present south-western sub-region presumably have ancestors who were Oromo; and at the time when the peoples of the Juba–Shebeli area were Oromo they probably exhibited the social complexity now occurring among the Soomaali of that area. These Juba–Shebeli people have a class system, since there are freemen and slaves, but, although the senior member of a senior local lineage, within the genealogical idiom, is accorded some respect, there is no aristocracy. With the elaboration of administration, however, under European governments, and with independence in Somalia and Kenya, a Soomaali elite is now forming. The Soomaali then have a class system of sorts, but with castes in addition.

Over a period of centuries, however, the pattern of small local communities has been complicated by attempts on the part of some rulers of city-states to incorporate neighbouring peoples, cultivators and pastoralists, into their centralized system of government. The most ambitious, and widely known, example of such an attempt was that of Ahmad Grañ in the sixteenth century, whose base was the city of Zeila and the territory of the coast called Adal. Although he involved great numbers of pastoralists, probably Afar, Oromo and Soomaali, in attacks far into the Ethiopian Highlands, the pastoralists became independent again, each community playing its own hand, and Zeila sank back to its earlier status as an autonomous city, with only a small area of jurisdiction in its immediate vicinity. A similar separation of city and surrounding peoples occurred after attempts in the nineteenth century by ambitious and zealous Soomaali war-leaders to extend the authority of Lugh and Bardera in the Juba valley.

Although the social systems of the Soomaali are complex by comparison with those of, say, the Maasai, and of other peoples in the Eastern Rift Coast region, they are, like these, essentially a large number of autonomous local communities, with a few city-states scattered among them. The Soomaali systems lack the scale and elaboration shown by the Interlacustrine states, and especially by the largest of them, in the period 1870–1900. Despite the apparent complexity, there are constant features in the shifting patterns of alliance and re-alignment, and these constant features provide a sure guide to the more fluid elements. City-states, cultivators and pastoralists are always present, although the links between them are repeatedly changing, while the caste groups are always clients, and never patrons.

The social systems of the city-states will be considered in the next chapter. They are more complex than those of the cultivators and pastoralists, among whom there is little social specialization. Priests are usually hereditory, members of special descent-groups with a long tradition of providing priests to their local communities. Furthermore, the priests are part-time specialists, engaging in either pastoral or cultivating work to earn most of their living. In the same way, the medical specialists are part-time, and are indistinguishable from other people, apart from the occasions when they are specifically engaged in diagnosis and cure. Informal war-leaders, who planned and carried out raids, have also been important, more so in the period before 1930 than they are at present, when central government restraints on raiding have become more effective.

Success in raiding, for cattle and camels, as well as for revenge killings, has been one criterion of overall prosperity for the peoples of the Horn, who are also concerned with the usual human requirements of an adequate food supply, good health and the birth of numerous children. Prosperity is under the control of God, who equally commands disaster, sometimes as a punishment for the wickedness of specific people. Although God is in overall control, there are other superhuman powers in operation. These take the form of spirits associated with uninhabited places, and some of which at least are seen by the people as manifestations of God Himself. In addition, people who are dead sometimes return as ghosts to trouble the living.

The Soomaali are unlike the other peoples of the sub-region in that all of them claim to be Muslims. Among other groups Muslims are very few; and among all of the peoples of the Horn there are very few who claim to be Christians. Being Muslim does not differentiate Soomaali very markedly from their non-Muslim neighbours, although many of them pray regularly, and they attend rituals at which the officiants are specifically Muslim. In many groups, the position of *qadi*, or Muslim ritual specialist, is hereditary, just as the priests were in the pre-Muslim period, and as priests still are among the Boorana and Bararetta. Indeed it is very likely that many of these families of *qadi* are the direct descendants of the priestly lineages of the earlier period. Furthermore, in many ways the modern Bararetta and Boorana must be similar in their ritual practices to the Soomaali of their pre-Muslim era, but there is no evidence that the early Soomaali, or their Afar neighbours, had age-sets which were as important to them as they now are to the Oromo groups of the Horn.

Neither the Boorana nor the Bararetta admit to being inferior to anybody, despite the claims to superiority of their pastoral Soomaali neighbours. At the same time the absorption of Oromo into the Soomaali in the past suggests the recognition of Soomaali pre-eminence, and such absorption is probably still going on where Soomaali and Oromo meet. Furthermore, the Boorana reckon themselves superior to the Rendile, and so do the Sambur, on the other side of Rendile country. In this case, the Rendile seem to half-accept the superiority of their two neighbours. Further south, the Bararetta look down on the Pokomo in the Tana valley, and this sense of superiority is shared by the pastoral Soomaali in the area east of the valley. Indeed throughout the Horn pastoralists rate themselves, and are rated by others, as being at the top of the prestige hierarchy, while pastoralists and cultivators alike rate the caste groups and slaves at the bottom. This social classification, however, cuts across the classification by ethnic groups.

Side by side with the rival claims of these groups, and the hierarchy of pastoralists, cultivators and castes, the cultivating Soomaali of the Juba–Shebeli area recognize the superior prestige of the Rahanwiin groups. By contrast, among the pastoral Soomaali, who are in any case spread over a vast area, the prestige attached to a particular group at a particular time is usually ephemeral, not only because of the rapidly shifting pattern of alliances, but also because a successful group, which attracts immigrants and clients, soon splits up into two or more groups, under the pressure of grazing needs and internal feuds. Only the name of the founder of such a successful group survives, in a genealogy, as a reminder of the group's former importance.

As has been indicated already, during the nineteenth century, and at earlier periods, some city-states were able to extend their authority over neighbouring groups; and all city-states, however unambitious their rulers, must have enjoyed some precedence in the eyes of their poor, ill-organized neighbours. At the same time, however, the fissiparous tendencies of the local groups, and especially of the highly mobile pastoralists, soon destroyed the larger alliances of the more successful cities.

Throughout this discussion of the peoples of the Horn, it has been necessary to refer to various historical changes. For the sake of clarity, it is convenient at this point to summarize them. For thousands of years most of the peoples of the Horn have been predominantly caucasoid in their physical type, as have neighbouring peoples in the Ethiopian Highlands and in Arabia. Cushitic languages have probably been spoken over the whole of the region since about the time of Christ, and possibly for longer. Although the outlines of events are still vague, because of a lack of archaeological and documentary evidence, the important features can probably be reconstructed. By the time of Christ pastoralists were well established in the dry foothills of the Ethiopian Highlands, and were spreading outwards into the Horn. The introduction of Arabian camels at about this time enabled the pastoralists to become more mobile, and to move into even the dryest areas. By A.D. 1000 the language of the dryest and hottest area of the Horn, near the Red Sea, was Afar; Soomaali was spoken throughout most of the present Soomaali sub-region; and Oromo was the main, and probably almost the only, language of the present Oromo–Soomaali sub-region.

Traders from south Arabia had been visiting the Gulf of Aden coast of the Horn since about 1000 B.C., in order to collect its incense-harvest, and Egyptian visits to that coast date back into the second millennium B.C. However, at that time the local peoples were probably hunters-and-gatherers. The first city-states on the incense coast, founded by Arabian immigrants, were already established by the eleventh century, and must date back to the first millennium A.D. In the south, the city-states of the Benadir Coast date from the tenth century, and perhaps no earlier. They were founded by Arabian immigrants, but soon attracted Swahili, in the wide sense, coastal East Africans from further south. Most pastoral Soomaali claim Arabian founding-ancestors for their lineages, and, although such claims are many of them strictly spurious, and are bids for the prestige of an Arabian ancestry, there must have been numerous Arabian immigrants, and many Soomaali really do have Arabians among their forebears.

The city-states, however, remained very local in their jurisdiction, although between 1527 and 1543 Ahmad Grañ launched a series of formidable raids, from his base in Adal, into the Ethiopian Highlands, during his *jihad*[6] against the states of that region. His efforts failed, however, with his death, and Adal built no lasting empire. When, during the nineteenth century, Soomaali preacher-warriors tried to build up states from the cities of Lugh and Bardera, in the Juba valley, they also failed.

By A.D. 1000, perhaps before the Benadir Coast cities were founded, a steady trickle of migrants had already begun to settle as cultivators in the lower Tana valley. They came from the Nyika area just to the south, where they already carried on hoe-cultivation; they spoke Bantu languages, or just one language, and they were negroid. Probably there were already cultivators in the valley, but they were Oromo and physically caucasoid. In the long run, by hybridization, the negroid features prevailed, and the sheer number of the immigrants, relative to the older settlers, ensured that a Bantu language replaced Oromo, with the result that there was now a sharp contrast between the negroid Bantu-speaking cultivators of the valley and the caucasoid Oromo-speaking pastoralists of the dry country.

Further north, in the Juba–Shebeli area, a similar process occurred at about the same period, around A.D. 1000, but here the results were different. Oromo cultivators were probably in the area before any Bantu-speaking migrants moved up the coast from the south. These settled in some numbers on the more productive land, cultivating by methods familiar to them in the Nyika and the Tana valley, and they intermarried with caucasoids in the area. As a result the population was gradually "blackened", and the effects of the process are still visible, but Oromo continued to be the language of the area, and the language or languages of the immigrants died out. There is no need to assume that the Juba–Shebeli area was ever a Bantu-speaking "island" like the modern lower Tana valley, although such a view has been put forward by Cerulli (1934)[7] and a number of other writers, who do not give enough weight to the fact that in the southern Horn it is the Bantu languages and the negroids who are the newcomers, and not the Oromo, nor Cushitic languages in general. The immigration of Bantu-speaking negroids actually continued into the nineteenth century, although by then most of them were slaves brought from the country of the Zigula, and of other groups in the hinterland of Bagamoyo, imported to the Juba–Shebeli area through the Benadir Coast city-states.

The Oromo language survived the immigrations of the Bantu-speakers in the Juba–Shebeli cultivated area, but it lost ground there to Soomaali, and has now been completely replaced by it. In the seventeenth century, the division of the Horn into three sub-regions, of which the southern was overwhelmingly Oromo, was beginning to change. Soomaali pastoralists were spreading southwards, and Oromo groups were beginning to join them, and to abandon their own identity. This expansion of Soomaali, and incorporation of Oromo, has continued to the present time, resulting in the situation described in this chapter. In the process, infibulation has spread southward, but the Oromo pattern of age-sets has survived in most of the southern sub-region. Northern Soomaali do not have age-sets, although they probably had them at an earlier period of their history. Just before 1850, the most southerly of the expanding Soomaali pastoralists reached the valley of the Tana river, thus coming into contact for the first time with the Pokomo, outliers of the Eastern Rift Coast region.

3. Notes

1. The Oromo are usually called "Galla" by European writers.
2. cvs stands for cultivars, i.e. cultivated varieties.

3. The Muslim era dates from the year in which the Prophet Muhammad fled from Mecca to Yathrib (now Medina), an event dated 622 according to the Christian era. A.H. is Anno Hejirae, by the year of the Flight, Hejira being the term in Arabic for that retirement to Yathrib.

4. M. Guthrie (1971). "Comparative Bantu", Vol. 4, pp. 48–51.

5. I. M. Lewis (1955). "Peoples of the Horn of Africa : Somali, Afar and Saho", pp. 51, 52.

6. Arabic for a war which is morally justified because it is fought in the interests of the Muslim faith.

7. I. M. Lewis (1955), op. cit., pp. 42, 45, 46.

4

The Eastern Rift Coast Peoples

Distinctive Features of the Region

As the name indicates, the region contains the Eastern Rift Valley and the highlands associated with it. From these highlands the land slopes away westward to the shore of Lake Victoria, while, on the east, another, and longer, slope stretches down to the Indian Ocean coast. The highlands are the distinctive features of the landscape, both in relief and vegetation, and they cross the region almost all the way from north to south. In the south they are interrupted by the Gogo plains, while in the north they fall away towards Lake Rudolf, in an area which belongs partially to the Savanna Stateless region (Map 10).

On the north and north-east, and transitional to neighbouring regions, are desert areas, with scattered thorny *Acacia* trees, part of the plant-cover of the Horn of Africa. Similar vegetation extends along the floor of the Rift Valley, and over the long slope from the highlands to the coast. This vegetation of the low areas, however, is continuous, and not therefore desertic, forming a dry woodland in which flat-topped *Acacia* species are prominent. In places, as between Nairobi and Arusha, there are extensive grassy plains, supporting large herds of zebra and wildebeest, and with only scattered trees. These grasslands are probably generated by burning and grazing, as has been indicated earlier.

The highlands, both east and west of the dry Rift Valley floor, are largely covered with cultivated areas, secondary scrub and wet forest. To the west of the highlands the lake-shore has a high rainfall, and in places supports lowland wet forest, but most of this has been cleared for cultivation. The lake-shore belt merges on the north-west into Soga and then Ganda country, which it resembles in vegetation, but not in social organization.

A striking feature of the region is the contrast between the wet and dry areas, with their different types of vegetation. Associated with this contrast, but not entirely coincident with it, is the uneven distribution of population (Map 6). There is a marked concentration of people near the lake-shore, and continuing into Soga and Ganda, in the next region. A second concentration occupies the southern slopes of Mount Kenya and, nearby high country. There is a third concentration on the southern slopes of Mounts Meru and Kilimanjaro, and in the Asu[1]–Shambaa highlands. Smaller concentrations occur at the southern end of the rift highlands, involving the Iraqw,[2] Langi, Rimi,[3] and Ilamba. These concentrations occur either in wet highland areas[4] or else on the wet lake-shore belt. Another concentration, the narrow band hugging the coast, is also in an area of high rainfall.

It will be clear from this summary, and from the map, that most of the region is thinly inhabited. The Maasai plains, for example, which occupy most of the centre of the region, have an estimated density of below three people per square kilometre. In such thinly peopled areas it is possible to travel for days, and gain the impression that no-one lives there at all. Even a flight over these areas in an aircraft often reveals few signs of human habitation.

While stressing the contrast between a few densely peopled "islands" and a "sea" of thinly populated territory, it is necessary to refine the picture and to point out that both types of settlement can be sub-divided. The greatest densities of population, sometimes two hundred and fifty per square kilometre, occur in parts of Gikuyu country and in some areas of Luhya and Luo country. Rimi and Asu areas, for instance, are less densely occupied. At the same time, Gogo and most of Kamba are thinly peopled, but not as thinly as Maasai.

Population distribution is not only partially correlated with rainfall amounts; it is more intimately linked to the land-use and to productivity. The areas of dense population are all occupied by peoples who practise intensive cultivation, doubtless originally through necessity. Cattle-dung is frequently used as manure in these areas, as in Iraqw and Langi, while the Davida,[5] Rwo (Meru), Chaga, Asu and Shambaa irrigate their plots as well as manuring. Furthermore, some of these intensively cultivating groups, the Davida, Chaga and Asu, have terraced their hillsides, a classic method of improving yields from highland soils. Higher reliability of rainfall alone, however, does not support a dense population, and it is conspicuous that the largest concentrations of people occur where the soils are well above the average for fertility. This applies to the alluvial soils of the Luo–Luhya areas on the lake-shore, and to the volcanic soils of Elgon, Kenya, Meru and Kilimanjaro. The other cultivators of the region put much less effort into their tilling of the soil. Gogo and Sandawa, for instance, do not even hoe some of the time but drop the seeds into dibble-holes without any other preparation. It is noticeable that these non-intensive farmers live in areas of lower rainfall or less fertile soil than their more intensive neighbours. In areas of high rainfall, and relatively high reliability, with good soil, extra effort is usually rewarded with extra output, but in the dryer areas of, say, Gogo and Kamba extra effort is usually wasted, because most years are not wet enough for the effort to have an effect on the crop. In these areas, live-stock provide a safer investment than crops.

This tendency, in the dryer areas, away from cultivation towards live-stock, reaches its limit in the groups with herds and flocks, but no crops. The classic example, whose prestige dominates the modern history of the whole region, are the Maasai. In addition, a more localized group, the Datoga,[6] are exclusive pastoralists. Apart from these two peoples, the pastoralists of East Africa live to the north and north-east. They are : the Turkana and their neighbours who are transitional to the Savanna peoples; and the Oromo and Soomaali groups of the Horn, already con-sidered in Chapter 3.

Mention of the Maasai introduces a complication. The language of the Maasai, Maa, is spoken not only by the pastoralists and by their northern representatives, the Sambur, but also by other groups who are not ex-clusive pastoralists. The Baraguyu are non-intensive cultivators as well as keeping animals, while the Arusha are intensive cultivators, growing bananas and coffee. There is even a hunting caste on the Maasai plains who speak the Maa language. Hence, all four modes of livelihood found in the region (outside the towns) are practised by people who speak the language. When I refer to the Maasai I shall mean the pastoral Maasai, and I shall refer to the Sambur separately, by name.

The fourth mode of livelihood has been mentioned in advance. A small number of groups, making up a tiny fraction of the population of the region, live by hunting-and-gathering. Apart from those of the Maasai plains already noted, there are the groups who call themselves Ogiek in the rift highlands of Kenya, and who are usually known by their Swahili name Wandorobo.[7] To the south of them, on the edge of the Eastern Rift Highlands in Tanzania, are the Hadza, of the Lake Eyasi basin.

These four different modes of livelihood form a mosaic, with the different modes occurring close to each other. To take one well known example, in southern Kenya, Ogiek, Maasai, Kamba and Gikuyu live within easy walking distance of each other, and follow each a different livelihood. One important feature that needs to be emphasized, however, is that the vast majority of individuals in the region live by cultivation, either intensive or not.

Without trying to give an exhaustive account of the crops which are the basis of the food supply for these people, it is important to list those which are most in use. The largest quantity of cultivated products consists of cereals, and, for most farmers, these are :

Maize   (*Zea mays*)
Sorghum   (*Sorghum bicolor*)
Bulrush-millet (*Pennisetum typhoides*)
Finger-millet   (*Eleusine coracana*)

Considerable acreages of wheat, barley and oats are also grown, but only by European farmers, or by African farmers who have adopted European farming practices. There is also some irrigated rice (*Oryza sativa*) near the coast. A number of leguminous crops are also important, and are usually grown interspersed with cereals, in the same fields :

Common beans   (*Phaseolus vulgaris*)
Hyacinth-beans (*Lablab niger*)
Cow-peas   (*Vigna sinensis*)
Pigeon-peas   (*Cajanus cajan*)
Ground-nuts   (*Arachis hypogaea*)
Bambara ground-nuts   (*Voandzeia subterranea*)

The other crops which are much cultivated are :

Cassava   (*Manihot esculenta*)
Sweet potatoes   (*Ipomoea batatas*)
Onions   (*Allium cepa*)
Tomatoes (*Lycopersicon esculentum*)
Pumpkins   (*Cucurbita maxima, C. mixta, C. moschata*)
Bananas (*Musa* cvs)
Coffee (*Coffea arabica*)
Castor   (*Ricinus communis*)
Sugar-cane   (*Saccharum officinarum*)
Tobacco   (*Nicotiana tabacum*)

Although a few mango-, pawpaw- and guava-trees can be seen in various places, fruit trees are rather rare.

The main domestic animals, apart from dogs, are cattle, goats and, a relatively few, sheep, as well as chickens. Apart from these, there are cats, of very little productive importance, and some occasional exotic domestic forms, such as Muscovy ducks and turkeys.

Most of the cultivating groups have cereals as their staple crop or crops, but on Mounts Meru and Kilimanjaro and in the Shambaa highlands the staple is bananas, that is cooking-bananas or plantains. This feature links these mountain slopes agriculturally to: the Nyakyusa hills in the Southern Savanna region; Soga and Ganda in the Interlacustrine region; and even to the distant Wet Forest region in the Congo Basin. However, there are no special cultural connections between these areas with banana staples.

Despite the great differences in density of population the whole region is marked by dispersed settlement, rather than nucleated villages, the difference being that in the densely peopled parts settlements are contiguous with each other over wide areas, whereas in the thinly populated parts of the region settlements are far from each other. There are, however, some instances of nucleated settlement. Conspicuous among them are the towns, such as Nairobi and Arusha, but there are also smaller concentrations, usually centred on a few shops run by Indians. The Maasai, too, show a form of nucleation because their settlements are arranged around the cattle compound, and hence are compact, but frequently moved.

Almost all the region has been marked by very small units of local loyalty, each comprising a settlement or a few settlements together. Social specialization has been slight, and it still is outside the towns. The conspicuous exceptions to this pattern in earlier centuries have been the city-states on the coast: Lamu, just in the Horn, Malindi, and Mombasa. Here, by contrast with most of the peoples of the region, long before 1800 there was centralized administration, taxation and heads of state, together with a considerable degree of social specialization. However, these city-states were in many ways outposts of the Near East rather than major features of East Africa.

The whole region is marked off from neighbouring regions to the west and south by the circumcision of the men, and by the excision of the clitoris among the women. At least some groups of Maasai, and some groups of Gogo, practise a more elaborate form of excision, cutting off the labia minora as well as the clitoris. Both circumcision and clitoridectomy are normal among the peoples of the Horn, as we have seen already, and it is as certain as can be, in the absence of historical documents, that both practices have spread into the region from the Horn, an event which must be examined further in Chapter 11. Also, before 1940 age-sets for the men occurred throughout the region, although at the present time they have faded out among most groups.

A final distinctive feature of the Eastern Rift Coast region has been mentioned already. Much of the dry centre of the region is occupied, although sparsely, by the Maasai, who have been central not only physically but also morally in the history of this area. Although always relatively few in numbers, the Maasai have been at the top of the prestige-pyramid of the region, without competitors, for some time, up to the period within living memory. In the last three decades, or slightly more, considerable numbers of their former admirers have found an alternative lode of admiration in the Europeans, with the new lures of money-earning jobs and, for some, executive power. However, Maasai prestige is still high in rural areas, that is, among most people of the region, and some awe for them may lurk in many of their ostensible denigrators among the elite. The theme of Maasai prestige will recur at different points in the next few chapters. At this stage it is only necessary to say that they have represented an ideal, exclusive pastoralism, without dirtying one's hands with hoeing, to which many farmers aspire, but which is excluded for most by the demands of survival, and therefore of a more mixed economy. The city-states along the coast, because of their organized power, must have enjoyed some local prestige; and the prestige and cultural impact of the Swahili increased in the nineteenth century as their caravans, and firearms, penetrated into the interior. Even so, the Maasai are the culturally dominant people of the region, so much so that, were it not for its invidious sound in the present political situation, the whole region could be called the Maasai region.

There are five sub-regions:

1. the Coast;
2. the Dry Plains;
3. the Wet Highlands;
4. the Wet Highlands Transition;
5. the Lake-shore.

These are not very different from each other in most features of culture, but are separated in terms of habitat and associated livelihood. The wet highlands, however, are further divided, because those nearer the coast have been affected by the traditions of kings, deriving from the Southern Savanna region.

The Coast Sub-region

To the east of the Maasai is the low-lying area near to the coast which is called, by European writers, the Nyika. It is an area of dry woodland, of repeated droughts and of sparse surface-water. Away from the coast itself population is thin. To the north-east the country becomes progressively dryer as it merges into the deserts of the Horn. On this coast the few rivers, rising in the wet highlands of the interior, are marked by the cultivated areas and occasional relict-patches of gallery forest which occur along their banks. The main river of the sub-region is the Galana, but to the north-east, in Oromo country, and in the Horn region, the Tana river forms an outlier of the Nyika, a thread of woodland and cultivated land through the desert. The Pokomo, in the lower Tana valley, are culturally akin to the peoples of the Nyika; and the archipelago of Lamu, just north-east of the Tana mouth, is another, but very different, outlier.

The difference between Pokomo and Lamu is an example of a striking contrast which characterizes the sub-region as a whole. Scattered along the coast there are rare, but significant, city-states, which have been mentioned already: Lamu, Malindi and Mombasa. Their wealth, organization and cosmopolitan contacts have contrasted strongly, over a period of seven centuries, or more, with the peoples who live over most of the Nyika area. These are cultivators, with very little social specialization.

The Pokomo are very distinct because they contrast with the Horn peoples who surround them, and to whom they were recently subject as clients. Their patrons were desert nomads, mostly caucasoid in physical type, while the Pokomo group are negroid in type, cultivators, and confined to a strictly circumscribed habitat, the land near the available water of the river. Here is an area where race, culture, livelihood and habitat neatly coincide, a rare event in East Africa.

Between the Pokomo and Oromo, in the north-east, and the Bondei, who are transitional to the next region southward, a number of groups are distributed along the coastal lowlands, among them the Giryama, Duruma, Rabai and Digo. These groups differ little among themselves in culture, and speak a single language.[8] The peoples of the city-states of Lamu, Malindi and Mombasa, although strikingly different from the coastal group in some ways, are connected to them through those rural populations of the coast, such as the majority of the Digo, who profess to be Muslim, although in most of their features they resemble other coastal peoples. Near the sea rainfall is higher, and the communities of this narrow zone make heavy use of coconut palms, which grow well on the coral-sands of the coast. In addition, they rely heavily on fish, which have been shunned till recently by most peoples of the region.

Although all coastal people who are Muslims are sometimes in East Africa referred to as Swahili, the term is used in a narrower sense of people who speak Swahili as their first language. More precisely, and more realistically, they must be divided into three: the Lamu group, speaking Amu (Kiamu); the Mombasa group, speaking Mvita (Kimvita); and the southern group, speaking Unguja (Kiunguja) and related dialects.

In order to appreciate the context of the city-states it is necessary to look further afield than the Coast sub-region. In the first place, Swahili is the principal language of other city-states and coastal areas beyond this sub-region. Unguja is the language of the islands of Pemba and Zanzibar,[9] just south of the Nyika, and also spoken on the neighbouring coast around Bagamoyo and Dar-es-Salaam. It is also the language of Kilwa, well to the south and on the coast of the Southern Savanna region. All these cities, strung out along the East African coast, are part of the changing patterns of trade in the Indian Ocean.

For a period of centuries, and probably for over two thousand years, people from Arabia, Iran and the west coast of India have visited the East African coast. Since the twelfth century at least ivory and black slaves have been big attractions to these traders, and since that time there have certainly been cities along the coast.[10] With the nineteenth-century increase in Indian Ocean commerce, coastal trade expanded into the East African interior, and in 1840 Sultan Sayyid Said of Oman moved his capital to Zanzibar. The cosmopolitan character of this new capital is exemplified by his bodyguard, most of whom were from Baluchistan, and by the financiers of the caravan-trade, most of whom were Gujarati, from the west coast of India.

It was Swahili who spoke Unguja who were most involved in the nineteenth-century penetration of the interior, and their dialect has become Swahili par excellence. It has given rise to a form which is spoken as far afield as Ganda and the eastern Congo Basin. Zanzibaris refer to this lingua franca of the interior, contemptuously, as Kibara, the language of the outback, of the upcountry. Not only have the East African city-states been linked for centuries, by trade, to other parts of the Indian

Ocean coast, outside Africa, but their links extended on the African coast to outside the area so far considered. In the north, there were other similar trading city-states on the coast of the Horn, such as Mogadishu; and, further south, by the fifteenth century, Swahili lived and traded at the city of Sofala, beyond the mouth of the Zambezi,[11] where the gold from the Rhodesian Plateau came out to the coast. By this time too they were trading with the people of the Comoro Islands, who were themselves already settled on the north-west coast of Madagascar, where many still live. The coasts from the Horn to Madagascar are thus all part of the history of the city-states. At the same time, in the period from the twelfth to the nineteenth centuries, these city-states were more like the extremity of the Near Eastern area than an outgrowth of the activities of the peoples of the Nyika, or further south.

Prior to their incorporation into wider, European, administrations, each city-state was self governing, although there was constant jostling for position in a league table of prestige, and some of the cities tried to gain, and retain, hegemony over others. For example, Kilwa's rulers, in the period from the twelfth to the fifteenth century, tried, possibly successfully, to hold Sofala as a satellite, and thus to monopolize the gold supply from the interior.[12] Each city-state had a ruler, who would be styled a governor by any ruler of another city who had pretensions to over-rule. These rulers behaved much like the kings of African states, or like the rulers of Near Eastern states. They were advised, flattered or dominated by councils, while the city was administered by a hierarchy of officials, whose most vital task was collecting the taxes, for which trading activities formed the readiest source. The city-government also provided a system of law-courts, with the ruler as ultimate court of appeal, and judicial business was conducted, in theory at least, according to Muslim practice.

To outsiders, and to East Africans also, one of the striking features of these coastal city-states was their formal submission to Muslim obedience. Mosques were, and are, striking features of their landscapes, and the Muslim festivals, for instance Ramadhan, are kept regularly. However, on the coast, as throughout the officially Muslim regions of the world, there is a great contrast between degrees of Muslim conviction within the population.[13] On the one hand, there have been the divines, officials and scholars, usually all the same people, and some of the rulers, who have prayed regularly, given alms, gone on pilgrimage, and directed their personal conduct with regard to divinely revealed morals. On the other hand, the great majority of people in the cities, and almost all of the rural professing Muslims, behave, and always have, much like the pagan population of the Nyika area. They make some deference to Ramadhan, however token, they rarely abstain from beer when it is available, and they pay great attention to their ancestors, and to spirits of the bush, even though they now call these *mashetani*, devils. Historically, they have been marked off by wearing a Near Eastern style of clothing, and by their submission to self-proclaimed Muslim rulers in the cities, whose stone architecture is observably of Near Eastern origin.

In striking contrast to the organization of the city-states are the coastal and Pokomo groups. Among them loyalties are extremely localized, each settlement being autonomous. The only social specialization at the time of first contact with Europeans, in the nineteenth century, was the common pattern of: informal war-leaders, hereditary priests, medical specialists and smiths. None of these specialized figures was full-time. The central rituals were, and for most of them still are, sacrifices of domestic animals to God and the ancestors. There are also the anonymous spirits of the bush and uninhabited places, who sometimes require sacrifices.

Unlike the Swahili, but like the other peoples of the region, there were age-sets for the men. In another sense, however, the coastal group were unusual in that they were transitional to the Southern Savanna region to the south. The Digo, Duruma and Rabai reckoned descent, until recently, both matrilineally and patrilineally, and were thus bilineal. Furthermore inheritance was matrilineal among the Digo and Duruma. Matrilineal descent and inheritance is usual in the Southern Savanna region, and was widespread, again till recently, just to the south of the Digo. However, most of the peoples of the Eastern Rift Coast region reckon descent and inheritance patrilineally, and already did so by 1890, and probably long before. The southern coastal peoples, therefore, seem to have combined traditions from the north with others from the south, and were bilineal as a result. The only other part of the region where bilineal and matrilineal features occur is in the south of the Rift Highlands, among Iraqw, Mbowe and Langi, who are also, in this respect, culturally transitional to the south. Unlike that part of the region, however, which is linguistically complex, the Pokomo and all the peoples of the coastal group speak Bantu languages.

The prestige of the Maasai extended, at least to within living memory, over the people of the coastal group; but the Pokomo, in the Tana valley, were clients of the Oromo, and looked up to them as a cultural ideal. The ideal remains much the same even now although Soomaali prestige is eclipsing Oromo in the area; and at the present time there is the all-pervasive alternative of the Europeans. For the Swahili, on the other hand, until European administration, there was the league table of the city-states, top position, and relative independence of each city, shifting through time. One constant feature has been that they have not bowed to pastoralists, Maasai, Oromo or Soomaali.

The Dry Plains Sub-region

Above the dry coastal lowlands the country rises gradually to the main plateau-surface. East of the Rift Highlands, this surface forms a vast expanse of plains, the territory of the Maasai, covered with dry woodland, interspersed wth grassland, which has only scattered *Acacia* trees, or no trees at all. Like the Nyika, these plains are marked by recurrent droughts, and they show an extreme shortage of surface-water. Apart from the Horn, they are the dryest part of East Africa, but they are the home of the most admired people of the region. In the north the plains run into the deserts of the Lake Rudolf depression and of the Horn. In the south, where there is a gap in the Rift Highlands, they penetrate westward towards the wetter, but still dry, plains of Nyamwezi. This westward lobe of the dry plains is largely occupied by the Gogo.

There are a few hunters in the sub-region, belonging to a specialized caste of Maasai, and there are areas of non-intensive cultivation, but most of the area is used as extensive grazing. Indeed most of the sub-region is occupied, albeit sparsely, by the Maasai themselves. They include in their territory the whole sweep of the plains east of the highlands, from the borders of Gogo country, in the south, to the Rift Valley in the north. The Sambur, almost identical culturally with Maasai, and classified by some people as a Maasai sub-group, continue the area of exclusive pastoralism northwards to the Karimojong'–Turkana group of peoples in the Lake Rudolf area. These peoples, set apart from their southern neighbours by the absence of circumcision, are transitional to the Savanna Stateless region. The Maasai themselves used to graze their herds and flocks right up through the northern Rift Highlands along the dry floor of the Rift Valley, vegetationally similar to the plains. From the valley floor they grazed up the slopes on to the neighbouring highlands. At the present time, however, they no longer do so, in accordance with the agreements of 1904 and 1911, made with the British administrators in Kenya, then the British East African Protectorate. Since that time the Maasai have kept out of the Rift Valley section around Lakes Naivasha and Nakuru. It is clear from their earlier distribution, however, even more clearly than from their present area, that they are people of dry country, and occupy the dry core of the region.

So striking is the position of the Maasai within the region that they have to be mentioned repeatedly in this account. They have impressed European visitors and residents in East Africa almost as much as they have their African neighbours. They figure again and again in the literature of East Africa, and in the Hollywood wildlife spectaculars. Probably the feature which most impresses Europeans is their effortless superiority, their transparent assumption that nobody is better than they are. Whatever Europeans' opinions, there is no doubt, as has been stressed already, that they are the key people of the whole region. Prior to European administration, the Maasai represented the centre of fashion for the peoples around them. Their long-bladed spears, their young men's long coiffured hair, and their wire ornaments on ears and limbs were found also, in varying degrees, among their neighbours. There is here, however, an historical difficulty : it is not certain that the Maasai originated these fashions. All that can be said with certainty is that the Maasai represented, in a high degree, the desirable way of life, and the appropriate culture, which was the ideal of all the peoples of the region, except for the Swahili.

There is, however, one feature which sets the Maasai apart, not only from most of their neighbours in the region, but also from all East Africans in other regions, and this is an aspect of their sexual morals. In nearly all East African societies the older generation hold an official attitude that people should not copulate before marriage. This is widely challenged in practice by members of the younger generation, who are not married, but as an official attitude it has general acceptance. It is remarkable, therefore, that the Maasai and the Nandi, of all generations, accept that young men and women ought to copulate unmarried, although no-one must become pregnant. This attitude looks like an assertion, albeit unconscious, that the Maasai are very different from other peoples around them, and a claim by the Nandi to be as good as the Maasai, in some respects.

The dry plains surround enclaves of wet highland country, such as Mounts Meru and Kilimanjaro, which are outside the sub-region, as defined here, but they also include two low-lying areas, which are tiny islands in a Maasai sea. Around the southern end of Lake Baringo live a small group called Tyamus. They speak the language of the Maasai, but live by farming and fishing, which is remarkable because of the widespread aversion to fish in the region.[14] Further south, on the western shores of Lake Natron, live the Sonjo, speaking a Bantu language, and cultivating intensively with the aid of irrigation. Both these groups are clearly defined in terms of habitat. Less clearly defined are the groups who speak and act as Maasai, and call themselves Maasai, but are disowned by the exclusive pastoralists because they cultivate, as well as herding. They are widely scattered on the borders of the Maasai plains, living usually in less dry areas than the pastoral Maasai, and thus in areas more suitable for raising crops. They occur in some numbers around the base of the highlands of the Transition sub-region, for example near Kilimanjaro, and also in Gogo and Burunge country further south, where they call themselves Baraguyu.

The Gogo and Burunge live on the area of dry plains which bulges westwards through the break in the Rift Highlands. They are rather desultory cultivators, but enthusiastic about their large herds of cattle, an attitude similar to that of the Kamba further north, and indeed of other groups. The Gogo habitat is the area of the plains intermediate in dryness between Maasai and the country of the Nyamwezi, who largely lack cattle. In the west, Gogo merge culturally towards the Nyamwezi, and Kimbu, having small states, each ruled by an hereditary line of kings. The Burunge live on plains similar to those of the Gogo but cut off from them by the wooded Chenene Hills. They have cultural links northwards to the Iraqw–Langi highlands, since they speak a language of the highly distinctive Iraqw family.

In the midst of these hills, where live most of the people who speak languages of the Iraqw family, is an area of dry plains near Mount Hanang. This is the country of the Datoga, who form an enclave of exclusive pastoralists in an area of cultivators. There are also a few hunters, the Hadza, who live in the wooded lowlands around Lake Eyasi, to the north of the Datoga.

The scale of social organization is small throughout the sub-region, and social specialization is limited to war-leaders, hereditary priests, medical specialists and smiths. The Hadza indeed, on the fringe of the region, lack any specialization except an ill-defined precedence of some men in a knowledge of medicine. Among the Maasai the smiths form an endogamous caste, as do the hunters; and there are hereditary specialized priests, the *oibonok* (plural), but their position differs from that of specialist priests in the other groups of the region. The most important among them are more powerful than the priests of other groups in that their advice is taken more weightily on day-to-day matters, for instance cattle raids. At the same time, however, they are feared, and even hated, in a way unfamiliar in the attitudes of other groups to their priests. The basis of this Maasai attitude probably lies in a tension between the real usefulness of the *oibonok*, which Maasai acknowledge from experience of their success in predicting future events, and the fear that the *oibonok* may use their position to gain excessive, by Maasai standards, executive power. The important *oibonok* are on their way to being kings, but the Maasai lack the administrative and factional machinery for limiting the power of kings.

The Maasai differ from their neighbours also in their total lack of any rituals associated with their ancestors. Only if a troubled ghost returns to haunt them do they perform any ceremony, and that to rid themselves of him. There are no regular sacrifices to ancestors, as there are among the Gogo, Burunge, Sonjo and Datoga. All the peoples, however, including the Maasai, acknowledge the sovereignty of God, and all, except the Maasai and Sambur again, recognize spirits of the bush, who occasionally cause trouble. Unlike most East African peoples, who bury their dead, the Maasai, Sambur and Datoga lay theirs out in the uninhabited areas away from the settlements, although the important *oibonok* and wealthy men are buried. Similar funerary practices were usual as late as 1920 among the Nandi, and their neighbours north as far as the Pokot.

Despite the cultural similarities between the peoples, there are very marked language differences among them. Maasai, Baraguyu, Sambur and Tyamus all speak the same language, Maa, a sub-group of the Nilo–Maa language family.[15] The Datoga also speak a language of this family, but of the Nandi–Pokot sub-group. Sonjo and Gogo speak Bantu languages, while the Burunge and Hadza speak languages of the small and localized Iraqw family.

It is unnecessary to emphasize that the Maasai are the dominating figures of the prestige hierarchy, although the Hadza live a kind of life too remote from pastoralism to be much affected. The Datoga, on the other hand, show now, and probably already showed in the last century, an independence of attitude to the Maasai which means that they form the centre of their own, localized, prestige hierarchy, in which different groups of Datoga compete with each other.

The Wet Highlands Sub-region

The hills north and south of the Datoga form one of the three clusters of the next sub-region. All three clusters, or sub-sub-regions, are on the margins of Maasai country, from which they are set apart by their greater altitude and higher rainfall. Above about 1700 metres the country carries, except where it has been cleared, woodland green all the year, while below this the woodland is deciduous, the trees dropping their leaves in the dry season. The most distinctive peoples of the region live in the higher, wetter, vegetation zone, and most of them are marked by considerable densities of population, the largest concentration being that of the Gikuyu. These wet-country peoples are also intensive cultivators, while the dry-country peoples, such as the Kamba and Sandawe, are marked by much less intensive cultivation, and by a heavier reliance on livestock. These lower-lying, dry-country, groups are intermediate in habitat between the wet-country peoples and the dry plains of the last sub-region. Gikuyu, Kamba and Maasai thus form a series, running downhill, to increasingly dryer, and, for human survival, more precarious, habitats. The sub-region also had a few hunters, the Ogiek, most of them in the western cluster.[16]

This western cluster contains the Nandi, Pokot and their neighbours, separated by the dry floor of the Rift Valley from the Mount Kenya cluster, comprising Gikuyu, Embu, Meru and Kamba. On the south-western edge of the Maasai Plains are the hills of the southern cluster, including the Iraqw, Rimi, Langi and some smaller groups.

Within the Mount Kenya cluster, the most numerous group are the Gikuyu, densely settled in wet highland country in the hills south-west of the eroded volcanic cone of Mount Kenya. On its southern slopes live the Embu, and on its eastern the Meru, on fertile volcanic soils, as are the Gikuyu themselves. These three peoples form a coherent ethnic and habitat unit, having an almost uniform culture throughout. The Kamba occupy a similarly homogeneous block of country, on the lower, dryer hills sloping away south-eastward from Mount Kenya, towards the Nyika.

To the west of the Gikuyu hills the floor of the Rift Valley is dry, providing grazing for Maasai herds until the agreements in 1904 and

1911. On the west, the hills rise again steeply from the valley floor, but, although the rainfall is relatively high, there is not the density of population of the wetter areas of the Mount Kenya cluster, which have the added advantage of highly productive volcanic soils. Although overall densities are low, however, there are pockets of dense population, and most cultivation is intensive. Nandi and Kipsigis, for example, irrigate their crops.

The most northerly people of the group are the Pokot.[17] In addition to the cultivating communities of the highlands, other Pokot live on the dry plains east of the highlands and are thus neighbours of the Turkana. As such, the pastoral Pokot are on the transitional fringe of the Savanna region, to be considered later. However, the Pokot of the plains are either of highland origin, or else they are descendants of plains people who joined the Pokot once these were on the plains. The prestige of the plains Pokot in the arid Lake Rudolf depression is high, and this probably accounts for their recruiting members from other peoples. In the present generation this prestige has been maintained by their success in the repeated cattle raids of the area, which have not yet been stopped despite some efforts by the Kenya and Uganda governments to do so. The Pokot are thus a very clear expression of the situation in the region, where high-prestige pastoralism, most flourishing on the dry plains, draws people away from their base in the wet highlands to found new settlements on the plains, and join in the raids and counter-raids for cattle.

On the margins of Pokot territory, in the highlands, are smaller ethnic groups, not markedly unlike the Pokot in culture. To the west are the Gony and Sabiny on the slopes of the extensive volcanic cone of Mount Elgon, named indeed after the Gony. To the south of the Pokot are the Markwet, and south of them are the Geyo and Tugen. The most southerly part of the cluster is occupied by the Nandi and Kipsigis, the Nandi rising to great eminence in the closing decades of the last century, when they raided as far as Mount Elgon and acquired a local military precedence over their neighbours. Culturally, however, the cluster is made up of peoples very similar to each other, and differentiated by the effects of distance apart, rather than by differences of habitat or background. In the period 1960–4 the Pokot, Markwet, Geyo, Tugen, Nandi and Kipsigis acknowledged their close similarities to each other when their politicians coined the collective term Kalenjin to describe them all. Speaking the same language as the Nandi and Kipsigis, but formerly very different in livelihood, are the Ogiek, also members of this cluster.

D

A much more complicated recent history is implied by the extreme linguistic complexity of the southern cluster, in Tanzania. The most northerly group here are the Iraqw, densely settled in a block of wet hill country, with the dry plains of the Datoga below them to the south. On the southern edge of the Datoga plains the country rises again into the hills of the Rimi, also thick on the ground, and intensive cultivators like the Iraqw. These three peoples, Iraqw, Datoga and Rimi, can recount memorized genealogies twelve generations deep or more, a depth rare elsewhere in East Africa, outside the Horn and the royal families of states. These three peoples, however, have no royal families, and the genealogies are those of different kin groups within highly localized communities. The incidence of these unusual genealogies in this area implies a shared history which has segregated these peoples to some extent from others in the region.[18] They probably form a grouping of the same sort as the Gikuyu, Kamba and Maasai, within which migrants have moved from one group to another, according to the dictates of famine or prosperity. These processes will have to be examined in some detail in Chapter 10.

East of the Rimi are the dry wooded hills of Sandawe country, dropping away southwards to the Gogo plains. The Sandawe, unlike the Rimi, are not intensive cultivators, and their way of life closely resembles that of the Gogo and also of the Burunge, on the dry plains east of the Sandawe. The edge of Burunge country is marked in the north by the hills which extend east from Sandawe, but are here occupied by Langi, intensive cultivators, some of them living in wet highlands. These continue northwards into the thinly-peopled hills of the Alagwa, and, north of them, the Gorowa, whose country runs into that of the Iraqw on the north-west. At the foot of the steep scarp which runs down from Iraqw to the flats of Lake Manyara, and at the south end of the lake, are the Mbowe,[19] living on an area which is an extension of the Maasai Plains, but which allows intensive cultivation because of water draining down from the highlands above. Along the eastern edge of the Langi hills, some Langi live in a similar habitat;[20] and the country of the Sonjo, out on the Maasai Plains, is also similar, a well-watered enclave in otherwise dry territory.

This southern cluster is the most linguistically complex area in East Africa. The Sandawe speak a Khoisan language, related to those of the Bushmen and Hottentots in southern Africa. Iraqw, Gorowa, Alagwa and Burunge speak mutually related languages of an isolated language family, whose only other members are Hadza and Ma'a. The widespread Bantu languages are represented by Rimi, and by the language of the Langi and Mbowe. As has been noted in the previous section, the Datoga, on their plains, speak a Nilo–Maa language. Further north, all the peoples of the western cluster speak closely related languages of the Nilo–Maa family; and all the peoples of the Mount Kenya cluster speak Bantu languages.

Although languages, habitats and ethnic identities fit so well together in the southern cluster, neither here, nor anywhere else in the region, is it possible to identify linguistic nationalism, of a kind familiar in Europe. Until the emergence of party politics, from about 1950 onwards, people who spoke one language had little sense of being united that went beyond recognizing that they spoke the same language. Raids, usually for cattle, were carried on between local settlements, irrespective of the language of raiders and raided. The one people in the region whose sense of unity went beyond this appear to have been the Maasai, an "aristocratic" people, who shared a common sense of superiority, but who had no common organization and among whom villages repeatedly raided, and continue to raid, other Maasai villages, as they would non-Maasai settlements.

Throughout the region, it must be repeated, the unit of loyalty was, and largely still is, the autonomous settlement. The age-sets which were general among the Wet Highlands peoples have faded out of activity since about 1940, but persist vigorously among the Maasai and Sambur to the present time. War-leaders have also faded out in the Wet Highlands clusters since European administration began, but the hereditary priests and the medical specialists persist, alongside the new doctors, teachers, officials and Christian incumbents.[21] The Mbowe are unusual in having hereditary rulers over five of their six ritual-areas, but these rulers are essentially combined war-leader priests, and on a very small scale. Sacrifices are the central traditional rituals, addressed to God, to the ancestors, and, where necessary, to the unpredictable spirits of the bush.

Maasai prestige is still registered by the peoples of all three clusters, even by the members of the new literate elites who feel they ought not to be impressed by people who do not wear European clothes. However, the high opinion in which the Maasai were held did not depend upon their ability to be militarily dominant. In the period 1880–1900 the Maasai of the Rift Valley were being raided persistently, and success-fully, by the Nandi of the hills to the west. As a result of their repeated successes, against their neighbours, the Nandi became the most feared of all the peoples of their area, and their experience of success accounts for their unreadiness to accept British administration, which their battered neighbours received much more enthusiastically. Hence there was a series of Nandi rebellions against the Government of Kenya, the first in 1905, the latest as recently as 1942. Through all this period, however, the Nandi did not replace the Maasai as supremely superior people. Superiority lay in the pastoral way of life and not just in repeated success in raiding. Indeed, even at their triumphant climax, the Nandi tacitly acknowledged Maasai superiority by recognizing as their supreme priest and prophet, over the whole of the Nandi, an *oiboni* (singular of *oibonok*) hereditary in an immigrant lineage of Maasai origin.

During the second half of the nineteenth century there were also changes in the Mount Kenya cluster. With Swahili traders penetrating the interior, the Kamba became involved in journeys to the coast, and some of them must have been drawn away from their admiration for Maasai by the rival prestige of the coastal peoples, with their cloth and guns. On an even smaller scale, in the southern cluster, during the present century the Rimi and Langi have been extending their territory by absorbing respectively Sandawe and Alagwa. They appear to have been doing this already in the nineteenth century. Certainly now they are each dominant in prestige over their relatively diminishing neighbours.

The Wet Highlands Transition Sub-region

From the dry plains in the eastern part of Maasai country there rise a number of highland masses which could readily be classified as a fourth cluster in the Wet Highlands sub-region. They need, however, to be distinguished because of the presence in part of their area of hereditary lines of kings. The states over which these rule are tiny, with only embryonic administrative patterns, but they nonetheless mark a transition to the royal traditions of the Southern Savanna region. In this respect the sub-region resembles the highlands south-west of Lake Eyasi, where the three small states of Isanzu, Iambi and Ilamba belong partly with the Sukuma–Nyamwezi states further west, and partly with the stateless peoples of the southern cluster. These three small states, however, have no tradition of clitoridectomy, unlike the Wet Highlands transition, and are considered with the Sukuma and Nyamwezi (in Chapter 7).

The habitats of the peoples of the transition zone are marked by wet highland forest, or rather the remnants of it still preserved after clearance, and by intensive cultivation. Mount Meru, a relatively young volcanic cone, forms the first element of the sub-region, its wet southern slopes inhabited by the Arusa, after whom is named Arusha, the town built by German administrators at the lower edge of Arusa country. Arusa speak the same language as Maasai, and are like them in all respects, except for their livelihood, since they are intensive cultivators of the fertile volcanic soils, as are their neighbours on the eastern slopes of the mountain, the Rwo.[22] These are very close in language to the Chaga on Mount Kilimanjaro, and some of their ancestors were immigrants from there. Kilimanjaro is separated from Meru by dry plains, grazed by Maasai herds, and, like Meru, it is a relatively young volcanic cone, rising straight up out of the plains. Unlike Meru, it is tall enough to be capped with permanent snow, but these high alpine zones are of little importance in the history of human settlement in East Africa. The Chaga live thickly on the well-watered southern slopes of the mountain. As with the Rwo and Arusa, their staple crop is bananas, and their intensive cultivation, on volcanic soil, also includes, as a cash-crop, coffee, of the arabica species. The other peoples of the transition highlands grow bananas and coffee, but only the Shambaa rely upon bananas as heavily as do these three groups on Meru and Kilimanjaro.

The northern slopes of Kilimanjaro are dryer than the southern, since the prevailing rain-bearing winds are from the south-east. On these northern slopes much of the vegetation is deciduous woodland, and the area is avoided by most Chaga, who favour areas wet enough to support forest which is green throughout the year. The thin population of the northern slopes contains some Ongamo,[23] concentrated in the north-eastern area, and speaking a language of the Nilo–Maa family, which appears to be a relict of a formerly more widespread language, or even group of languages.

A third mountain-mass lies east of Kilimanjaro, the Taita Hills, marked again by dense population on its better watered southern slopes. Since they have no kings or states, the Davida and Sagala[24] groups who live there could be included with their neighbours the Kamba, in the Wet Highlands Mount Kenya cluster, but, as has been emphasized elsewhere, the distribution of peoples does not lend itself to neat demarcations of regions and sub-regions. Some peoples just are in transition zones.

The fourth element in the transitional sub-region consists of the Asu hills and the higher land to the south-east, forming the country of the Shambaa. On the northern, and dryer, slopes of the Shambaa hills live a small group called the Ma'a, who are remarkable for speaking a language which has the pattern of Bantu languages, but a vocabulary including a component from the Iraqw family.[25] The people who spoke the original Ma'a have, presumably, adopted increasingly the speech forms of their neighbours, and it is probable that in time the process will continue, and the remaining Ma'a merge into the Shambaa. Historically, however, the Ma'a are very important since they are evidence of an Iraqw language elsewhere than in the southern cluster, and it seems likely that all the people of the Asu–Shambaa hills spoke languages, or else a single language, of the Iraqw family before immigrants arrived speaking Bantu languages. It will be necessary to return to this theme in Chapter 11. A conspicuous feature of the sub-region is that the apparently relict languages, Ma'a and Ongamo, have both survived on the dryer northern slopes of their respective highland masses, where cultivation is less intensive than on the wet southern slopes. Presumably the pressure to change, resulting from numerous immigrants, has been less intense where the potential of the land is less attractive to immigrants.

Apart from Ma'a, Ongamo and Arusa, which is a form of Maa, the languages of the transitional hills are Bantu. Below the Shambaa hills, on the coastal lowlands, are the Bondei, transitional to the coast sub-region, and south of the Bondei, along the coastal lowlands again, are the Zigula, Zaramo and other groups on the edge of the Southern Savanna region, where all the languages are Bantu.

The peoples of the transitional hills are organized on a small scale, and, before the establishment of European administration, each settlement or group of settlements raided its neighbours. The area was, however, unusual, compared to the rest of the region, because of the presence of royal lines and the rudiments of state organization. Only the Davida and Arusa showed the classic pattern of the region : spontaneous war-leaders, hereditary priests, medical specialists and smiths. The other peoples all had, in place of the spontaneous war-leaders, hereditary rulers. Apart, however, from the Shambaa, who were united under a single monarch, the people of each ethnic group were divided into a number of tiny "states", each with its own ruling line. Although each king usually "ruled" more than one settlement, they were little different, except for their hereditary position, from war-leaders among other groups. Indeed, in the period 1880–1900, the followers of most of the Chaga kings were not as numerous as those of each of the more successful war-leaders among the Gikuyu.

The transitional position of these peoples is brought out still more by the exceptionally large, for the sub-region, state of Shambaa, where the ruling family in office during the nineteenth century, and until 1963, originated from among the Zigula, on the coastal lowlands. The Zigula, and the Shambaa also, were affected by contact with the Swahili. By 1890 the King of Shambaa professed to be Muslim, and wore the robes of a prosperous Swahili merchant. The relatively large size of his realm, despite its loose organization, permitted and encouraged the development of a court, with specialized functionaries, and also the beginnings of a regional administrative hierarchy. Shambaa could be classified as the most northerly state, on the east coast, of the Southern Savanna region; but it is not necessary to argue about the precise allocation of the peoples of transition zones. Like the groups to the south of them, the Shambaa had no age-set organization, but the other peoples of the sub-region had age-sets similar to those of their neighbours. By 1960 only the Arusa still retained the practice. For all the peoples, however, sacrifices were the central rituals offered to God, the ancestors and, when necessary, the spirits of the bush. The only major change in this pattern has been the abandonment of sacrifice by most of the Chaga, who profess to be Christian.

The Chaga are also conspicuous for their enthusiasm for European ways, in other directions. They have for some decades run a very prosperous coffee-selling co-operative; they have a high proportion of their children in school; and they are by far the most numerous ethnic group in the civil service of Tanzania, as well as providing a high proportion of school-teachers. Their success has made them unpopular among most other groups in Tanzania, who come into contact with them as officials. They are thus in a position of successful unpopularity similar to that of the Gikuyu in Kenya, another densely settled people of wet highlands.

Prior to European administration, however, the Chaga were engaged in rivalries for prestige between their tiny kingdoms, as were the other groups. On Mount Meru the little kingdoms of the Rwo were overshadowed militarily by the Arusa, and over the whole sub-region hung the prestige of the Maasai. By 1800, and possibly long before, however, the Shambaa had turned to the Swahili as their ideal of excellence. Indeed, whatever their earlier ideals, they may never have been part of the Maasai prestige-orbit. Once they emerge into historical records, by the beginning of the nineteenth century, they are peripheral members of the same zone as the Zigula and Zaramo to the south (Chapter 7).

The Lake-shore Sub-region

The Shambaa are living in highlands just above the Indian Ocean coast. At the opposite margin of the region the Rift Highlands drop down towards the shore of Lake Victoria. From north to south a series of rivers flow from the highlands into the lake, carving out a series of valleys between ridges of subdued relief. In the north the gentle slopes of the huge squat volcanic cone of Mount Elgon rise gradually away from the lake-shore lowlands; while in the north-west the lake-shore zone continues into the similarly dissected country of Soga and Ganda. Rainfall is abundant and, for East Africa, reliable, supporting in places wet lowland forest, although over much of the sub-region this has been cleared for cultivation. Similar rainfall conditions and vegetation follow the lake-shore round into the Soga states and beyond into Ganda.

On the eastern side of the Soga states is the area which, in the late nineteenth century, Soga and Ganda called Bukedi, the country of the naked people. The peoples of this area were seen by their western neighbours as immensely inferior to the groups of the Interlacustrine region, with their state organization, kings and bark-cloth robes. Certainly the peoples of Bukedi lacked these features. Not only were they divided into a number of ethnic groups, but none of these was united, each settlement being autonomous in a manner familiar throughout the Eastern Rift Coast region.

The northern part of the Lake-shore sub-region, of which Bukedi is the western face, is largely inhabited by peoples of the Luhya group. Luhya is a modern term, not in use in 1900, which grew up to denote peoples in western Kenya who all spoke one language, although they had formerly no sense of unity, and recognized a diversity of groups among themselves, such as the Kusu, Hanga and Logooli. European administrators and missionaries recognized the linguistic unity of the group, and coined a common name for them before they did themselves. However, when, around 1960, it became clear to local leaders in Kenya that the British Government would grant Kenya independence in the near future, the unity implied in the common term Luhya became extremely valuable to politicians in the area, since they needed to group a large number of voters together as a counter-weight to their neighbours, and looming rivals, the Luo, who already had a name for all of themselves. In this account the Luhya include not only the people usually so grouped in western Kenya but also very similar peoples across the border in Uganda, the Saamia, Nyuli and Gisu. The Gisu, for instance, although today conscious of being separate from the Luhya, since these are in Kenya, and the Gisu in Uganda, are historically the same people as the Kusu, who have indeed a form of the same name. Both Kusu and Gisu live on the lower slopes of Mount Elgon.

Inside the area of the Luhya group there are two peoples who do not belong to it, speaking different languages and not practising circumcision. These are the Adhola and Tesyo, both of them descended in part from immigrants who spoke Nilo–Maa languages. On the north the Luhya group are bordered by the upper slopes of Mount Elgon, inhabited by the Sabiny and Gony of the Wet Highlands sub-region; and on the east they are bordered by the hill-mass and the Nandi of the same sub-region. On the south, however, the country does not change noticeably, but a very distinct ethnic group occupies the lowlands around the Kavirondo Gulf.[26] These are the Luo, who extend southward along the lake-shore, their territory crossing the boundary into Tanzania. Luo do not circumcize, unlike any of their neighbours. To the east of them, away from the lake-shore itself, are the Gusii.

South of the Gusii, and reaching the lake-shore south of the Luo, are the Kuria, and south of them a group of small peoples, all resembling the Kuria closely. They include the Jita, Zanaki and Nata; and, out on an island in Lake Victoria, are the Kara, culturally part of the Interlacustrine region. The next island and the nearby mainland are inhabited by the Kerewe, also part of the Interlacustrine region, and, like the Kara, densely settled. On the mainland, these small peoples, at the south end of the Lake-shore sub-region, border the Sukuma states. The sub-region is therefore marginal to the region in an extreme sense since it runs into the Southern Savanna in the south, while in the north it borders both the Interlacustrine and the Savanna regions.

Throughout most of the Eastern Rift Coast major linguistic differences between peoples do not correspond with other cultural differences, but on the lake-shore such a coincidence of features does occur. The Luo and the Adhola, who both speak Luo, do not circumcize, and neither do the Tesyo. All the other groups of the sub-region circumcize, and all speak Bantu languages. The Luo language belongs, on the other hand, to the Nilotic sub-group of the Nilo–Maa languages,[27] while Tesyo speak the same language as the Teso, in the Nilo–Maa family, but in a different sub-group from Luo. Both Tesyo and Adhola are near the non-circumcizing peoples of the Interlacustrine and Savanna regions, being outliers of the second, but the Luo form an island of non-circumcizers in an area where circumcizing is normal. Furthermore, during the later nineteenth century, and up to about 1950, considerable numbers of Luhya were joining the Luo, and their children were then not circumcized. On Rusinga Island, for example, the names in genealogies have a Luhya form two generations before the present, but now all the names are Luo, and all the people speak Luo, and do not circumcize. The end of the drift from Luhya to Luo coincides with the awareness, by themselves, of the unity of the people now called Luhya. Indeed in the disturbances associated with party factions during the period 1960–4, Luhya sometimes captured Luo and forcibly circumcized them, a reversal of the recent historical process of assimilating to the Luo.

In addition to the absence of circumcision in some areas, the peoples of the lakeside itself, whether Luo- or Bantu-speaking, catch and eat fish. Thus they, like the Swahili on the Indian Ocean coast, do not observe the prohibition on fish which, until recently, occurred among all the other peoples of the region. The lakeside peoples, it is important to stress, were catching and eating fish in the nineteenth century, when their neighbours to the east were not. By the present generation the ban on fish, identified with snakes, and on eggs, which also marked the region, has greatly relaxed, but in 1900 the lake-shore and sea-shore peoples were the only exceptions. It is true that they were the peoples with the strongest incentive not to keep the ban, since they had access to the largest fish stocks in or near the region; but it is also important that they were near to alternative scales of prestige to that which focussed on the Maasai. The coast peoples were aware of Arabian and Persian standards, and wealth, while the lakeside groups were near the Interlacustrine states. Nearness to large bodies of water gave them access not only to large quantities of fish but also to alien centres of prestige.

The scale of organization was, and largely still is, small. One settlement raided another, irrespective of language, and the specialists, none of them full-time, were the war-leaders, priests, doctors and smiths, so widespread elsewhere. Sacrifices, by lay individuals or part-specialist priests, were addressed to God, the ancestors and, sometimes, to spirits of the bush and, a local variation, of the lake. One exceptional feature of organization is the small kingdom of the Hanga, in Luhya country. By 1890, a minor king, Mumia, was ruling from the place now called, after him, Mumias. He was made relatively wealthy by the caravan trade, but his administration was minimal, his court vestigial, and Hanga differ little in other respects from other Luhya. As usual, minor kings do not look very different from spontaneous war-leaders, but culturally and historically it is worth noting that the Hanga are near to the Soga states, and the kingly traditions of the Interlacustrine region. A source of inspiration is near at hand for a would-be king, and the Hanga resemble the Chaga, and other peoples of the Wet Highlands Transition sub-region, in moving towards kingly state organization, however minimally.

Eating fish, the presence of a minor king and the lack of circumcision all emphasize that on the lake-shore we have reached a frontier zone of the region. The ideals associated with the Maasai, and with circumcision, clitoridectomy and age-sets,[28] are here challenged openly by the Luo. Until recently, their challenge was so successful that they were gathering recruits from neighbouring Luhya groups. Locally, the Luo were at the top of their own prestige-gradient, and they did not apparently look up to anyone else further afield. The habitats of all the groups of the sub-region are very similar, except that some peoples have access to the lake while other do not. Historically, it seems that the different ethnic groups from the Kusu to the Zanaki differentiated out in situ on this lowland area between the lake and the highlands. The Luo are so different from the others because some of their founders arrived as immigrants, colonists, certainly from further north, in the Savanna region, probably in the eighteenth century. Since then they have absorbed local recruits, and are today one of the most numerous peoples of East Africa. Possibly their initial prosperity was based on the rich fishing of the Kavirondo Gulf. Whatever the details, the movements of Luo-speakers will be reviewed in Chapter 11.

In the south of the region the small groups such as Zanaki and Nata live near the Maasai, but also near the Sukuma states, themselves still subject to Maasai attack where they border the Maasai Plains. From their age-sets and local organization, it is clear that these small peoples have bowed towards the Maasai and not the Sukuma. The states of the Sukuma are small, and not militarily very frightening, although their cattle herds are impressively large. Whatever the reasons, the Sukuma have not impressed their north-eastern neighbours as much as have the Maasai.

Until the arrival of European missionaries and administrators, the whole region was marked by the precedence of the Maasai, who probably did not originate the cultural ideals, but who represented them, as a living

example of how such ways could be practised. For most peoples cultivation was essential, but the ideal was still herds and only herds. How the
ideal arose is obscure, but by 1900 the details were established, and
accepted by all the peoples involved. These formed a mosaic of habitats,
livelihoods and languages. Some groups farmed intensively, in the wet
areas, others farmed less intensively, a limited number, including notably
the Maasai, were exclusive pastoralists, and an even smaller number were
hunter-gatherers. Although the ethnic groups were relatively permanent,
and remained in one habitat over a period of generations, individuals
moved from one group to another under one pressure or another. The
largest detonator of movements from one group to another was famine,
usually the result of drought. In times of famine, many people moved to
better favoured habitats, and many of the migrants did not move back
to their people of origin.

   One of the unusual features of the region is the patchwork quilt of
languages of unrelated families. Although the peoples speaking these very
different languages resemble each other in most features of their culture,
the languages provide evidence which can be used to unravel some of
the movements of peoples in and near the region, and to identify some
of the processes by which different elements of culture have been mixed
together in helping to form the present culture of the region. An
examination, however, of these processes, and of the history of the
formation of the present peoples, must wait until Chapters 10 and 11.

4. Notes

1. These people are called "Pare" by Swahili and Europeans.
2. These people are called "Mbulu" by Swahili and Europeans.
3. These people are called "Turu" by Swahili and Europeans, the full form
   of the Swahili name being "Wanyaturu".
4. Wet highland areas are defined in terms of their vegetation, which
   reflects the balance between precipitation and evaporation. For instance,
   Iraqw country has relatively low rainfall, but much lower evaporation
   than nearby lowland areas, such as Mbowe.
5. Usually called "Taita" by Europeans.

6. The Datoga are called "Taturu" by Swahili and Europeans, and must not be confused with "the Nyaturu", that is Rimi. Of the Datoga the largest, and best-known, sub-group are the Barabaig, whose name is sometimes used by Europeans to refer to all Datoga.

7. Although hunters-and-gatherers in 1900, and still regarding themselves as hunter-gatherers at the present time, the Ogiek have during this century begun to cultivate a little and to keep livestock.

8. During the period 1960–64 the peoples of this group increasingly used the term Midzichenda to denote themselves collectively and in contrast to all other ethnic groups in Kenya.

9. In addition to Kiunguja, there are two other dialects on Zanzibar, closely related to it. They are Tumbatu (Kitumbatu) and Hadimu (Kihadimu). Closely related to them is Kipemba, the main dialect of Pemba island. M. Guthrie (1971). "Comparative Bantu", Vol. 2, p. 50.

10. For a survey of the sources for the history of the coastal city-states : R. Oliver and G. Mathew (Eds) (1963). "History of East Africa", Vol. 1. Chapters IV, V and VII.

11. Sofala's role as the port of this section of the coast has now been taken by the town of Beira, founded by the Portuguese.

12. This sort of league-table situation is common in areas with a number of neighbouring city-states, and can be seen in the Peloponnese in the fifth century B.C., or in Mesopotamia in the third millenium B.C.

13. The same is equally true of traditionally Christian areas, such as Europe.

14. Another fish-eating group of Maa-speakers are the Molo, who live at the southern end of Lake Rudolf, north of the Sambur. Their country is too arid for farming, and they rely entirely on fish. The inadequacy of this diet probably accounts for the prevalence of rickets among the Molo.

15. The Nilo–Maa languages are, according to Greenberg (1963), part of a much larger group, the Shari–Nile, itself part of a Nilo–Saharan family : J. H. Greenberg (1963). "Languages of Africa".
    Tucker and Bryan (1956) are not convinced of the links between Nilo–Maa and the other groups. A. N. Tucker and M. A. Bryan (1956). "The Non-Bantu Languages of North-Eastern Africa", pp. 150–153.

16. During this century, the Ogiek, whose ancestors were cultivating peoples, have increasingly added cultivation and keeping livestock to their gathering and hunting, and so now resemble the Nandi and Kipsigis more than they did in 1900.

17. They are usually called "Suk" by Europeans in East Africa.

18. Oliver, in Oliver and Mathew (1963), op. cit., p. 203, notices this linking of Rimi and Datoga. In one respect the Rimi are very distinctive. They are convinced that some of their number can turn themselves into lions, which then kill people. Ordinary lions, say the Rimi, never kill people.

At intervals of about ten years there are outbreaks of killing, which are attributed to lion-men. At these times also certain people are accused of acting as managers of lion-men, arranging murders in return for fees. The last outbreak was in 1966.

19. In Swahili, "Mbugwe" (Wambugwe).

20. The Iraqw and Mbowe are bilineal in descent, and the Langi were till recently matrilineal in descent and inheritance. These matrilineal elements in their culture link these three groups to the Southern Savanna region, which is not very distant from them, and these groups are thus comparable to the Rabai, Duruma and Digo on the coast. This culturally transitional aspect of the Iraqw, Mbowe and Langi will be examined in Chapter 11.

21. Smiths too continue to forge iron weapons and implements, but now with imported iron, from European sources. They have abandoned smelting, which is no longer worth the effort now that there is so much imported raw material available. Until this influx of European-produced iron, however, the only people in the southern cluster who smelted the ore were the Langi, and they provided all their neighbours, except the Maasai, with crude iron, as well as exporting some weapons and implements ready-made.

22. The Rwo are called "Meru" by Swahili and Europeans, and must not be confused with the Meru on Mount Kenya.

23. The Chaga call them "Ngasa".

24. I refer to these two dialect-groups collectively as Davida. They are usually both called "Taita" (i.e. Davida) by European writers.

25. A. N. Tucker and M. A. Bryan (1956). "The Non-Bantu Languages of North-Eastern Africa", pp. 72–4.
The Shambaa call the Ma'a "Mbugu".

26. Both Luhya and Luo are repeatedly called "Kavirondo" in accounts of this lake-shore zone. Sometimes they are differentiated as "Nilotic Kavirondo" and "Bantu Kavirondo", i.e. Luhya. "Kavirondo" is, however, a derogatory term, and is avoided here, as it is by both peoples themselves.

27. These are the group of languages which Greenberg (1963), op. cit., calls simply Nilotic, a confusing term because Nilotic has been used for decades as referring only to the Jieng', Naath and Luo languages, which are only a part of Greenberg's Nilotic languages.

28. Most of the peoples of the Luhya group did not have age-sets, even in 1890, another mark of the frontier position of the sub-region.

5

The Savanna Stateless
Peoples

Distinctive Features of the Region

North of the Eastern Rift Highlands, the East African Plateau drops
away to the Lake Rudolf depression, an area of desert, inhabited by
exclusively pastoralist peoples, such as the Turkana, similar in some ways
to the Maasai. In other respects, however, they are less distinctive culturally than are the Maasai, and are more like the groups living to the
west of them, where the rainfall increases, and the vegetation changes.
From this better watered area, the territory of, among others, the Acholi
and the Otuho, the northern savanna, or sudan belt, stretches westwards
as far as the Atlantic Ocean (Maps 8, 11).

Over most of this huge extent the surface is gently rolling or nearly
level plateau. There are a few areas of hills rising above the generally
subdued landscape, but they are widely separated from each other. Just
west of the middle Nile are the Nuba Hills, and west of them, on the
northern edge of the savanna, the extensive hills of Darfur, with the
Massif des Bongos to the south of them, in the Central African Republic.
From here it is about fourteen hundred kilometres westward to the
Plateau in Nigeria, and even further from here westward to the Futa
Jalon, in Guinée. These hill areas, however, are only at about the height
of the general plateau surface of East Africa, and over half the savanna
is below 500 metres. The only areas near the savanna, and beyond East
Africa, which are high, and wet, enough to resemble the highlands of
the East African Plateau are the great mass of the Ethiopian Highlands,
and, much further west, the highland-range in Cameroun.

The vegetation of the savanna is a mosaic of dry woodland, parkland

and grassland, with some extensive areas of swamps, for example in the upper Nile valley. Rainfall decreases northwards from the Wet Forest region, which bounds the savanna in the south, to the Sahara, and the vegetation changes gradually in the same direction. In the south there are patches of wet forest, especially along the rivers, while in the north the plant cover thins out through the Sahel zone to the true desert.

The distribution of peoples, and of cultural types, over this great belt is complex, and reflects a complex history of migrations, cultural imitation and the aggrandizement of the larger states. Along the southern margin of the Sahara, in the Sahel zone, is a long line of kingdoms extending from the Atlantic to the foot of the Ethiopian Highlands. Another line of kingdoms stretches from the Nile–Congo watershed, near the East African Plateau, westwards to the Atlantic, along the wetter zone of the savanna nearest to the Wet Forest. This second line, however, consists of only tiny states through most of the Cameroun and Central African Republic section of its length. Between these two lines of states, which meet at some places, for example at the Atlantic end, are a large number of, often small, ethnic groups, characterized by the absence of state organization and of kings. These stateless peoples are rather like the filling in a sandwich, with the lines of states as the two slices of bread. Furthermore, the appearance they give, of being squeezed between the two ranks of states, is not illusory. In the last two hundred years various states, on both flanks, have raided the smaller societies in the middle of the savanna and have incorporated some of them, temporarily or permanently, into their territory. This process has doubtless been going on for much more than two hundred years, and it is likely that we are watching the Savanna Stateless region in the course of its disappearance.

The encroaching states of the savanna must be divided into four regions (Map 8) on the grounds of their cultural diversity. Only the states of the Nile–Congo watershed are near enough to East Africa to need much attention in this account, and they have been characterized in the first chapter. They are mostly ruled by Zande royal families. Much further west are the famous kingdoms of the West African coast, Benin, the Yoruba states, Dahomey and Ashanti; and, further west still, are the Mande-speaking kingdoms of the upper Niger. On the dryer northern margin of the savanna are the Song'ai and Hausaawaa states, and, further east, Bornu, Wadai and Darfur. These are all very distant from East Africa, and the peoples of the Savanna Stateless region nearest to the East African Plateau were those least affected, in the whole region, by

the expansion and intrusion of any states during the nineteenth century.
On the grounds of diversity again, the Savanna peoples without states
have to be divided into a number of sub-regions. Despite the great extent
of the region east to west, however, there is a fundamental unity of
culture throughout, and there is strong evidence that these peoples are
the cultural descendants of the oldest established cultivators of tropical
Africa, a theme which will be reviewed in Chapter 11. The sub-regions
which have to be recognized are, from the west :

1. the Black Volta;
2. the Togo–Dahomey Hills;
3. the Nigerian Plateau;
4. the Eastern Belt;
5. the Jieng'–Naath;[1]
6. the Nuba Hills;
7. the Edge of the Ethiopian Highlands;
8. the Lake Rudolf Dry Transition.

We are concerned only with the Lake Rudolf dry area, which has been
mentioned earlier, and with the Eastern Belt, although in this sub-region
only with the more easterly peoples. The whole sub-region extends westward to Lake Chad. It is distinguished from the other sub-regions largely
by the lack of the special features which set the others apart. For instance,
the Lake Rudolf Dry Transition is marked by its arid habitat and the
exclusive pastoralism of its inhabitants.

Population is rather sparse over much of the Eastern Belt, although
there are moderate densities in and near the valley of the Shari River,
involving peoples of the Sara group. Further east, densities above the
mean for the sub-region occur on the highlands to the west of Lake
Albert and of the Albert Nile, an area forming part of the rim of the
East African Plateau. Also, where the sub-region approaches the Interlacustrine states and the eastern shore of Lake Victoria, in the area close
to Lake Kyoga, the Teso live at moderate densities. In this distribution,
wet highlands, lake-shores and river valleys are the critical factors in a
thickening of population. To the east, in the Lake Rudolf sub-region, the
dry country supports only a very sparse population, comparable to that
of the Horn, to which the sub-region is transitional.

Like the peoples of the Horn, and like the Sambur of the Eastern Rift
Coast region, who are their neighbours to the south-east, the groups near
Lake Rudolf are exclusive pastoralists. Their livestock are cattle, goats

and sheep, while the Turkana have some camels, evidence of their contact with the Boorana, who live in the western deserts of the Horn.

Cattle, sheep and goats are also kept by the peoples of the Eastern Belt sub-region, although they are none of them exclusive pastoralists as are their dry-country neighbours. Some of them, for instance the Diding'a, are would-be pastoralists, somewhat like the Kamba and Gogo further south, with their interest focussed on their herds, but obtaining much of their food by cultivation. Cultivation is indeed the main productive activity throughout the sub-region. The principal crops are the same as in the Eastern Rift Coast region, without coffee but with the addition of cotton (*Gossypium herbaceum*), which is an important cash-crop in many areas. Those peoples who live near suitable rivers or swamps fish to increase their food supply, but there are few groups exclusively engaged in hunting-and-gathering.

Throughout both sub-regions the largest autonomous units are small, two or three hundred people at the largest, and mostly smaller in fact. With such a scale of organization, social specialization is predictably slight. War-leaders still occur in places, and there are smiths, medical practitioners and priests.

Age-sets occur in both sub-regions, but only in the east of the Eastern Belt, and not further west. There is no clitoridectomy, and circumcision too is largely absent, although in the second half of the nineteenth century some peoples began to adopt circumcision, as did the western Jieng' in the sub-region to the north. West of these Jieng', the people of the Kpala (Kresh) and Yamegi (Kara) groups who began to circumcize did so presumably in imitation of the various Arabic-speaking raiders who were capturing slaves in the area.

Although the peoples of the Eastern Belt have been the neighbours of large kingdoms for centuries, in the nineteenth century there was a great intensification of contact between the stateless peoples and their more powerful neighbours. In the south the Zande states continued to increase in number, and the total area which they occupied increased in size. As a result of the successful attempts by ambitious members of Zande royal clans to set up their own kingdoms, in hitherto non-Zande territory, a number of small ethnic groups were absorbed into the Zande states. More dramatic, however, was the large scale raiding for slaves from the north.

The Egyptian Government began to expand its territorial control up the Nile valley into Nubia after 1800. Their interest in the areas to the south of them were part of the same expansion of commerce which eventually led the Sultan of Oman to move his capital to Zanzibar. As in East Africa, however, government efforts were outstripped by the activities of private trader-adventurers, lured by the ivory and potential slaves of the south. Egyptians and Nubians were engaged in the trade, and as the century wore on the Arabic-speaking groups even further up the Nile valley became involved in slaving and ivory-collecting. Camel nomads from the desert areas and cattle-herding groups, often collectively called Baggara, began to take part, and the kingdom of Darfur became a base for traders who penetrated south into the stateless belt.

Like the government of Zanzibar, the Egyptian Khedive eventually reversed his policy on slavery, under British pressure. He also established an administration, in the middle and upper Nile valleys, whose senior officials were Europeans, and whose efforts were expected to suppress slave-raiding. Egyptian intervention had, however, generated widespread resentment among the various Arabic-speaking groups, and the rebellion of the Mahdi in 1882 was sweepingly successful, destroying the frail Egyptian administration in less than three years. For the stateless peoples, this victory involved further raiding without now any attempt by anybody to stop it, until a British expeditionary force defeated the Mahdi's followers, under his successor, in 1898, at Omdurman. Even before the Mahdi's victory, however, the most southerly governor of the Khedive's empire, the Silesian-born Emin Pasha, had established an administrative post at Wadelai, in the valley of the Albert Nile, near the southern edge of the sub-region.

Most of the nineteenth century, therefore, was for the stateless peoples disturbed and frequently blood-stained. Even the Acholi, only just north of Nyoro in the Interlacustrine region, were visited by Arabic-speaking traders, who tried to dominate them, but it was groups further to the north-west who suffered most. The Yamegi, Kpala and Banda, south of Darfur, were raided repeatedly, as were the Jieng' further east. These areas are thinly populated at the present time, and the deportation or killing of so many of their inhabitants possibly had a long-lasting effect on the population. On the other hand, it is more probable that population was always thin, and that the raiding had little long-term effect. However, the raids certainly drove many people to move from one area to another, in a search for safety, and the ethnic groups of the area south of Darfur have been greatly altered since 1850. Some named groups have disappeared, others have been formed. The confusion is only lessened by the relative homogeneity of culture in all the groups, however recent their origin. To the south-east of the Jieng', and near or on the East African Plateau, the peoples of the region were much less affected; and the peoples of the dry country in the Lake Rudolf depression were not affected at all.

Although these peoples of the Lake Rudolf sub-region bowed to no-one, it is by now clear that the Eastern Belt peoples were much affected by the power of outsiders. Circumcision was borrowed by the Yamegi and Kpala from the various Arabic-speaking raiders, and was later adopted by the western Jieng'. At the same time various groups to the south of the Jieng' were being incorporated into the Zande states, which were spreading over a wider extent of the watershed area than before. Even further south-east, the Acholi were troubled by raiders and traders, but were more impressed, or at least some of them were, by an old neighbour, the kingdom of Nyoro, one of the Interlacustrine states. Some of the Acholi leaders of the late nineteenth century regarded themselves as some kind of voluntary vassals of the kings of Nyoro.

Circumcision then, where present at all, is an innovation in the Eastern Belt, but there is another practice widespread in these two sub-regions, and indeed further south in East Africa. This is the knocking out of two or four of the lower incisor-teeth, itself a gesture linked to initiation of the young men. In the period 1880–1900 this practice was found among almost all the peoples of the Eastern Rift Coast region, and it persists among the Maasai, and other groups less ready to switch to a European standard of excellence. Knocking out the incisors is an old practice on the eastern savanna, and it is probable that it spread southwards to the East African Plateau.

Another practice also is probably old on the eastern savanna, although it has been abandoned during the present century in deference to European taste. In the period 1880–1900, however, women of the Sara group of peoples distended their lips to the size of plates by the insertion of, progressively larger, round flat pieces of wood. This custom has been the delight of European cartoonists, who have repeatedly shown African women adorned in this way. Still just in the Eastern Belt, the distended lips recurred among the Bira near the highlands west of Lake Albert; and large numbers of peoples between the Bira and the Sara have small, inconspicuous plugs in their lips. The enormous plugs, however, appeared yet again much further south, in the Ruvuma–Nyasa area. Probably the custom spread south through eastern Africa from the eastern savanna, and was once more widely practised, but by 1880 had died out in all but a few areas.

It is also very likely that some groups of languages have spread southward from the eastern savanna to East Africa, but not necessarily at the same time as other practices. The Luo language of the Nilotic group certainly has travelled in this direction, and it is most probable that the Maa language moved south from the Lake Rudolf depression. More doubtful is the origin of the Nandi–Pokot group of languages, which may have antecedents on the eastern savanna, although the modern languages of the group came into being in East Africa. Similarly, the Karimojong'– Turkana group of languages near Lake Rudolf may have their antecedents somewhere to the west on the savanna. It is certain that Karimojong'–Turkana, Maa, Nandi–Pokot and Nilotic languages are all related to each other, and have ultimately a common origin. What is not so certain is how, if at all, they are related to other groups of languages.

It is possible that nearly all the languages of the Eastern Belt and Lake Rudolf sub-regions belong to a single family, the Shari–Nile. If this is so, the Sara group of languages, Maa, and most of the languages on an arc between them are mutually related. It may be, however, that these languages are not one family but a series of smaller language families, strung along the savanna, and with some borrowing of words between member-languages of different families.[2] Even if all these languages are mutually related, it is certain that the language of the Zande, spreading northwards to the nearby stateless peoples of the Eastern Belt, is not related to any of them. It probably belongs to the Niger–Congo family, as do the Bantu languages and most of the languages of West Africa. Furthermore, there are a number of small groups of languages, and even isolated languages, scattered along the Sahel zone and nearby areas, which cannot be fitted into other, larger, families. The Nuba Hills, for example, have a very fine collection.

The Lake Rudolf Dry Transition Sub-region

In the dry country near Lake Rudolf the language situation reflects the complexity of the whole region. Apart from the Dasanech, who speak a Cushitic language closely related to that of the Konso in the nearby hills, the pastoral peoples of this sub-region speak a language belonging to the Nilo–Maa group. Bordering the sub-region are the "Tepes", on three separated areas of wet highlands, whose language belongs to a very small group, presumably once less restricted in area. The Lake Rudolf depression resembles the Horn of Africa in its low rainfall and desert vegetation. In the west a few water courses run down from the Eastern Rift Highlands, actually from the country of the Pokot and their neighbours. To the west of the depression the East African Plateau rises over 500 metres above the lake, but at this edge the plateau's vegetation is sparser than further west. On the north-west there is no such dramatic change of altitude, but the vegetation changes gradually to the grassland, dry woodland and swamps of the savanna. The north and north-east are bounded by the Ethiopian Highlands, with their foothills dry, but well watered higher up; and on the east are the deserts of the Horn.

East of Lake Rudolf the people are Boorana, but the western part of the depression is occupied by the Turkana, exclusive pastoralists, like the Sambur to the south-east, and the plains Pokot on the south. Above the escarpment to the west are the would-be pastoral Karimojong', their herds repeatedly harried by the raids of the hill Pokot, living in the highlands to the south. On three outposts of these highlands, Mounts Nepak, Debasien and Moroto, live the "Tepes",[3] numbered only in hundreds, and cultivating in wet forest. West of the Karimojong' the vegetation changes to less dry savanna, and the country is occupied by Acholi, Lang'o and Teso.

There is a much more striking cultural change in the north, where the foothills of the Ethiopian Highlands mark the boundary zone of the NANE Major Cultural Region. Through this boundary zone the Omo River flows into the northern end of Lake Rudolf. The people who cultivate the area along the lower valley of the river are Nyang'atom, speaking the same language as the Turkana, while there are other Nyang'atom, exclusive pastoralists, wandering over the dry plains between the lower Omo and the Turkana. The remaining people of the sub-region are the Dasanech,[4] east of the Omo, but raiding widely from their base-territory. As has been noted already, they speak a Cushitic language, related to those of the Horn, and to the majority of languages in the Ethiopian Highlands. There is another people in the lowlands, and again they speak a language close to Konso. These are the "Arbore", just north of Lake Stephanie, now dried up, but they are cultivators, and transitional to the hill-peoples above them, of whom the nearest are the "Amar".

The largest social groups are on a subdued scale in the sub-region, often not above fifty people, and social specialization is correspondingly slight. There are spontaneous war-leaders, that is raid-leaders, now as in the past, since raiding for cattle continues to the present time. Medical specialists occur in all the groups, and there are specialized priests. God is supreme, and neither Nyang'atom nor Turkana take any notice of their ancestors, nor of any other spirits, except troublesome ghosts. All their sacrifices are thus to God alone, and they resemble in this respect the Sambur and Maasai further south. Dasanech, however, sacrifice also to their ancestors, and, when necessary, to spirits of the bush, as do the peoples of the hills just north of them. They do not, however, have kings as do most of the peoples of the Ethiopian Highlands. The men of all the groups in the sub-region are divided into age-sets.

During the twentieth century the Dasanech have built up huge herds of cattle, and a formidable military reputation, by repeated raids on their neighbours. They have been able to acquire guns from Amharic-speaking Ethiopians, who have appeared in the area north of Lake Rudolf in increasing numbers since 1900, following the expansion of the empire of Shoa by Menelik. These guns have helped the Dasanech raid the peoples of the foothills, such as the "Amar", as well as the Nyang'atom and Turkana to the west. In addition, they have seized cattle from the edge of the savanna country, in the area of the Toposa. Technically, their activities have occurred in the territories of three governments, those of Ethiopia, Kenya and the Sudan; but in an area so remote from the respective capitals these raids have been largely carried out with impunity.

Further south, although less sensationally successful than the Dasanech, the Pokot have been raiding vigorously into Turkana and Karimojong' territory. The plains Pokot have been responsible for repeated raids on the Turkana in Kenya, and the hill Pokot have descended to the plateau again and again to raid the Karimojong' in Uganda. Such raids are the continuation of earlier exchanges, dating back into the nineteenth century, and probably for centuries before that. The modern ethnic groups were probably formed more recently than the beginning of cattle-raiding, and there is no indication that the Pokot and Dasanech have always been so successful relative to their neighbours. During this century the Pokot have not had the access to firearms which has been such a feature of events on the edge of the Ethiopian Highlands, but neither the Kenya nor Uganda Governments have been able to stop the raiding.

The Lake Rudolf sub-region has cultural and historical connections southwards to the Eastern Rift Coast region, eastwards to the Horn and northwards to the Ethiopian Highlands. For example, camels have come in from the Horn, while the language of the Dasanech is linked to those of the nearby highlands. Southwards, Karimojong' and Turkana are locked in raid and counter-raid with the Pokot, and there is every indication that the Maa language, so important in the recent history of the Eastern Rift Coast, spread on to the East African Plateau from what is now Turkana country, probably in the seventeenth century. Above all, however, the links of the area are westward to the savanna, and the sub-region is the arid eastern face of the Savanna Stateless peoples.

The Eastern Belt Sub-region

Westwards the dry woodlands, grasslands and swamps of the savanna are, in the south, on the East African Plateau. This is here conspicuously dissected by the Rift Valley, containing Lake Albert, and by the broad swampy valleys of the Albert and Victoria Niles. To the north the country drops away gradually, most of this lower country being in the Sudan, while most of the plateau area of the sub-region is in Uganda. Still further to the west the plateau, and its associated highlands, drop westwards down into the Congo Basin, while the country north-west of the plateau forms the watershed between the Congo and the Nile. This is the area of the Zande states. The watershed zone, and the lower country just north of the plateau, sink away still further as one goes northward; and to the west of the Ethiopian Highlands is a great basin, full of swamps and numerous tributaries of the Nile. This is the country of the Naath and the Jieng', another sub-region.

Returning to the south, Karimojong' country is bounded on the north-west by the subdued hills of the Abuor, who have specialized in smithing, and in the period around 1900 provided iron weapons and implements to the Karimojong', and also to the Acholi. The Abuor actually speak Luo, the same language as the Acholi, and the Luo of the eastern shore of Lake Victoria. Since about 1930 the need for smelting iron has died away with the increased supplies of mass-produced iron and steel from Europe. Like other smithing peoples, such as the Langi and the Ke, the Abuor have largely abandoned smelting, but continue to specialize in forging tools and weapons.

The Karimojong', Jiye, Dudutho and Toposa are very similar to each other, and all speak languages closely related to Turkana. They are cultivators but would-be pastoralists, with more enthusiasm for their herds than for their crops; and they are a version of Turkana living in better watered country, where there is some point in planting a crop since it might come up, whereas in the Lake Rudolf sub-region it usually would not. The Dudutho appear to be absorbing two small peoples who are their neighbours. In wet hills on the edge of the plateau are the Ik, cultivators, but also hunters until recently. The other small group are the Upale, again in wet hills, but this time on the western borders of the Dudutho, although a few of them live near the Ik. It is not yet certain whether these small groups will be finally absorbed by the Dudutho, but they seem to be losing their identity at the present time.

The hills of the Upale continue northwards into yet more hills, again bordering the plateau. They are the area of the Diding'a and Larim, cultivators but would-be pastoralists, like the Jiye, Dudutho and Toposa. There are some differences of habitat here. Whereas the Diding'a and Larim are in wet hills at the edge of the plateau, the Dudutho and Jiye are on the plateau itself, as are the Karimojong' further south-east. The Toposa, however, are below the plateau, as are the Turkana, also to the south-east, in the dryer country. Although the "fit" is not absolute, there is a close connection between habitats and ethnic groups in this area.

North of the Larim we reach the lower country again, with a group of Anywak settled below the hills, and then north of them the Murle in the area of small streams near the Pibor River.[5] There are more Anywak to the north of the Murle, along the River Sobat, the main Anywak country; and to the west of both Murle and main Anywak are the Jieng' and the Naath. The southern group of Anywak are probably colonists from the main area along the Sobat. They are Luo-speakers, and their dispersal is part of a much wider Luo-language diaspora, whose southern members are the Luo on the eastern shore of Lake Victoria. The distribution of the Luo language must be considered in its historical context in Chapter 11.

The Anywak of the main area, along the Sobat, have a tradition of kings and a royal clan. There are also convincing traditions among them that they were once a united kingdom, although at the present time they are divided into numerous autonomous villages. Such royal traditions could easily have been borrowed from the Ethiopian Highlands just above them, but the presence of a single kingdom, symbolic if not very administratively effective, among the Cholo (Shilluk), also Luo-speakers, and just north of the Naath, raises some doubt as to whether this was the course of events. It is more likely that the Cholo and Anywak are cultural relics of a period when all the Luo-speakers were in one area, now in Jieng'–Naath country, and were ruled by kings, inspired originally from the states of Nubia. If this were so, the expansion of the Jieng'–Naath culture, absorbing the Luo-speakers in the process, reasserted kingless societies over kingly in the area. We shall have to look at this process again in Chapter 11.

The well-drained low country, west of the southern Anywak and of the Larim and Diding'a, is occupied by Otuho, all speaking a single language, but divided into a number of self-defined groups, such as the Lolopit living on Lafit (i.e. Lopit) Hill, and the Logoriuk (Lokoya), on Lueh and Lyria Hills. West of the Otuho is the riverine country along the Nile, inhabited by the Bari group of peoples. Like the Otuho they are divided into a number of named groups, such as Mundari and Nyangbara, but they all speak a single language. One group, the Kakwa, are found among the Madi higher up the Nile valley, and even on the plateau to the west among the Lugbara. These Kakwa appear to be colonists from further north, and indeed the history of the Bari section of the valley seems to be one of migration of Bari-speakers upstream, probably from what is now Jieng'–Naath country. In the process the earlier inhabitants adopted the Bari language. It is clear that the upper Nile valley, and nearby areas, have been the scene of considerable migration and cultural transformation in recent centuries.

Whereas the languages of the Nilo–Maa group, which includes Bari and Otuho, have been involved in various expansions of territory in this period, the languages of the area west from the Albert Nile do not appear to have expanded, and the group as a whole seems to be losing ground. This group, Moru–Mangbetu,[6] includes the language of the Madi, who live beside the marshy valley of the Albert Nile, with the very similar Lugbara on the plateau to the west of them.

Further south, on the highlands, are the Bale and Ke,[7] west of Lake Albert. Like the Abuor, further east, the Ke specialize in smithing, and they live among the Bale, who rely upon them for forged implements and weapons. Furthermore, both groups, by 1900, had small local kings, who were members of Aluur royal lines, and who had originated from the little states in Aluur country, also on the plateau.

South-west of the Bale live the Bira, on the plateau in savanna dry woodland and grassland, but speaking a language identical with that of the Bira further to the west, and themselves a classic people of the Wet

Forest region. The Bira of the plateau, but not those of the wet forest, are among the peoples whose women used to wear the huge lip-plates which have been discussed earlier in this chapter. Their language is Bantu, unlike that of the Bale, and must have reached the plateau with migrants out of the wet forest to the west, where the majority of languages are also Bantu. On the other hand, those huge lip-plates probably arrived from the north, that is from the main area of the savanna.

Bira belongs to the same sub-group of languages as Rwanda and Rundi,[8] in the Interlacustrine region, themselves situated on the highlands well above the wet forest of the Congo Basin. Most of the languages of the sub-group, however, are in that wet forest, and it is extremely likely that they originated there. If so, then migrants from the wet forest carried the ancestral language of Rwanda and Rundi up on to the Western Rift Highlands, just as some Bira migrants carried their language up on to the plateau further north. At the same time, movements from the wet forest uphill on to the East African Plateau are not the only migrations which have affected the area. This complexity of migration-movements must be examined later, in Chapter 11. Below the Bira are the peoples of the wet forest, to whom they are culturally transitional, peoples such as the Lese and Bali to the west, and the Amba to the south.

North of the Bira and Bale, west of the Lugbara, and living in an area of savanna vegetation on the Congo–Nile watershed are the Logo, also speaking a language of the Moru–Mangbetu group. West of the Logo, however, the cultural situation is complicated by the expansion of the Zande states. The Avukaya and the Moru themselves, peoples very like the Logo, are embedded in an area of Zande kingdoms, although they retain their identity. Indeed the Moru are also in a zone where Jieng' culture seems to be still expanding towards the watershed. Further northwest, and with Zande states to the south of them, are some small groups of Luo-speakers, some of them the so-called Jur (Jieng' for strangers), who call themselves Luo, and the others the Turi and their neighbours. These latter peoples speak Jieng' as a second language, and are gradually, it seems, becoming Jieng', just as further south various groups are becoming Zande.

All the small peoples between the Zande and the Jieng' give a strong impression of gradually losing their identity. In the long term, therefore, the Jieng'–Naath sub-region and the Forest-edge region, with its local representatives, the Zande kingdoms, may meet on the northern slope of the watershed, cutting off the Logo all the eastern groups of the sub-region from its more westerly peoples. The pressures on these small, and apparently disappearing, groups are not identical, since some are being absorbed into kingdoms, and then imitating the royal clan and other nobility, while others are remaining small autonomous settlements, with no aristocracy, but are increasingly regarding themselves as Jieng'. In both cases, however, the high prestige of expanding peoples is attracting other groups into their fold.

The Bale too are being affected by foreign pressures, although the presence of Belgian and British administrators, in the period 1900–60, has rather dulled the edge of Aluur prestige. In 1900 some Bale and Ke local groups were each ruled by a minor king of Aluur origin. These kings were welcomed into the country because of their effectiveness in performing rituals for ensuring rain at the right times. Since 1900, however, some Bale and Ke have complained to European officials that the Aluur royalty imposed themselves against the wishes of the local, stateless peoples. These complaints were made some generations after the event, and in 1900, as far as can be judged, Bale and Ke communities, without kings, were still ready to welcome newly arrived Aluur princes. Given the high prestige of effective rain-ritual throughout East Africa, it is highly credible that Aluur with a reputation as specialists in this direction were indeed very welcome. It is true that the specialists were ambitious members of royal clans unlikely to succeed to the kingship in their own minor states. This does not alter the fact that Bale and Ke, as well as Aluur princes, gained from the arrangement. Subsequent complaints could spring from the basic ambivalence of power, which makes people fear what awes them, and also from the lessening of Aluur prestige in the light of overwhelming European power. The whole process is illuminating in terms of the emergence of royal clans at different places and times in East Africa, and this theme is examined again in Chapter 10.

The Aluur themselves, as we have just seen, have royal clans, and are divided into a number of minor states. They thus seem out of place in the region, as do the Anywak at its north-eastern edge, and, like the Anywak, the Aluur speak Luo. It is possible that the tradition of kings arrived from the north with the Luo language, at a time probably in the fifteenth century when Luo-speakers were moving up the Nile valley. On the other hand, the Aluur kings may have arisen locally by inspiration from the more magnificent kings just to the south, in Nyoro and the other states of the Interlacustrine region. Indeed it is highly plausible that two traditions of kingship, Luo and Interlacustrine, both probably of Nubian and therefore ultimately Egyptian origin, meet in Aluur royal clans.

Across the Nile valley, to the east, and still on the plateau, the Acholi also have small local kings. Like those of the Aluur, they are more like glorified priests than kings in a European, or Interlacustrine, sense, but they were war-leaders in the period 1880–1900, as well as performing rain-rituals, and so were kingly, if on a very modest scale. By that period, moreover, some of their achievements were not so modest. In 1899 Awich, of the Payera kingdom, was lord of the whole area from Kitgum settlement to the Victoria Nile. His "empire" was transitory, but it was real, and the whole situation was changing because of the arrival of guns, Arabic-speaking traders, European officials, and other foreign, and new, factors. The same factors, as we have seen, were also affecting other parts of the sub-region, often disastrously. Acholi was relatively prosperous at this period, compared to the areas south of Darfur, for instance.

Between the Acholi and the Aluur is the wide swampy valley of the Albert Nile. Just below the Aluur, however, there are a group of Luo-speakers who distinguish themselves as the Nam (Jonam, with the prefix). Another group of Luo-speakers are south of the Acholi, actually on the borders of Nyoro. They call themselves simply Luo (in full Jopaluo). Both groups are very similar to Acholi and Aluur, and are virtually local sub-divisions of them, but they are significant as recognizing their own separate identity, which is also correlated with a habitat-difference.

Across the Victoria Nile from the Jopaluo, and south of the Acholi, are the Lang'o, also Luo-speaking, and extending southwards to the swampy shores of Lake Kyoga. South-east of them, in this swampy country near the lake, are the Lang'o Ikokolemu;[9] and east of them are the Teso, also with a southern boundary-zone touching the swamps of Lake Kyoga. The language of the Teso is very close to that of Karimojong' and Toposa, while the Lang'o Ikokolemu, like the Lang'o themselves, speak Luo. People in this area say that migrants have arrived here from the dryer country to the east and the north-east, and there has indeed been immigration in this direction over a long period, probably for centuries. Over a long period also, it is worth emphasizing here, other migrants have been moving into the area, bringing the Luo language from down the Nile. For the inhabitants of the dry country one lure of the zone north of the Lake Kyoga swamps is the more reliable rainfall, and the abundant surface-water, at least in the south.

The Lang'o indeed, and also the Acholi, are would-be pastoralists, rather like the Jiye, Dudutho and Toposa, but the Lang'o Ikokolemu and Teso are more intensive cultivators, thickly settled and making use of the better returns possible in the lake-shore zone. In terms of habitat they resemble their neighbours in the other regions just south of Lake Kyoga, the peoples of the eastern shore of Lake Victoria, and the Soga states, in the Interlacustrine region.

Even the "states" of the Aluur and Acholi were on a very restricted scale, apart from some ephemeral "empire"-building by a few of the rulers among the Acholi. Throughout the sub-region the largest social groups were small, and social specialization was slight. Aluur and Acholi had kings who had both ritual and military functions, but in most of the groups war-leaders and priests were separate people; and in all groups there were the usual medical practitioners and smiths. Priests and doctors are still flourishing, but administrative centralization has made war-leaders less necessary, while the rulers' position, for instance among the Acholi, has, as usual, been changed by their involvement in European administration. Sacrifices, however, still have to be made to the ancestors, and sometimes to spirits of the bush. GOD is supreme.

There are two social specializations which have considerable historical significance. Age-sets are formed among the peoples in the east of the sub-region, but not further west. The Aluur, Madi, and some of the western Bari group are without age-sets, but east of this line of peoples age-sets are general, as they are in the Jieng'–Naath sub-region to the north. Given the importance of age-sets in the recent history of the Ethiopian Highlands and of the Horn, and given the way in which they die out westward and southward from these regions, it is most probable that in this part of Africa they originated in the Highland–Horn regions and spread outwards from there. The impact of these regions does not, therefore, at present spread to most parts of the Savanna Stateless region. In the same way it is highly probable that endogamous castes of smiths and hunters, found in north-eastern Africa, and also in the Eastern Rift Coast region, were first established in the Horn or the Ethiopian Highlands, later spreading from there. Castes of smiths and hunters occur among the Bari group of peoples, and there is also an endogamous caste of landless clients, known as *dupi*. Again the Bari group seem to be the limit of north-east African cultural influence in the upper Nile valley at the present time.

It was noted earlier that the classification of languages in this sub-region is not widely agreed. A high proportion of the languages in the east of the sub-region are of the Nilo–Maa group, and it is possible that the others may belong with these in a single Shari–Nile family. If they do not, then the independent language-families in the east of the sub-region include two which are very small. Ik, Upale and "Tepes" make up one family, and Diding'a, Larim and Murle are a major part of the second. West of the Nilo–Maa languages, Madi, Lugbara, Bale, Logo and their neighbours form a cohesive group, in the Moru–Mangbetu family, and then there are other families further west, but still in the sub-region : the Banda–Gbaya–Ngbandi family and the Bongo–Barma family. Furthermore some languages further west are probably not related to either of these groupings.[10] In other words, without a Shari–Nile family the language situation is very complex indeed.

From what has already been said about the social organization of the peoples in this sub-region, it can be seen that competition and prestige were on a small scale, except for the intrusion of peoples from other areas. The Jieng' are culturally close to all the peoples of the sub-region and they were increasing in numbers and territory at the beginning of this century, and apparently are still doing so. The small ethnic groups on their southern border have imitated them, and then gradually become simply Jieng'. This situation is complicated still further by the prestige-gradient within the Jieng'–Naath sub-region, where the most admired people are the Naath and not any of the Jieng' groups.

Further south, the military strength of the Zande states enabled them to absorb small ethnic groups entirely, and these have become, or are becoming, Zande. The whole of the Jieng' and Zande areas, with the zone between them, was subject in the nineteenth century to repeated raiding by various Arabic-speaking groups, whose guns and clothing were the envy of many local people, much as the Swahili traders, and raiders, had a similar impact further south.

Towards Lakes Albert and Kyoga, however, there was relative calm. Bale and Ke looked up to Aluur, who were themselves overshadowed by the relative magnificence of the king of Nyoro. Moreover, Acholi rulers, although competing among themselves, sometimes submitted difficult judicial decisions to the king of Nyoro, as if to an appeal court, over-arching their own minor jurisdictions.

5. Notes

1. The Jieng' and Naath are usually called respectively "Dinka" and "Nuer" by European writers.
2. J. H. Greenberg (1963). "Languages of Africa". He puts the case for the existence of a Shari–Nile (Chari-Nile in his spelling) family, pp. 85–129, and wants to include this in an even larger Nilo–Saharan family, pp. 130–148. However, Tucker and Bryan (1956) express caution about grouping together even the eastern part of Greenberg's family. A. N. Tucker and M. A. Bryan (1956). "The Non-Bantu Languages of North-Eastern Africa", pp. 150–153.
3. "Tepes" is not their own name for themselves.
4. These are the people whom the Amharic-speaking Ethiopians call "Geleba", and who are often called "Murle" in European writings. The name "Murle" is confusing, because of the presence of another group, who call themselves Murle, in the southern Sudan.
5. There are also some Murle on the Boma Plateau, in the foothills of the Ethiopian Highlands.
6. Tucker and Bryan (1956), op. cit.;
   Idem (1966). "Linguistic Analyses of the Non-Bantu Languages of North-Eastern Africa".
7. These are the "Lendu" and "Okebo", respectively, of most European writers.
8. M. Guthrie (1971). "Comparative Bantu", Vol. 2, pp. 42–44.
9. These are usually called "Kumam" by Europeans.
10. Tucker and Bryan (1956, 1966), op. cit., give details on all these groups of languages.

6

The Interlacustrine States

Distinctive Features of the Region

In the south the country of the Lang'o and Teso runs into the swamp basin of Lake Kyoga, which here separates the Savanna region from the Interlacustrine states. Most of this region is well watered by African standards, and the landscape is predominantly green throughout the year, a marked contrast to the savanna. The greater part of the area is a dissected plateau with its surface a little above that of Lake Victoria. Many of the valleys, like those which drain into Lake Kyoga, are marshy, and are avoided by farmers. In the west, however, the country changes, rising to the highlands which flank the Western Rift Valley, with its string of lakes (Map 12).

Both plateau and highlands would support wet forest, although of different types in the two areas, and there are stands of forest in various parts of the region. Much of the wooded cover, however, has been cleared, and is now replaced by cultivation, or by grassland or bushy country, in areas formerly cultivated.

However, through the centre of the region runs a dry belt, or, more precisely, a series of dry pockets which separate the lake-shore populations from the peoples of the north and west. One of these dry pockets is in eastern Ankore, on the western borders of Ganda. These sections of the Dry Zone were probably the only areas, apart from the swampy valleys, which did not carry wet forest before clearance, and they are important in the history of human settlement in the region. Despite the presence of highlands and plateau, however, there is not the dramatic contrast of wet country and dry country which is so marked a feature of the Eastern Rift Coast region.

E

Even so, population distribution is uneven, with a huge concentration of about six million people in Rwanda, Rundi and their borders. The other large concentration of people is in Ziba, Ganda, and Soga, towards the lake-shore. These two large concentrations coincide with the areas of highest rainfall reliability, respectively in the volcanic highlands and near Lake Victoria. There is a third, small, concentration, in the Ruwenzori Mountains, but the people involved, the Konzo, belong to the Wet Forest, and will be mentioned in that context later. Again, however, they are in an area of volcanic highlands and of high rainfall reliability.

Most of the people of the region are cultivators, but there are some specialized herders, and even a few professional hunters. However, it is not possible here to differentiate ethnic groups by their livelihood, as it is in the Eastern Rift Coast region. There, people with different livelihoods have often been differentiated also by language, as with the Maasai, Gikuyu and Ogiek. Also the vast majority of any one group's members have followed the livelihood of the group. For instance, adult Maasai men do in fact, as well as theory, herd cattle, although new job opportunities have changed the picture in most ethnic groups. By contrast, in the Interlacustrine region, the social patterns, in the nineteenth century as well as currently, have been much more complicated, and specialized livelihoods have been part of a class system.

As will be emphasized repeatedly in the present chapter, the dominant feature of the organization of people within the region was the state, moulded around the king. Almost all the peoples of the region have been tax payers since long before living memory. Indeed the only exception are the Chiga of the Uganda–Rwanda border zone. The great majority of the tax payers also hoed the soil, and paid their dues in produce or by corvée labour. The herders were not separate ethnic groups, but specialists within one of the states or another, that is, they were always subject to a king, most of whose subjects were cultivators. In terms of ethnic identity, within any one state, cultivators and herders belonged to one people, and it is even proper here to say one nation. Hunters were only important in Rwanda and Rundi, where hunting was associated with one caste, a theme which will recur later. Hunters too, however, belonged to the same nation as their cultivating and herding neighbours. The one exception to this general pattern occurs in Ganda, where most of the herders are Ankore immigrants, who have been hired by Ganda cattle owners. Herding does show, however, one sign of specialization of habitat within the region. The Dry Zone has a sparse human population, but

a large cattle population, relative to the rest of the region, and the concentration of herders is correspondingly high.

The main domestic animals, apart from dogs, are cattle, sheep and
goats, while the main crops are the same as those which have been noted
for the Eastern Rift Coast, but with some differences of emphasis. The
outstanding change from that region is the large area where bananas
are the staple crop. Throughout the whole of the lake-shore zone, from
the Soga states, through Ganda, to the Ziba states, bananas are the main
food of the people who form that concentration of dense settlement.
Inland the density of population, and the importance of bananas, fades
out into the Dry Zone, thinly peopled and relatively pastoral. Coffee
is a major cash-crop, the arabica species (*Coffea arabica*) growing abun-
dantly in Rwanda and Rundi, as in Gikuyu and Chaga country in the
region to the east. The wet lowlands of Ganda also support coffee bushes,
but of the robusta form (*Coffea canephora*). A crop which is not mentioned in the account of the region east of Lake Victoria is cotton, the
other major cash-crop of Ganda, and abundant also in Soga.

The farmers who grow the bananas, coffee and other crops were, as
has been stressed already, the subjects of a number of states spread
throughout the region. For the sake of clarity it is best to begin with an
account of the situation around 1890, and then to go on to outline some
modern changes. At the earlier period the only people who were not
subject to a king were the Chiga. Everywhere else, the king was the
symbol of the whole of his people. In theory, at least, he was the head
of the army, a national levy and not a professional force; he made the
laws, enforced them, and was the court of final appeal, all again in theory
at least. In practice, in each state, the king was surrounded by a group
of ministers, and his authority was delegated in different parts of his
realm to the members of a hierarchy of officials. In theory, the king
owned all the land and all the livestock; the ministers and the provincial governors were his tenants; and they had tenants, who had tenants,
who sometimes had tenants of their own.

The social pattern was thus that a large number of small, tenant
farmers produced the food and other raw materials of the state, largely
for themselves but also to feed, and otherwise support, a relatively small
unproductive class of officials, including, at the top, the king. The key
to the whole system was taxation. Minor officials gathered the produce
of the farmers in their area, took a portion of it in lieu of salary, and,
in theory at least, passed on the remainder to their local superior, who

was expected to pass it on up the hierarchy after taking a portion, again in lieu of salary. At the same time the officials were land-owners, and the produce they received was owed to them, while what they passed on was their own taxes owed to their superior. In such a system the king's position was precarious, since it was easy for the major tenants to hold back their taxes, on which his position depended. The king's army was provided by troops mustered by his major tenants, who depended for their supply of troops upon their own tenants. In addition to troops, the officials, who were also land-owners, were responsible for the supply of labourers for public works projects, such as roads, where they occurred, or for building a royal residence. Although historians of Europe usually insist on defining the term very minutely and in a restricted sense, there is every reason to call this Interlacustrine system of social order, and government, feudal. It is analogous to the condition of England and France in the twelfth century.

The amount of wealth available to the king and his ministers varied with the size of the state, and also with the condition of the country. Local rebellions, for instance, cut off the supply of taxes to the king. When the taxation system was working fully, however, the large states were wealthier than the small, and their kings could afford patronage on a more munificent scale than the rulers of their smaller neighbour-kingdoms. In the larger states, such as Ganda and Rwanda, there were thus some full-time musicians, dancers, smiths and priests, as well as officials. In the central and southern parts of the region there was an additional social complication. The peoples of the Ziba–Ankore and Rwanda–Rundi sub-regions were divided into castes, and, in theory, the members of one caste were not allowed to marry those of another. In most of the states affected, there were only two castes, but Rundi had as many as five. There were, however, no age-sets, and no circumcision or clitoridectomy.

In a feudal, in the wider sense, system of authority, national political processes have an aspect which is almost international, because the autonomous power of the provincial governors allows them to behave like states within the state. Wars of secession are frequent, the central government is liable to be taken over by a faction with its power-base in another part of the country, and the death of the reigning king usually leads to a succession crisis, and frequently to civil war between rival claimants, supported by rival factions. The recurrence of factional strife, and succession disputes, opens the way for intervention by neighbouring states, themselves prone to internal dissension, but ready to fish in troubled waters in order to strengthen the hand of factions likely to ally with themselves. This general characterization of feudal systems in action applies closely to the Interlacustrine states in the second half of the nineteenth century. By 1890 the two main contenders were Rwanda and Ganda, who intervened repeatedly in the affairs of the Ziba states, and notably in Karagwe.[1] The other very large kingdom, Rundi, was torn at this period by factional squabbles, and was, for practical purposes, a cluster of independent kingdoms, whose rulers nodded in insubstantial obeisance to the king of Rundi.

Since 1890, European administration has prevented secessions, civil wars and the intrigue and invasions of the earlier period. The kings and their major feudatories have themselves been overshadowed by the European officials of the administration, and have received salaries as functionaries within the bureaucratic hierarchy. Taxation was made more predictably regular, and the commitments of government extended to public health, education and agricultural services. In the process, however, the splendour of the ruling families was dimmed, by their lack of supremacy and sovereignty. As a result, various governments have since found it possible to abolish the roles of the kings, without provoking too great opposition. The Rwanda Government ended the office of king in 1961; in 1963 Tanzania removed official recognition from all rulers within the country, including those of Dzindza and Ziba. Uganda followed the same course as Tanzania in 1966, and in the same year Burundi abolished the monarchy. The one ruler whose reputation in his own country is largely undimmed is the Kabaka of the Ganda, whose office underwent a renaissance of prestige in the years 1953–4. The president in power in 1966, Obote, deposed the Kabaka and divided Ganda administratively to lessen the effect of their patriotism, but the threat of such a large kingdom, even if kingless and officially divided, still worries the rulers in Uganda's capital.

The region is divided into three sub-regions :

1. the Ganda–Nyoro;
2. the Ziba–Ankore;
3. the Rwanda–Rundi.

Of these the Ganda–Nyoro area is on the northern part of the plateau near Lake Victoria, while the Ziba–Ankore sub-region fills the southern part. The third sub-region, the Rwanda–Rundi, is coterminous with the highlands of the south-west. It is also distinguished by the presence of more than two castes, and of the caste-names Tuutsi, Hutu and Twa. In the Ziba–Ankore sub-region, there are only two castes, called throughout Hima and Iru; while the Ganda–Nyoro sub-region has no castes, or else only traditional vestiges of them. All the peoples of the region speak Bantu languages.

The Ganda–Nyoro Sub-region

The northern states of the region occupy a dissected plateau-surface, most of it well watered, and with some patches of the original wet lowland forest still standing. In the west the region fades out at the foot of the high, forested Ruwenzori Mountains. As has been noted already, in Ganda and Soga, on the lake-shore, the staple is bananas, but on the far side of the Dry Zone, in Nyoro and Tooro, although bananas are grown, they are less prominent, because less favoured by the climate.

South-east of Lake Kyoga, peoples of the Luhya group, such as the Saamia, occupy country similar to that of the Soga, whose small states border them to the west, and who inhabit the green country between the swamps of Lake Kyoga and the shore of Lake Victoria. On the west, their boundary is the course of the Nile as it flows out of Victoria towards Kyoga. This broad river, in its rocky course, was a strong enough barrier to allow the differentiation of the Soga from the Ganda. However, the barrier was not sufficient to prevent Ganda kings from treating the Soga states as vassals by the nineteenth century.

Ganda has been mentioned repeatedly as one of the giant states of the region. Its core, in terms of people and produce, is the lake-shore zone between the Soga and the small kingdoms of the Ziba. It is bounded in the north-east by the Kyoga swamps, but most of its northern border is made up of the Dry Zone, where bananas only flourish in the stream-valleys, and where population thins out. On the far side of the Dry Zone is Nyoro, engaged during the later nineteenth century in a series of wars with Ganda, which was apparently still expanding at that time. The establishment of European administration prevented us from discovering how the Interlacustrine states would have fared in their dealings with each other, had they been left to themselves. Nyoro, which had re-absorbed rebellious Tooro by this time, held off Ganda, which was much bigger, in the period 1880–1900, but the Ganda rulers of the nineteenth century had other frontiers to worry them as well as the Dry Zone. In the south they claimed hegemony over the northern Ziba states, but here ran into competition with the equally expansionist kings of Rwanda. Both governments, for instance, tried to impose their own candidates, from the local royal family, upon Karagwe, whenever a succession dispute arose there, as it did, for example, in 1878. Even further south, the Ganda court intervened in the affairs of the Dzindza, on the southern shore of Lake Victoria. Here their fleet of war-canoes gave them access which Rwanda could not rival, and the same fleet carried their claims to suzerainty across the lake to the state of Kerewe on its south-east shore.

The story of Ganda, although largely obscure, is one of increasing size and power from the eighteenth century, and possibly before. By 1870 it was unique in East Africa as a nation-state, of great internal homogeneity, whose people not only spoke a single language, but which included most of the people who spoke that language within its borders. To Europeans it is a classic nation-state. By the same period its administration was as centralized as an agrarian, basically feudal, state can become, and it even had a postal system of runners and state-maintained roads, or paths, which none of its neighbours could boast. Such centralization, however, in an agrarian state, is fragile, and the period 1890–1900 was marked by civil wars, but also by a rapid reassertion of central authority by the winners. In the south, the power of Rwanda would presumably have halted the Ganda frontier, although by then most of the Ziba states would have lost their autonomy to one or other of the giants. Soga, Nyoro and Tooro could have been culturally absorbed to the Ganda language and style of administration, but in 1900 they were still distinct, and they still are.

Possibly Ganda was at full size anyway by 1870. With no horses, effective control of outlying provinces was more difficult than for the Romans or the Chinese, and Ganda might have disintegrated rather than expanded. What is remarkable is the size of the kingdom, even without its dependent states, in 1870, with a probable population of over half a million. It was bigger than the majority of states of the region, and vastly bigger than the little autonomous settlements of the Luhya group east of Soga. In the absence of detailed historical records, the process of initial state formation and of state expansion in the region is obscure, but at some stage the competition between petty kings in a local league must have sparked off a series of bids to be top of the league, and to stay there. In other areas, such as the Near East and Europe, this process occurred and is well documented; in this region the process must be guessed, but it is unlikely to be otherwise. Once the desire for hegemony, and permanent hegemony, had become fashionable, the high productivity of the plateau helped the would-be empire-builders, and the best-watered lake-shore belt favoured expansion along itself, rather than into the Dry Zone.

The story of Ganda is intertwined with that of Nyoro, on the other side of the Dry Zone. Nyoro seems to have been displaced by Ganda as the top state of the northern part of the region from the eighteenth century onward. The king-list of Nyoro seems to take the kingdom back to the thirteenth century, and probably further. King-lists are unreliable in a number of ways, but it seems probable that there have been kingdoms on the Interlacustrine plateau for a thousand years, and probably much longer.

Nyoro is bounded on the south-east by the Dry Zone, and on the north by the thinly peopled valley of the Nile. This area, much of it swampy and full of large game-animals, is inhabited, where at all, not by Nyoro but by Luo (Jopaluo), similar to the neighbouring Acholi. On the north-west is Lake Albert, but the boundary with Tooro, in the south, is not clearly associated with a change in the landscape. Tooro, however, had only seceded from a greater Nyoro in the period 1830–40, and was summarily reincorporated. Its autonomy under the British Protectorate dates from the settlements of 1890–1900, when the suspicion of British administrators for Nyoro led them to give the benefit of the doubt to Tooro, and to Ganda, both claimants on Nyoro territory.

If one regards Nyoro and Tooro as one ethnic group, then this greater Nyoro occupies a clearly defined habitat, bounded: in the east by the Dry Zone; in the north by the Nile valley; and on the north-west by Lake Albert. The south, Tooro, is bounded on the west by the Ruwenzori Mountains; and its southern border is the swampy valley of the Katonga River, which separates it from Ankore. This greater Nyoro is a belt of well watered country, the western analogue of the Soga–Ganda–Ziba belt, and it is continued southward in western Ankore. The Nyoro living beside Lake Albert can supplement the produce of their farming with fish, a feature in which they also resemble the lakeside Soga, Ganda and Ziba, east of the Dry Zone.

The Ruwenzori Mountains are covered with wet highland forest and are inhabited by a distinct ethnic group, the Konzo, who, however, also extend well to the west, into the similar forest on the nearby highlands in Zaire. Immediately west of the Ruwenzoris, in lowland forest, are the Amba. Unlike their eastern neighbours on the plateau, the Konzo and Amba have no kings or states; and, apart from the still precarious attempts at central administration by the governments of Uganda and Zaire, they live in autonomous settlements. Furthermore, they circumcize, again a striking contrast with the Interlacustrine peoples, and they belong culturally in the Wet Forest region to the west, with peoples such as the Bali and Lese.

Until recent changes, the sub-region was marked by kings, courts and regional administrators, as has been discussed already. In addition, there were, and are, smiths and medical specialists, as among stateless peoples, and there are also priests serving local shrines, again familiar from stateless peoples. European medicine was introduced into the sub-region by Christian missionaries, from 1877 onward, but in this area of states the missionaries had an effect not seen in the regions so far considered.

At the Ganda court, factions identified themselves as allies of the British, Anglican, missionaries, or of the French, Roman Catholic, missionaries. Both factions had their attention fixed partly beyond East Africa on possible aid they might receive from different European countries, Britain, France or Germany. The horizons of Interlacustrine power-politics were expanding. Another faction, professing to be Muslim, relied for support on Swahili traders. Between 1890 and 1894 a series of brief but fierce civil wars left the Inglisa, pro-British, victorious, but British administration, from 1894 on, resulted in compromises which ensured that Roman Catholic and Muslim nobles were guaranteed, and even entrenched in, certain fiefs. These events led to a polarizing of Ganda into Roman Catholic and Protestant, with a minority claiming to be Muslim. Some whole districts were predominantly Catholic or Protestant. The other states of the sub-region, as well as Ankore and Chiga, caught up in the administration of a protectorate based on Ganda, and often ruled by Ganda officials of the Protectorate Government, took on the same factional labels. Despite the strength of this partisan feeling in the period 1900–60, there is evidence that it is waning in the course of events since Uganda became independent in 1962.

Within the sub-region there are no castes, a feature which sets this area apart from the two sub-regions further south. However, the names of castes, Huma and Iru, are known in Nyoro and Tooro, even though people there are not all allocated to a caste, and there are no rules of endogamy in force. A probable explanation of this situation is that the caste-procedures have died out in Nyoro–Tooro, although they were once there. It is also possible that castes existed at one time in Ganda and Soga, although there is no trace of them in the period from 1880 onward.

There is another distinction between this sub-region and the other two. The royal families of Nyoro and Tooro are called Bito, and they are descended, it can safely be inferred, from immigrants who moved into the area from the north, some centuries back, and probably in the fifteenth century. How their leaders became kings is not known, presumably by forcibly deposing the ruling dynasty of the period. The immigrants spoke Luo, and belonged to a group ancestral to the present Acholi. Nyoro used to knock out their two lower middle incisor teeth, unlike other Interlacustrines, and this reflects imitation of the habits of people to the north of them. Elsewhere in the sub-region, some Soga royal lines claim to be Bito, but the Ganda royal house makes no such claim. In Ankore, and further south, the term Bito does not occur, and there is no indication of contact with any peoples of the Savanna region.

God is assumed to be the source of all events by Nyoro, Tooro and Soga, who also recognize the need to sacrifice to their ancestors, and to spirits of the bush and of the lakes. Their cosmic pattern is very similar to that of most East African peoples, but the Ganda are remarkable in this respect. At the present time, a high proportion of Ganda assume God's unity and presence, as do other East Africans, and most Ganda profess to be Muslim or Christian. Some Ganda, however, recognize a number of deities, Katonda and Musoke, for example, and in 1870, presumably, almost all Ganda recognized these. It is true, as some modern Ganda monotheists stress, that Katonda was supreme, co-ordinating the activities of all deities (called *balubaale*).[2] What is remarkable, however, is that no other East African people even approached dividing the unity of God. To find a parallel in Africa it is necessary to travel as far as the Yoruba states, on the west coast.

In various parts of the world the differentiation of divine power into a number of distinct, and personal, forms only occurs in conjunction with elaborate social specialization, but Ganda is only one of the complex societies of the Interlacustrine region, and all the others are implicitly monotheistic. There is, therefore, some evidence here that the Ganda are strikingly different from neighbours whom they otherwise resemble closely. Their sacrifices, for example, are directed, by those who have not given them up, to their ancestors, and, occasionally, the other spirits, of the bush or lakes.

From this discussion of the sub-region, it will be clear that Ganda has played a dominating part in the period since 1800, and that Ganda's position at the top of the prestige-gradient was assured at the time that the Uganda Protectorate was confirmed by the treaty of 1900. With large numbers of officials in the Uganda civil service, they are possibly still the envy of their Interlacustrine neighbours, but events since 1962 have made it clear, to Ganda and their neighbours alike, that power in the area today is vested in the Uganda army; and the army is not an instrument of Ganda supremacy.

From the considerable obscurity of the oral traditions, it is at least clear that Ganda's high position was relatively new in the nineteenth century. Through much of the previous century, and perhaps back to the fifteenth, Nyoro had been more important than Ganda. However, not only had the Ganda occupied Nyoro's old role at the top of the prestige-gradient, but they were differentiating away from the older traditions and forms of the northern Interlacustrine region. For example, their cosmic pattern, with its plurality of deities, is unique in East Africa, let alone the Interlacustrine region. Furthermore, the absence of castes was probably a social innovation made by the Ganda; and Soga had already followed them in this respect, while in Nyoro–Tooro the castes were being allowed to die, following Ganda example. Also, by 1860, Ganda's administration was the most ruthlessly streamlined in the region, to the extent that it is tempting to drop the word feudal, and begin to talk about bureaucracy. The Ganda were thus not just the militarily most powerful state of their area, as Nyoro, and perhaps other states, had been before them. They were administrative innovators, the loss of caste reflecting the emphasis on centralized power and promotion. In these conditions, conscious superiority had unconscious effects, in changing their cosmic pattern. This process of unconscious differentiation, in order to demonstrate difference and superiority, has been already invoked to account for the peculiarity of Maasai sexual morals. Any recourse to unconscious processes can be criticized harshly on the grounds that it is an escape from observable facts. The view that Ganda peculiarity springs partly from their sense of superiority, and of specialness, does, nevertheless, fit the available facts.

However, the prestige situation in the sub-region was not simple. The Nyoro king, during the later nineteenth century, was repeatedly asked by members of different Acholi groups to adjudicate disputes which were very difficult for them to handle themselves, and which were best submitted to a neutral arbitrator. This implies that the Acholi were impressed by the power of the Nyoro, overshadowed though it might be, on its Dry Zone frontier, by Ganda.

The Ziba–Ankore Sub-region

Southwards from Tooro and Ganda, the dissected plateau surface continues along the western side of Lake Victoria. The three zones also continue down the western side of the Lake, the wet zone near the shore, the Dry Zone inland, and another wet zone on the west. There is a difference, however, in that the western wet zone, south of Ankore, is occupied by the Western Rift Highlands, in the next sub-region, and not by the plateau surface. Patches of wet forest survive, but much of the original tree cover has been cleared; and the eastern wet zone, near the lake, supports extensive groves of bananas, the staple crop of the Ziba, who live in that zone.

The state of Ankore is in the western wet zone, and also in the Dry Zone; and it is separated from Tooro, also in the western wet zone, by the marshy valley of the Katonga River. Although the productive heart of Ankore is the western, wet, area, the eastern section of the state, in the Dry Zone where it borders western Ganda, is a major grazing area, with large numbers of cattle. A high proportion of Ankore living here are cattle herders, and belong to the Hima caste. In this division between a wet agrarian west and dry pastoral east Ankore comes nearer than any other part of the Interlacustrine region to that separation between livelihood areas which is so marked in the Eastern Rift Coast region. The people of the Dry Zone, however, are Ankore, like those of the west, and not a separate ethnic group.

The west of Ankore occupies the end of the western wet zone on the plateau. Beyond here, to the south, the Western Rift Highlands project far eastwards, and are largely covered by the states of Rwanda and Rundi. The northern end of these highlands, however, are unusual in the region, being devoid of state organization before its establishment by European administrators. This is the country of the Chiga, wet, thickly-populated, and covered with a dense spread of autonomous settlements, whose members only started paying taxes to a central government well after 1900. The Chiga speak the same language as the Ankore, from whom they differ in habitat and organization. There is no evidence that they were ever part of any Interlacustrine state, and they are organizationally closer to the peoples of the Wet Forest region than to the states of the plateau. However, they do not circumcize, unlike the Konzo, another stateless people on the Western Rift Highlands. Chiga cultural ties lie with the plateau peoples below them, but their organization survives from a much earlier period of Interlacustrine history.

On the southern edge of the Chiga, inside the present state of Rwanda, there are people who speak Rwanda, but who in 1900 showed little loyalty to the Rwanda kings, and retained memories of autonomous settlements, like those of the Chiga. They had been incorporated into the Rwanda kingdom by the expansion of "feudal" land-tenure and of taxation to them, during the eighteenth and nineteenth centuries, as part of the military outreach of the kings, which also brought these into conflict with Ganda in the Ziba states.

These occupy the plateau between the Rwanda highlands and Lake Victoria, their population decreasing inland from the well watered lakeshore to the Dry Zone. In the north they are separated from Ganda and from Ankore by the marshy valley of the Kagera River. In the south, their country passes gradually into the territories of the very similar Dzindza, and of the Shumbwa. In this zone, the peoples are transitional to the dryer Sukuma–Nyamwezi sub-region of the Southern Savanna region. The Dzindza, divided like the Ziba into a number of small states, occupy the southern shore of Lake Victoria, west of Smith Sound. South of the Dzindza are the Shumbwa, transitional to the Nyamwezi.

The Dzindza had in fact formed a united kingdom at one stage, but this united phase had ended in 1860, when the king Ruhinda II died, and his sons dismembered the state in their scramble to each ensure a patrimony for himself. At the present time large numbers of western Dzindza are identifying themselves as Ziba, while eastern Dzindza is increasingly occupied by Sukuma settlers, moving in from the east and south. Probably the Dzindza are in the process of disappearing, their members being recruited into other groups. The Shumbwa appear to be in a similar position. At the present time, they resemble Nyamwezi, but there are indications that once they were clearly distinct from them. Notably, they show an interest in cultivating bananas which is markedly unlike the farming habits of the Nyamwezi. Both Sukuma and Nyamwezi are expanding peoples, their prestige high in the last hundred years, and the Shumbwa and Dzindza may be simply joining neighbours they cannot beat. Behind this acquiescence, however, so markedly unlike the tenacious clinging to identity of most East African peoples, there is probably a physical factor. Their territories seem to be drying up, with the result that their cultivation practices are increasingly less effective. In these circumstances, they are at a disadvantage when in contact with peoples well adapted to dry conditions, such as the Sukuma and Nyamwezi. If this is so, then the Dzindza who leave for Ziba country are taking an elegant way out, by re-settling in an area suitable to the continuing of their old way of life. Whatever the factors behind the changes, in this zone, south of the Interlacustrine plateau, the Southern Savanna region is encroaching on the Interlacustrine region, a reminder that we must not assume that cultural boundaries are permanent.

From the eastern part of Dzindza, now filling with Sukuma, it is a readily practicable canoe trip to Kerewe, much of it an island but with part of its territory on the neighbouring peninsula. The state of Kerewe is marked by dense population and intensive farming, including the stall-feeding of cattle. The population history can be guessed, with a high degree of probability, although the people themselves have not memorized anything so mundane. On the island the relative safety from raids allowed people to settle over a long period of time; the rainfall is relatively reliable, as on the eastern lake-shore nearby; and, as a result, population began to build up. Eventually, land became scare and cultivation was intensified, as in other high-density areas. Population then increased further, and it was necessary for some people to move to the nearest part of the mainland, where many stayed clustered together for defence, and retained the traditions of centralized kingly rule, and of intensive cultivation. Any who went beyond this mainland enclave became absorbed into people culturally very different, such as the Jita and Zanaki, with no royalty and with much less intensive farming. A major factor in the security of the island and, later, of its mainland colony was centralized kingly government, derived from the states on the west shore of the lake, as oral traditions state clearly.

The Kerewe are thus on a frontier of the region where it meets the Maasai-centred Eastern Rift Coast, on the lake-shore, and here represented by Jita, Nata, Kuria and others. Furthermore, the Sukuma, on the mainland south of the lake, belong to yet a third region, the Southern Savanna. This south-eastern corner of Lake Victoria will be examined again when the Sukuma are discussed, in Chapter 7.

Except for the Chiga, the peoples of the sub-region showed the familiar pattern of king, court, regional administrators, taxes and local law-courts. There were also smiths, medical specialists and priests, who all persist, alongside European medicine and Christian priests and pastors. God is above all, the sacrifices being offered more immediately to the ancestors and the spirits of the bush and lakes.

The names of the castes Huma and Iru have already been mentioned among the Nyoro and Tooro, although there are no effective castes among these groups. Further south, however, in Ankore, Ziba and Dzindza, the people are divided between the two castes, the name Huma occurring in its more widespread form Hima. In theory, each caste is endogamous, although they probably never have been exclusively so, in practice. Each caste too has a stereotype of habitual livelihood and of bodily appearance. The Hima, who are much less numerous in each of the states, are characterized as cattle-herders, pale-skinned, and with fine facial features. The Iru, on the other hand, are said to be cultivators, dark-skinned (*Iru* means dark in all the languages involved) and with coarse features. The Iru are ugly, while the Hima are lovely; beautiful people are also top people; and the Hima, socially superior to the Iru, own and tend the cattle, which are admirable, desired and beautiful. It is a neat system, but it does not correspond with what is going on. Hima and Iru are often indistinguishable in appearance, although some Ankore really are more fine-featured and more pale-skinned than others. Furthermore, cattle ownership is not confined to the Hima, nor are all Hima too proud to dirty their hands with hoeing. Neat-minded traditionalists will tell you that in the past things were much tidier, but it is not certain that they were. Theory and practice may always have been out of step.

One element of the social order, at least, fits the theory. The royal families in all the Ankore–Ziba sub-region are Hima, but even here sceptics will ask : once a family is in power, who will dare say that they are not Hima? The castes of this sub-region, and the next, have been the basis of some elaborate constructions of the history of the region, involving cattle-keeping caucasoids who overran the area from the north. Whether there ever were such people must be examined later in this chapter.

By 1880, Ankore was overshadowed by the power and prestige of Ganda, and the stateless peoples of the highlands, on the southern borders of Chiga, were being absorbed by the Rwanda kings, with whom their relations were probably love-hate : they resented paying taxes, but they were impressed by the power of the Rwanda king and nobles, and resorted readily to the courts to have their disputes adjudicated. It is likely that the Chiga were similarily impressed by the power of Ankore, secondary though this kingdom was to Ganda. As has been mentioned already, in the Ziba states, and especially in Karagwe, Ganda and Rwanda clashed in their rival bids to acquire satellites. The Ganda were more successful overall, and they also intervened between 1860 and 1890 in the states of Dzindza, beyond the reach of Rwanda diplomacy, as was Kerewe, another Ganda potential satellite. All the peoples of the sub-region formed a zone of Ganda outreach, and their rulers must have looked nervously towards the Ganda court, while those Ziba who were near the Rwanda foothills had to look that way as well. Meanwhile, in the south, the transitional Shumbwa were gradually being absorbed culturally by the Nyamwezi, an alternative centre of prestige.

The Rwanda–Rundi Sub-region

By 1890 the stateless Chiga were on the edge of the area loyal, at least in theory, to the kings of Rwanda. From Chiga country the Western Rift Highlands stretch southwards to the northern end of Lake Tanganyika; and on the west of the Rift Valley similar highlands run parallel, dropping down to the Wet Forest region in the Congo Basin. Most of the highland wet forest, which must once have covered these hills, has now been cleared, for cultivation, and possibly also specifically for grazing. Certainly, at the present time, large areas are under grassland, which is perpetuated by the grazing of cattle, preventing regeneration of the forest.

Almost all the people of the sub-region live in these densely populated highlands, but on the south there is an area of plateau, much lower-lying, dryer, and merging into the country of the Nyamwezi. Most of this plateau area is covered with dry woodland, similar to that of Nyamwezi, and there is an extensive zone of swamps near the Malagarasi River. The people of the area are in most ways more like the Nyamwezi than the Rundi and Rwanda, but they are transitional between the two groups and have strong cultural and historical ties to the highland peoples.

The Republic of Rwanda, successor to the kingdom, occupies the highlands east of Lake Kivu. With a population of three million, it is an overcrowded country, large numbers of Rwanda emigrating, for some decades past, to work, and settle, in Ganda and other areas. The factional fighting, with its attendant suspicion between castes, from 1959 to 1965, has driven tens of thousands of refugees into neighbouring territories, but land remains scarce, and population continues to increase.

Pressure of people on land, and consequent emigration, has been a feature of Chiga country also; and, to the south of Rwanda, Rundi shows a similar situation. Throughout these highlands, volcanic soils and relatively high rainfall have supported the increase of population, which has led in its turn to pressure on the land. This has prompted intensification of farming, with heavy use of cattle-dung as fertilizer, and the result has been an even larger population, now enhanced further by the great reduction in the incidence of epidemic diseases, such as smallpox, an effect of European medicine, as elsewhere in East Africa.

Burundi, with a population of some two and a half million, is in most respects a double of Rwanda. Since 1966 it too has suffered from faction-fighting which has tended to set the castes against each other, and refugees have left for neighbouring countries, including Rwanda, some of whose own refugees have been in Rundi since 1963. The border between the two states, now fixed, shifted before European administration with the victories and defeats of the rival armies along the frontier.

West of the Rift Valley, in country very similar to that of the two giant states, is a string of smaller kingdoms, now incorporated into the Republic of Zaire. Separated from each other by distance rather than by any changes in the habitat, they are from north to south: Hunde, Haavu,[3] Nyabungu, and Fuliiro. Although they possess royal families, and are each divided into two castes, these peoples are transitional from the Interlacustrine region to the Wet Forest below them. To the south, these highland states connect, through the Bembe, with the kingdoms of the Southern Savanna region.

It has been noted already that in the south Rwanda and Rundi themselves have a transition-fringe to the Southern Savanna states. In addition, further north, there are two small states, in the eastern foothills of Rwanda and Rundi, and transitional to the Ziba and Dzindza. The Shubi and Hangaza, the people of these two states, have only two castes, like the Ziba and Dzindza, but resemble the Rwanda and Rundi in that one of their castes is named Tuutsi. In the dry southern fringe itself are the Ha, divided into several states, and to the south of them are the Vinza, and the Jiji. The name of their country has been given to the settlement, Ujiji, which was the lake terminal of the grand caravan route from the coast. Its place has now been taken by Kigoma, the terminal of the central railway line. All three peoples are marked by the division of the population into two castes, of which the socially superior is called Tuutsi. On the eastern borders of Vinza country, in the swamps of the

Malagarasi River, there are specialized Vinza who live largely by fishing, and spend most of their lives in their canoes.

The sub-region was marked by states and kings, prior to the reorganizations after 1960, and the pattern of administration was similar to that of the rest of the region: ministers at court; regional administrators; taxes; and law-courts, over which presided the local official who represented the central government. Smiths, medical specialists and priests also occur, as usual. God is the source of all events; and sacrifices have to be made to the ancestors and to spirits of the bush. The arrival of Roman Catholic and Protestant missionaries, from around 1880 onward, has resulted not only in large numbers of people professing conversion, but also in some political labelling, as in Ganda. In both Rwanda and Rundi the noble families became largely associated with the Protestant missionaries, and the Roman Catholics came to be seen, to a large extent, as the ministers of the common people. Although the association was not as neat as rumour had it, when aspiring politicians in both countries challenged the ruling groups, from 1959 onward, they saw the Roman Catholic missionaries as allies.

The outstandingly distinctive feature of the sub-region, apart from the great size of Rwanda and Rundi, is the degree of differentiation of their castes. Rwanda are divided into three castes, each supposed to be endogamous. It is tacitly agreed, probably even by the present ruling elite in Rwanda, who would like to hear otherwise, that the prestige order from the top is: Tuutsi, Hutu, Twa. In 1900, certainly, this was the accepted order. Each caste has attributes which were openly discussed in 1900 and are still widely accepted. The Tuutsi are very tall, graceful, with pale brown skins and fine facial features. They are privileged, and obliged, by the command of God, to own and tend the cattle, and to rule. Certainly, the royal family was Tuutsi, and so were most of the major land-owners who were the upper rank of the administration. Hutu, by contrast, it was said, are much shorter, stocky and clumsy in build, dark-skinned and with coarse faces. They are ordained to be cultivators, dirtying their hands at hoeing; and they must be content to be tax-payers, and not to aspire to high office. There is clearly a strong parallel between this contrast of Tuutsi and Hutu, and the contrast between Hima and Iru in the Ziba–Ankore states. There is, however, the difference in Rwanda that a third caste occurs, not paralleled in the other sub-region. This third caste are the Twa, said to be small, very dark, very coarse-featured and startlingly ugly, their work especially hunting and pottery, although they also formerly provided the bodyguard of the king. They are, anyway, only a tiny fraction of the population. In the Rwanda scale of prestige, as in Ankore, beauty went side-by-side with honour.

This neat hierarchy did not work according to its ideal form in the day-to-day running of Rwanda. For example, the Twa bodyguards of the king did not exist in the ideal scheme. According to that, they were far too degraded and sub-human to fulfil so important a function. Furthermore, individual Hutu repeatedly rose to high office, and often married Tuutsi women. Presumably, the children of such marriages were Tuutsi, and the descendants of all eminent Hutu ultimately became Tuutsi, so that there was always an approximate coincidence of the ruling elite with a wealthy section of the Tuutsi caste. Most Tuutsi, however, must have been poor, many of them at a time landless and without cattle of their own. At the same time, a proportion of Hutu were rich in land and cattle, and held responsible positions in local administration. In practice, Rwanda seems to have worked much like most kingdoms in all parts of the world. Talent and wealth provided an avenue to higher social position; and astute kings knew well, as they did in England, earlier, that their most reliable allies against the entrenched nobility were capable members of the class just below the aristocracy.

Perversely, Belgian administration, between 1919 and 1959, seems to have slowed down, although completely unwittingly, the upward flow of lower class, usually Hutu, talent; and in the faction-fighting which preceded independence, during 1959–62, and thereafter, Hutu and Tuutsi became terms increasingly identified with, respectively, aspiring talent and entrenched privilege. Once this had occurred, it was possible for wealthy Hutu to condone the massacre of poor Tuutsi by poor Hutu, in 1963, by shrugging off all Tuutsi as exploiters. Actually, it was the clique around the young king Kigeri V who were the group clinging desperately to power, which they hoped would become absolute once the Belgians had left. Most Tuutsi, as always, were far from the elite.[4]

The same contrast between a rigid theory of caste, and a more flexible practice, occurred, in the period 1900–20, in Rundi; but here there is a difference from Rwanda. Instead of three castes there are five : Twa, Hutu, Hima, Tuutsi and Ganwa. The Hima are described conventionally in the same terms as the Tuutsi, or as the Hima in Ankore; but there is a striking contrast with Rwanda in the symbolic position of the royal clan, the Ganwa, who form their own caste, not identified with Tuutsi, as in Rwanda, nor with any other caste. This symbolic aloofness emphasizes that the royal clan is apart from the factions and lobbying of every-day life. Not surprisingly, in practice, the Ganwa have formed their own factions to press rival claims to the throne.[5]

On the dryer fringe of Rwanda and Rundi, as we have seen already, there are only two castes, the socially more esteemed always called Tuutsi. This pattern occurs among the Shubi, Hangaza, Ha, Vinza and Jiji. In all these cases, the lower caste is called simply by the ethnic name, for instance Ha or Vinza. They are thus less specialized than the two-caste Dzindza and Ziba, who have a separate name for each caste; and it is probable that these groups borrowed the habit of calling their nobles Tuutsi from Rwanda or Rundi, or, alternatively, were taken over by Tuutsi nobles, in the manner of the Norman Conquest in 1066.

Whatever the course of events, the prestige of Rundi, based upon its size and power, is strong enough in these dryer fringe states for Tuutsi to mean something to the local populations at the present time. In the late nineteenth century also, the two giant states overawed the smaller king-doms on the western highlands overlooking the Wet Forest. At this period, furthermore, Rwanda was aiming to obtain Karagwe as a satellite, and to intervene similarly in other Ziba states. Rundi was not so adventurous at this period, probably because the state was in practice divided into a number of autonomous fiefs, each virtually a kingdom in its own right. The king of Rundi ruled his own fief but could exert little pressure on his immediate subordinates, who were in practice his equals. Even in such a divided condition, however, Rundi was strong enough not to be eroded by Rwanda, whose kings were expanding their territory in the north. Furthermore, Rundi had not always been so divided. It appears to have been more cohesive in the reign of Ntare Rugaamba (c. 1795–c. 1852).

Rwanda and Rundi are remarkably similar in terrain, population size, territorial extent and culture. They give the impression of being twins, an impression strengthened by the similarity of the stems of the names, both sharing the pattern r-nd-, which may be insignificant but, if so, is certainly extraordinary. The use of a prefix with the name of Rundi, hence Burundi, while there is no prefix in the name of the other state, hence Rwanda, looks like a simple example of deliberate, if only partially conscious, self-differentiation. A comparable example probably occurs further north, where breakaway Tooro has dropped a prefix long normal in the name of the original state, Bunyoro.

Piecing together numerous clues in the memorized king-lists of the two countries, a number of writers have been able to produce a convincing general picture of the stages by which the two states increased in size, to reach their present boundaries. In the process they absorbed other countries, once their equals, the size perhaps of the smaller states of the western fringe, such as Haavu. The names of these absorbed territories are preserved, probably, in the names of some of the modern provinces, just as in England the names of formerly independent states, such as Essex, Kent and Sussex, are preserved as county-names. What seems to have been the original territories of Rwanda and Rundi are not far apart, and another possibly significant fact is that the king-list of Rwanda is longer than that of Rundi. The longer list goes back to perhaps the fourteenth century, possibly much further, while for Rundi there are only nine names, against twenty-six for Rwanda. The Rundi rulers probably go back only to the seventeenth century. There is, therefore, a possible solution to the similarity between the two states. At some time after the process of swallowing neighbours was begun, Rwanda and Rundi were one state, but Rundi seceded, probably in the seventeenth century. From that point onward Rwanda expanded largely on its northern frontier, Rundi on its southern. Such a secession would fit the available facts, and is paralleled by numerous examples in different regions of the world, including Tooro, nearby. There is one further detail: Rwanda have five names for their kings, each taken in turn, so that the king-list contains groups of five names. In Rundi there are four regnal names, and the king-list has clumps of four. Could this be self-differentiation again?

The Origin and History of the Kingdoms

The king-lists provide a body of information which cannot be paralleled in the kingless areas of East Africa. It is true that the Iraqw, Datoga and Rimi have long genealogies, with some details of events, mostly major famines, but they lack the quantity of detail found in the memorized chronicles of the larger Interlacustrine states. Even so, these oral traditions are poor compared to the written records of the Near East or China, the names of the kings being accompanied by notable campaigns and conquests, but lacking the snippets of incidental comment which sometimes give a hint to the reader of written chronicles that events were not as the official version seeks to show. Apart from the lack of detail, king-lists passed from one court genealogist to another sometimes miss out a king's name altogether, especially if he is a failure of some kind, for instance by losing a battle against an enemy-people. Ironically, the rewriting of history is easier when there is no writing. This disappearance of names from lists makes hazardous the common exercise of estimating the average length of reigns in written chronicles, and then multiplying the average so obtained by the number of names back in order to obtain a "precise" date for a particular ruler. However, most kings are remembered, and not forgotten, and the method has a crude validity.

Such a procedure will not, however, take us back to the beginning of royal states in the Interlacustrine region. There is no certainty that any recorded list goes back to the beginning of the state to which it is attached, nor is it likely that any modern state has its roots as far back as the earliest formation of states in the region. A parallel is worth quoting: in the British Isles there have been kingly states, fairly certainly, for four thousand years, but the kingdoms of England and Scotland are only about a thousand years old. They arose on territory, and with a backlog of tradition, which they inherited from earlier states, probably more than one generation of them.

In the Interlacustrine region, states are certainly younger than in the British Isles, but the archaeological evidence is extremely scanty, and any reconstruction of the past must be very tentative indeed. It is worth introducing an outline of a reconstruction here, in order to set the scene for the necessary refutation of some illusions which have played a large part in writings about the region. I shall not attempt to show all the processes by which I arrive at these tentative conclusions, because this would distract attention from the main themes, but it will be necessary shortly to mention certain critical details.

In the early centuries A.D. the region was inhabited by cultivating peoples, with cattle, sheep and goats, as well as a few of their present crops, notably sorghum and bulrush-millet. Culturally, they were probably similar to neighbouring peoples in areas now outside the region, on the savanna and in the Eastern Rift Highlands. In other words, the region had not yet differentiated out from its neighbours. The scale of organization was small, with each settlement autonomous; and there were doubtless the familiar part-time specialists: war-leaders, priests and doctors. By the time of Christ also, smiths had probably appeared, and iron tools and weapons had largely replaced stone. The Bantu languages may not by that time yet have reached the area along the northern edge of the Wet Forest from the west, and, if not, then the people spoke languages related to the ancestors of Lugbara and Madi. Physically, the people were negroid in general appearance but many of them showed evidence of a caucasoid admixture, because for some centuries negroid immigrants from the west had been trickling into an area inhabited for millennia by caucasoids.

The first kingdoms were tiny, established around the time of Christ by war-leaders whose positions became permanent, and who each, undeliberately and gradually, acquired the aura of unifying symbols for their own people, a process which occurs wherever kings appear. The mysterious spark which changed war-leaders to hereditary, divinely sanctioned, rulers must have sprung, as everywhere else, from the members of a group feeling that they needed a visible, and living, focus for the sense that they belonged to a group. Very often such a need is felt when people are threatened by others more powerful militarily than themselves, but this is not likely in the region at that period. There were modestly impressive kingdoms in Nubia, in the middle Nile valley, and also in the Ethiopian Highlands, but none of them would have been able to exert any pressure on the Interlacustrine peoples. The swamps and dry woodlands of the Savanna region (as it has become), and the deserts of the Lake Rudolf depression, separated these earlier Interlacustrines from the nearest threatening states and kings, with their armies. Perhaps it was just a collection of unusually visionary and talented men living near each other at the same time who established the tradition of a glorified war-leadership.

It is likely, however, that the founders of the first tiny states were not starting entirely from scratch. There had been kingdoms in the lower Nile valley for over three thousand years, and in the middle Nile valley for over a thousand. Probably some knowledge of these states had reached the Interlacustrines. Some of them may even have travelled down the Nile valley, and seen them for themselves. Possibly there is evidence for such contact in the Shooting of the Nations ceremony, performed by the king of Nyoro, and strongly reminiscent of the Sed ceremony among the Egyptians of the dynastic period.[6] It is necessary to be careful here, however, because all peoples with kings see them as defenders of the realm, and such ceremonies, showing the king striking down his nation's enemies, could have arisen spontaneously and independently.

Once a king had emerged in one group of settlements, then others followed suit in self-defence. Small kingdoms, each of a few settlements, proliferated across the region. Once this mosaic of small kingdoms had occurred, then a league-table emerged, each vying with others in their own area to be the champion, and after a time successful champions began to absorb their less successful neighbours. In self-defence again, other states had to respond to this threat to their continued identity, and so they in their turn absorbed their weaker neighbours. This process is documented in the Near East and in China, as well as in other long-literate areas, and there can be little doubt that it occurred here, on the Interlacustrine plateau.

Kingdoms thus grew bigger, and fewer, while at the same time others were growing up at the fringes, among stateless peoples now threatened by the new powers. After a period of increasing in extent, however, the region covered by the states reached roughly its present size. In the north, further expansion was hindered by the sparser population, resulting from lower rainfall. The same factors inhibited for a time state formation in what is now Nyamwezi. Sparse population, the result of the adverse habitat, also halted the spread of states westwards, down into the wet forest of the Congo Basin; but there is no readily discernible physical factor to prevent a spread of states eastward to the lake-shore below the Eastern Rift Highlands. Here it was probably the prestige of stateless pastoralists, such as the Maasai, and their predecessors, who kept the peoples from adopting kings, together with the fact that no king was able permanently to overrun this zone.

The increasing size of the states involved a corresponding increase in the degree of social specialization. The courts of the kings offered increasing patronage for musicians, dancers and story-tellers; and husbandry became more intensive and more specialized. As a result herding was separated from hoe-farming as an occupation, and the main part of the population, outside the court, split into two castes, the cultivators and the herders. Herders were concentrated where conditions favoured them, especially in the Dry Zone, not needed for cultivation and free for extensive grazing. Although less productive than cultivation, herding carried much more prestige, since it associates people with cattle, powerful, productive, and symbols of prosperity, which itself implies divine approval. The precedence of the herder-caste over the cultivators followed from this basic pattern of prestige. If kings and nobles were associated with either caste it would have to be with that of the herders. Actually, members of the elite did not, and do not, dirty their hands with cattle any more than they do with hoeing, but the symbolic association is still there. Throughout sub-Saharan Africa, kings and strong men are symbolized as bulls. The same precedence of cattle ensures that in the Eastern Rift

Coast region the exclusive pastoralists have been the most admired groups. In the Interlacustrine region, on the other hand, the contrast between wet and dry areas is not as marked as further east, and it is unlikely that cultivating and pastoral groups differentiated out there before the increasing social specialization within the states.

These processes of growth, specialization and caste formation were well advanced after about a thousand years of development, that is by around 1000 A.D. By this date there were states approaching the size of modern Nyoro and Ankore; and the nuclei of the modern kingdoms probably already existed. The king-list of Nyoro, again probably, takes the story back to the thirteenth century, and that of Rwanda to the fourteenth, and both must have roots which are earlier still. According to the Nyoro traditions, in the thirteenth and fourteenth centuries a state called Kitara, which they claim is Nyoro, was head-state of a league which contained all of the present Ganda–Nyoro sub-region. By that period it seems likely that the present sub-regions were beginning to differentiate out.

Certainly the special shared history of the states of the northern sub-region continued, leaving the other two largely aloof. In about the fifteenth century new dynasties were established throughout much of the sub-region. They were founded by Luo-speakers, somewhat like the present Acholi, and probably the same people. In Nyoro the dynasty was called Bito, and survived until 1966. Similar dynasties came to power in a number of the Soga states, but the Ganda may not have changed dynasty at this time. Bito dynasties presumably came to power by conquest in a manner similar to that of the Norman Conquest of England, in 1066, with one elite largely replacing another. These new rulers came from peoples with weak, or no, state-traditions; they were "barbarians" and were largely absorbed to the culture of the states, much as the Manchu dynasty in China became Chinese in culture from the seventeenth century onward.

As we have already seen, the long (according to Nyoro) precedence of Nyoro faded in the eighteenth century, and Ganda emerged not only as the top state of the hegemony, but as an innovator, fiercely centralized, somewhat bureaucratic, and with a more streamlined social order, in which the old castes withered away. Caught in Ganda's orbit the Soga states, and later even traditionalist Nyoro, followed suit.

Further south, the Ziba–Ankore sub-region had a different history. No Bito, nor any of their kind, seem to have taken over here, but they may have tried, and the sub-region was less affected, in the nineteenth century, by the impact of innovating Ganda. One notable feature, apart from the survival of Hima and Iru castes, is the presence in all the states of the sub-region of dynasties who claim descent from a man called Ruhinda. It is not possible to ascertain the full significance of this alleged common descent. Conquest could account for it, or a long series of diplomatic marriages, as in the case of the Habsburgs in Europe; or perhaps it is not historically true that all the royal lines are descended from Ruhinda. They may just claim to be so descended because he is an auspicious person to claim as an ancestor. One conclusion is safe, and that is that the states are closely linked to each other by tradition, and have a cohesive history as well as a modern cultural unity.

The third sub-region, physically separated from the others by its highland habitat, also has a history which sets it apart from the other two. It is possible that all, or most, of the royal families are inter-related, but there is no putative common ancestor such as Ruhinda. The Tuutsi caste, however, is found throughout the area, even on the dry apron-fringe to the south. Here, there is evidence of long contact with the highlands since the languages of the Ha and Vinza are very closely allied to Rundi and Rwanda.[7] A large element in the populations here are probably the descendants of migrants down from the overcrowded hills. The major theme of the highlands' history is the emergence of Rwanda and Rundi as the dominant states, and their probable splitting apart, as has been suggested earlier in this chapter.

An outline of the probable history, or prehistory, of the region, over the last two thousand years, sets these states more firmly into their context. At one stage the peoples of this region had no states, and were more like their present neighbours on the west, north and east. In addition, it is useful to review the history of processes, because of some traditions which have arisen, and persisted, in the ethnological accounts of the region. Meinhof (1912)[8] and Baumann (1948)[9] are the major writers involved, although many others have agreed with them, and many more again have treated them as authoritative. Their version of events can be summarized briefly. At some stage the region was inhabited by cultivating peoples, speaking Bantu languages, negroid in appearance, and devoid of state organization and of kings. There came, from the north-east, pastoral, Cushitic-speaking, caucasoid invaders who overran the earlier inhabitants, established themselves as a ruling elite and caste, and established also an administrative hierarchy, with a king at the apex, in each new state thus formed. I have introduced refinements here, for the sake of clarity, because both these important writers used the term "Hamitic" to cover both a language group and the physical type of the Horn caucasoids.

This version of the processes of state- and caste-formation is widely divergent from that which I offered earlier, and it is necessary to comment upon the differences. The first observation which I need to make is that no-one has yet discovered states established by one stateless people conquering another. States are formed either by endogenous developments, such as probably happened at the beginning in this region, or else by people with a state tradition over-running people without one, and ruling them for a time, as happened, for example, in Finland, originally invented by its Swedish aristocracy. The Horn of Africa pastoralists lack kings or states, and so do the peoples of the Lake Rudolf depression, and of the Savanna to the north of the Interlacustrine region. Also, they seem always to have lacked large states, and possibly even tiny ones. Invaders from the north, with experience of kings and states, would have had to come from as far away as the Ethiopian Highlands or from the Nubian area of the middle Nile valley. They may have arrived from here, but there is no evidence that anyone did so directly until the nineteenth century.

Indeed, the Interlacustrine peoples themselves have no records of immigrants from the north, except for the founders of the Bito group of dynasties, affecting only the north of the region. These came to states already old and elaborate; they were not exclusive pastoralists; and they were negroid, and spoke a Nilo–Maa language, Luo. Other migrations that are remembered are short-distance movements inside or near the region. The Rwanda claim simply that they have always been where they are.

A third objection to the migrations from the north is based on the languages. Earlier in this chapter, it was noted that all the languages are Bantu. Furthermore, it can be added here, their vocabularies are massively Bantu. There are now words of English, French and German origin, borrowed only recently, and occasional Arabic stems borrowed, also recently, via Swahili. In Nyoro and Tooro, furthermore, there are some words of recognizably Luo origin, borrowed from the conquerors. Immigrants from the Horn, however, would at no time have spoken Bantu languages, and neither would any immigrants from the Ethiopian Highlands, the Lake Rudolf depression or the savanna. Any groups, therefore, arriving in the region from one of these areas would have spoken a language markedly different from those at present spoken there, and they cannot have failed to leave a distinguishable trace in the form of loan-words. The prestige which they, as rulers, would have enjoyed among the subject-peoples would have ensured, according to all the known analogous situations elsewhere, that the local people would have copied their customs, including their speech. One such analogous situation is England in the period after 1066 when, over a span of three centuries, French words passed into the English language in great numbers. Anyone arriving in England to study the customs and oral traditions of the people, and without any access to written documents, would be struck by the vast number of words of French origin now in use, and he might well start looking for an event of the type represented by the Conquest. On the plateau and highlands between the lakes, however, there is no trace in the languages of any borrowed elements which make it necessary to seek a conquest, or any immigration from far afield, apart again from the Bito example.

The strong feature, however, of Meinhof's argument has not been considered. According to the evidence at his disposal and also facing Baumann, the castes of the region, represented in most of the states under one set of names or the other, were not just social categories. Rather, they were racial units, their members distinguishable from those of other castes by their appearance. On the one hand, the Hima and the Tuutsi were caucasoid (to use the terms of this book), while the Iru and Hutu were negroid. The Twa, where they occurred, were different again, being a pygmy form of negroid, distinguishable by their small size. These differences in appearance, corresponding to differences of social esteem, and in political power, could, Meinhof assumed, be most readily interpreted in terms of waves of invaders, the Twa being the earliest inhabitants, and the Tuutsi, and Hima, the latest arrivals.

There is a major objection to the physical evidence, and that is that the differences in appearance are not marked, or even, much of the time, visible at all. It is certainly true that some of the individuals of the region, although still negroid, are more caucasoid than others. Such differences are not, however, neatly correlated with caste boundaries. There are some Twa in Rwanda and Rundi who are very short; and some Tuutsi from Rwanda are startlingly tall, as much as seven feet six inches, in some cases. Most Rwanda and Rundi, however, are much the same size as each other, irrespective of caste, and the same is true of Ankore and the Ziba states. Meinhof, and other early writers in the area, were swayed by the nature of the ethnographic evidence. There had been no detailed surveys of the differences between the physical types or the castes, but there was evidence on the social systems, and the local people who spoke to the European visitors had stressed the connection between high social status and admirable appearance. They had in fact repeated stereotypes which were genuinely part of everyday speech and assumptions among the peoples of the region.

Like other East Africans, the Interlacustrines regarded light brown skins as more handsome than dark brown, and they still do so. Regular faces, with finely-modelled features, are also admired, and large size is equated with majesty and importance, as it is in other parts of the world. Interlacustrines are, therefore, admiring the same features as their caste-less neighbours when they give the ideal types of the socially superior castes, either Tuutsi or Hima. It is not clear, however, how this type, rather than any other, has come to be the standard of East African bodily excellence. Pale brown skins and rather sharp facial features presumably derive from the populations who covered the northern half of the area before negroid immigrants began to filter in from the west (see Chapter 11) and to interbreed with the earlier peoples. It is, at the same time, unlikely that priority would give these features any claim to excellence, and still less likely that they would be remembered as excellent, for that initial reason alone, over a period of two millennia or more. Probably the East African peoples just do find paler skins[10] and the other features attractive, in terms of design and appearance, without reference to any historical priority or social precedence. Given such a taste, however, it follows spontaneously that these admired aspects of peoples' appearance should be attributed to the highest social group in any state, rather as princesses in European fairy-tales are always beautiful, and princes always handsome.

It remains true, nevertheless, that some Twa in Rundi and Rwanda really are very short, and some Tuutsi amazingly tall. The Twa probably have intermarried, over a long period, with pygmy groups in the Congo Basin, an understandable affinity for a caste specializing in hunting, and some Twa would thus show some pygmy features. The Tuutsi, on the other hand, or rather those among them who have formed the true aristocracy, have been able to exercise a wide choice when searching for wives for their sons, and have been able, if they wished, to concentrate on wives with the right bodily appearance. Over a period of a thousand years, this amounts to a form of selective breeding, as with racehorses or cocker spaniels, and some of the nobility have come to show the desired features to a high degree. The same effect has probably come about in aristocracies in other parts of the world. It must be stressed, however, that all Rwanda and Rundi look much alike, rather than racially different.

Meinhof and the other writers who invoked state- and caste-formation by invasion were probably affected by the events of their own period. Modern state-boundaries and administrative hierarchies were established after 1890 by Europeans, who formed a ruling caste, truly endogamous *vis-à-vis* the indigenous peoples. They were culturally distinct from these, and they looked very different from them. This remarkable increase in the scale of East African administration, which dwarfed Rundi, Rwanda and Ganda, the former giants, was, however, a new and unprecedented change. Apart from some possible distant inspiration from Nubia, the formation and growth of the Interlacustrine states was a thoroughly endogenous process.

6. Notes

1. For convenience, I use the term Ziba to include, not only the people who call themselves by the term, but also the neighbouring, and culturally very similar, Nyambo, of Karagwe. Ziba and Nyambo together are called "Haya" by Swahili.
2. There is a close analogy here with Zeus, in the pre-Christian Aegean, and with Odin in pre-Christian Scandinavia.
3. The name of their country, Buhaavu, is the origin of the name Bukavu, now given to the town known until 1960 as Costermansville.
4. Lemarchand gives a very lucid and detailed account of events, and their underlying causes, in Rwanda and Burundi, in the period 1959–68. R. Lemarchand (1970). "Rwanda and Burundi".
5. Lemarchand (1970), op. cit. pp. 324–342, 366.
6. See, for example, C. G. Seligman and B. Z. Seligman (1932). "Pagan Tribes of the Nilotic Sudan", p. 18.
7. M. Guthrie (1971). "Comparative Bantu", Vol. 2, p. 44.
8. C. Meinhof (1912). "Die Sprachen der Hamiten".
9. 1948 is the date of the French edition of "Volkerkunde von Afrika".

Baumann was writing on this subject already during the decade 1920–30.

H. Baumann and D. Westermann (1948). "Les Peuples et les Civilisations de l'Afrique".

10. East Africans, by contrast, do not find attractive the blotchy, semi-transparent looking complexions of most northern Europeans.

7

The Southern Savanna Belt of States

Distinctive Features of the Region

At the southern edge of the Interlacustrine states, there is a transition-zone, the country of the Ha, Vinza and Shumbwa, where the rainfall decreases southwards and where we approach the country of the Nyam-wezi. Their territory, occupying much of the west of modern Tanzania, is part of the huge Southern Savanna region, which stretches right across Africa between the Indian and Atlantic Oceans (Maps 8, 13). Most of the region is rolling plateau surface at between 1000 and 1300 metres, dropping only on the coasts, and in the lower Zambezi valley. There are, however, two major areas of highlands.

The eastern highlands area has been described briefly already, when introducing the East African Plateau. It is in the form of a Y, the three limbs of the letter joining at the northern end of Lake Nyasa. The western limb extends from the southern end of Lake Tanganyika and the eastern bounds the East African Plateau on its south-eastern edge. The two limbs join in the high mountains north of Lake Nyasa, and from there the high-lands continue southwards, flanking the lake for some distance. In the west of the Southern Savanna region there is a second, and more compact, highland area, in Angola, somewhat to the north of the Kalahari.

These two highland areas, with more abundant and reliable rainfall than the rest of the region, carry wet highland forest, although this has been cleared over large areas. Over most of the region, however, the vegetation is remarkably uniform from coast to coast, consisting of *miombo* dry woodland, with *Brachystegia* species frequent as dominants. Rainfall decreases from the edge of the Wet Forest region southwards towards the Kalahari and the dry south-west of Africa; and the dry conditions here extend northwards along the coastal belt to the west of the Angola highlands. Hence, to the west and south of these highlands the *miombo* woodland fades out into desert conditions, with only scattered thorn trees.

Over most of the region population is very sparse, less than three people to the square kilometre over thousands of square miles. Although there is some concentration of population in the highlands, this is not very marked except around the northern end of Lake Nyasa. From there dense population continues south very close to the lake's shores; and at the south end, continuing into the valley of the Shire River, is the only area of extensive dense population in the region. Apart from that, in the wet country of the Nyanja group of peoples, there is no part of the Southern Savanna to compare with Rwanda and Rundi, or with Luo, Luhya and Gikuyu country further north. On the southern shore of Lake Victoria, however, where the Southern Savanna touches the two regions to the north, there is a concentration of people in the country of the Sukuma (Map 6).

The people of the whole belt are cultivators, except for a few hunting-and-gathering groups around Lake Bangweulu, and in the Luangwa trench, all of whom are called "Twa" by their cultivating neighbours. At the same time, hunting is very important to all the groups outside the few densely-settled areas. Not only is it a source of meat, but hunting takes up a great deal of men's attention, and has elaborate associated rituals over most of the region. Fishing is important to the cultivating peoples who live near the lakes, although there is a marked difference between the two largest lakes. Lake Nyasa is surrounded by dense populations, and is fished from all its shores, while Lake Tanganyika, apart from its northern end, is in sparsely peopled country, and the steep slopes down to the lake surface provide few sites for settlements.

Over most of the region, farming is not intensive, much of it being shifting cultivation, with the woodland cleared, and the debris burned, before a crop is planted. Such clearings are cultivated for only a few years. In the zone around Lake Nyasa, with its dense population, there is, predictably, much more intensive cultivation, necessitated by pressure on the land. At the northern extremity of the lake, in the wet volcanic highlands of the Nyakyusa, the staple crop is bananas, and the cash-crop coffee. It is a southern counterpart of Chaga country on the well watered, and again volcanic, slopes of Kilimanjaro.

F

The crops of the region are very similar to those already detailed for the Eastern Rift Coast region, with a little more rice grown, for instance among the Nyamwezi, Bena and Ndamba. In addition, cotton is a major cash-crop among the Sukuma, and the unusual features of Nyakyusa country have been mentioned already.

Livestock, on the other hand, is conspicuously scarce over much of the region, although there are concentrations of cattle in the wet high-lands and in two border regions. One of these is Sukuma country, close to the Interlacustrine states and also to the lake-shore of the Eastern Rift Coast. The second cattle-rich border zone is at the opposite extremity of the region, south of the Angola highlands. Here, in country which becomes increasingly arid as it approaches the Kalahari and Namib deserts, live peoples, such as the Nyaneka and Kwambi, culturally transitional to the pastoral Herero and Hottentots of the dry south-west. Unlike these two groups, they are cultivators, but not enthusiastic cultivators, their attention being focussed on their herds and flocks. Among these groups the young men coiffure their hair in long tresses, larded with sheep-fat and ochre, in a manner remarkably reminiscent of Maasai and their neighbours, far to the north-east. The two areas seem to share a common widespread tradition, which has survived only among these strongly cattle-centred groups. There are, however, no exclusive pastoralists in the Southern Savanna region.

The vast majority of peoples of the region have traditions of kings and of states, although the actual size of the kingdoms varied, in the nineteenth century, from the domains of the Mwaant Yaav of the Lunda, with outlying provinces and tributary states, to the autonomous villages of the Makonde, near the lower Ruvuma valley, with the "king" no more than a hereditary village headman. The hunting-and-gathering groups, the "Twa" of the Luangwa and Bangweulu, had no rulers, as is usual for such groups, but there were also cultivating peoples who lacked even the minimal tradition of royalty preserved by the Makonde. On the southern central borders of the region live the Lenje, Ila, Tonga, Totela and Subiya, as stateless as any Gikuyu or Iraqw, despite the culture which they largely share with their king-ruled neighbours. Some of the peoples who have arrived as immigrants to make up these groups have apparently lost their traditions of royalty in the process, but the critical factor must be the Bushman culture of other forebears of these peoples. There are still Bushman bands not very far to the south, and Bushmen were once the only inhabitants of Ila–Tonga country. Bushman traditions have here diluted the otherwise kingly customs of the region.

The degree of social specialization varied, around 1900, with the size of the state. Those peoples who had no state organization at all, such as the Tonga and Ila, had the usual part-time war-leaders, priests, doctors and smiths, while the Makonde and their neighbours were similar, except that they had hereditary war-leaders, in the form of very minor "kings". Larger units, however, such as the Bemba kingdom or some of the larger Nyamwezi states, had a nobility, clustering around the king's court, even though the abundance of cultivable land made land-grants, with "feudal" tenure, unworkable. The same factor obstructed the formation of a tight-knit governing hierarchy even in the large Luba and Lunda states, but here the nobility were more numerous, and the courts wealthier, and so better able to patronize musicians, dancers, wood-carvers and smiths.

There were no castes, as in the Interlacustrine states, and no age-sets over most of the region, although they did occur in some areas, as among the Lele,[1] on the edge of the Wet Forest.

Clitoridectomy does not occur, and circumcision, where now present, is not earlier than the nineteenth century, and is practised only by Muslims, for instance among the Yao and Nyamwezi.

Two other cultural features illustrate relations between regions. The carving of statuettes and of masks in wood is a striking feature of the peoples of the west coast of Africa from the Ivory Coast to south of the Congo mouth. Such carving occurred in the nineteenth century inland as far as the Lunda and Luba, and also as far as the Lega in the Wet Forest. It was, however, confined to the wetter northern part of the Southern Savanna, where the larger, and wealthier, states occurred; and the carvings were less numerous so far from the west coast. Surprisingly, the carving of wooden masks and statuettes reappeared among the Makonde, on the east coast, evidence presumably of a spread of traditions, and possibly craftsmen, right across the region from ocean to ocean.

A striking discontinuity has already been recognized in the hairstyle of Kwambi and Maasai young men, and there is an even more unusual far-flung discontinuity in the enlarging of women's lips, already noticed in Chapter 5. Although no longer a practice, it was customary still in the period 1880–1900 for the women of some groups east and south of Lake Nyasa to distend their lips to the size of plates with the aid of discs of progressively greater size. The groups in question were the Matambwe, Makua, Yao and Nyanja. This same practice occurred at that period among the Bira west of Lake Albert, and, much further away, among the women of the Sara group south-east of Lake Chad. Furthermore, the Mursi, of the Omo valley, north of Lake Rudolf, still distend the lips in this way. Since the practice, in this extreme form, is unknown elsewhere in the world, these four separated areas must represent a common tradition; it is highly improbable that African peoples started such an unusual custom independently on more than one occasion. Before the late nineteenth century the practice may have been more widespread, but even in its known distribution there is evidence of the extent to which cultural elements could be diffused over sub-Saharan Africa. By contrast with these elements of cultural diversity, all the languages of the region, from coast to coast, are Bantu.

Although we are only concerned with a more detailed consideration of the peoples in and near East Africa, it is essential to review the whole region in order to set these north-easterly groups into perspective. The area can be divided into five sub-regions :

1. the Sukuma–Nyamwezi States;
2. the Fipa–Hehe Highlands;
3. the Southern Belt of Minor States;
4. the Mbundu Highlands;
5. the Belt of Major States.

Sukuma, Nyamwezi and their neighbours occupy the southern half of the East African plateau, and have a modern history of abandoning matrilineal for patrilineal descent and inheritance. Their southern boundaries are marked by the "arms" of the Y-shaped highland zone with its centre at the northern extremity of Lake Nyasa. This highland zone is the habitat of the peoples of the Fipa–Hehe sub-region, who have also abandoned matrilineal descent and inheritance. They are distinguished from their lowland neighbours within the region by the presence of a considerable population of cattle. To the south of them are peoples of the Southern Belt of Minor States, the only sub-region which extends from coast to coast, and distinguished from the others by its lack of very distinctive features. It can readily be sub-divided, for instance the stateless Ila–Tonga group can be separated out, but on the whole there is considerable cultural uniformity throughout its great length. We shall only be concerned with the peoples of its north-eastern area.

Outside the East African Plateau area altogether is the Mbundu High-lands sub-region, occupying the highlands of Angola and their fringes. Like its eastern analogue, it is distinguished by a considerable cattle-population. Also beyond the borderlands of the East African Plateau, but approaching much nearer than the Mbundu Highlands, is the Belt of Major States, which stretches from west of Lake Tanganyika as far as the Congo mouth on the Atlantic. The name is chosen because all the largest states of the region, with the exception of the Lozi and the Bemba, occurred in this belt on the southern edge of the Wet Forest. Although not all the states were large, and although states fragmented and coalesced over time, this sub-region saw the largest scale of taxation, administration and court patronage in the region. By the nineteenth century the important states were those of Lunda and Luba dynasties, but at an earlier stage there had been a large state also on the southern bank of the Congo's lowest reach. The river indeed received its European name from this state.

In diplomatic contact with the Portuguese from the late fifteenth century onward, the kingdom of Congo disintegrated into a number of much smaller states by the end of the sixteenth century. The presence of the Portuguese at the mouth of the Congo during the seventeenth, eighteenth and nineteenth centuries doubtless prevented any other state in that area from growing to the size necessary to take Congo's place.

In the southern belt the only known kingdoms with a claim to be any-thing but tiny were those of the Lozi and Bemba. By 1890 the area inhabited by Bemba was worthy of a Lunda or Luba state further north, although the population was sparse. The administration too was minimal. Each provincial governor was effectively a reigning king, and the flow of taxes to the capital, and of largesse outward from there, less than in the larger Luba and Lunda kingdoms. Bemba then was not on the scale of the largest northern kingdoms, but it is a reminder that symbolic kingdoms of some size can occur in areas with very sparse population. Its present dynasty derives from the Luba area, and doubtless arrived, perhaps in the seventeenth century, determined to increase the scale of in this thinly peopled Southern Savanna region.

The Lozi kingdom, on the other hand, was fully on the scale of the kingdoms further north. One factor here must be the arrival, in 1838, of Sotho raiders from the south, who took over the state in a sort of "Norman Conquest". Even their expulsion as a ruling group, in 1864, left the Sotho language in the area, and the new rulers continued the scale of administration which derived from the "grand ideas" which the Sotho had themselves drawn from the empire-building which had been going on in south-eastern Africa in the early nineteenth century. A second factor, however, must be the site of the centre of the kingdom in the Zambezi valley, so that its core area is well watered and productive, although in a sub-region largely marked by recurrent drought and deficient surface water.

It cannot indeed be accidental that the large and wealthy states were concentrated into the wetter part of the plateau, next to the Wet Forest region, while the dryer south was marked by tiny states, or stateless peoples, apart from the Bemba and Lozi. Although population is not dense in the wetter north there are more people to the unit area than further south, a factor which would have provided more accessible taxes once there was a will to collect them on a grander scale. With more taxes, the hegemonies built up would have been less fragile than in the south, and less purely symbolic than with the Bemba. The inspiration to build larger states, however, may have come from outside the region, and it is very likely that this Belt of Major States, as it can now be called, played a critical role in the spread of kingdoms into the Southern Savanna in the first place. We must return to this theme in Chapter 11.

The Sotho invaders of Lozi were not the only immigrants from the south during the nineteenth century. From about 1825 onward Nguni-speakers, from south-eastern Africa, raided up to the north of the Zambezi, and settled in a number of places around Lake Nyasa. From this period onward also Swahili were travelling inland to Lake Tanganyika, and the Congo Basin, and the Nyamwezi were involved, probably already by 1800, in journeys to and from the coast. As the intensity of trading, in ivory, slaves and other commodities, increased during the century, Nyamwezi penetrated further westward to the Katanga plateau, and probably, with Swahili, into the Wet Forest. On the Katanga plateau, indeed, a Nyamwezi, Msiri, set himself up as king in an area where most rulers were Luba, and established a new state, a practice very frequent in this thinly-peopled Southern Savanna region.

Increasing trade affected other groups further south. The Yao, east of Lake Nyasa, established their own caravans to the areas around the lake; and the peoples of the Nyanja group, thick on the ground and relatively defenceless, became a major source of slaves, to be driven down to the coast. Further south still, the role of the Yao was played by the Portuguese, that is by the black Portuguese of the lower Zambezi, families which had become established as local aristocrats during the eighteenth century, and who now raided up the valley, for slaves, more ambitiously than hitherto.

On the west coast also, the nineteenth century was a period of commercial, if predatory, expansion. Again the Portuguese, many of them black, were involved in deeper penetration of the interior from their old base along the coast from the Congo mouth to Luanda. South of them were the states of the Mbundu, in the highlands, who themselves became increasingly involved in trading as the century wore on. Inland from both the Portuguese and Mbundu were the Chokwe, connecting the interior with the coastal groups, and acting as middlemen in the slave- and ivory-traffic. They played in the west of the region the role filled in the east by the Nyamwezi; and Chokwe and Nyamwezi trader-adventurers met in Katanga, well known already for its rich copper ores.

One of the less dramatic effects of the travelling and trading was the changing of direction in descent and inheritance in many areas. When the region was introduced in the first chapter, one of its characteristics which was emphasized was the widespread occurrence of matrilineal inheritance and descent, in contrast to the other regions nearby. Not all the peoples of the region were matrilineal in these respects during the nineteenth century, but they probably all were at an earlier time, perhaps the beginning of the seventeenth century. Around 1800 the only people patrilineal in descent and inheritance were the Luba, and a few groups imitating the Portuguese in the Luanda and lower Zambezi areas.[2] The rulers of the Lunda states or provinces also reckoned descent patrilineally, either imitating the Luba or themselves of Luba origin. At an earlier date the Luba had probably changed from matriliny because of conquest of their states, and possibly considerable immigration at the same time, by "barbarians" from the stateless Wet Forest. If this was the process, it cannot be dated, but it was a "Norman Conquest" type of change, similar to that of the Bito takeover in Nyoro.

At the present time almost all the peoples of the Sukuma–Nyamwezi and Fipa–Hehe sub-regions follow the patrilineal mode, but this is a recent situation, and matrilineal features still occur. In the early twentieth century some Nyamwezi royal families were still matrilineal in succession, and on the east of Nyamwezi, in the hills above the Wembere swamps, the little states of Isanzu, Iambi and Ilamba were still matrilineal in all respects until recently. Slightly to the east of them, and in the Eastern Rift Coast region, matrilineal features occur among the Iraqw, Mbowe and Langi, and, south-eastwards from the Iraqw–Langi group, matrilineal features also survive among the Kaguru, Nguru, Ruguru, and Vidunda.

At the beginning of the nineteenth century the neighbours of these four peoples, including the Zigula and Zaramo, were also matrilineal, but changed during the century, impressed by the increasing power and wealth of the Swahili. This process continued far into the interior, where the Nyamwezi, ready converts to the new ways, formed secondary centres of change, so that people impressed by the Nyamwezi imitated them, and so indirectly imitated the Swahili. A further pressure towards patrilineal procedures came from the Nguni. These were probably the critical impulse to change among the Bena–Sango group of highlanders, and also among the Fipa and their neighbours.[3]

These changes in descent, inheritance and succession are indicative of prestige gradients in the east of the region, but the Swahili were not important, or even known, over the west or much of the central area. In 1500 the kingdom of Congo was the top state of a cluster of kingdoms around the mouth of the river, but, with its disintegration into various minor states by 1600, it was the Portuguese who stepped into the high prestige role in this area, their imitators including the Ngola people, who have given their name to the territory of Angola. In the nineteenth century the Portuguese continued, and increased, their high status, while to the south the Mbundu were at the top of their local prestige gradient, with the individual Mbundu states competing with each other in an internal league. Like the Mbundu and Portuguese, the Chokwe were engaged in the slave-trading, and, like them also, the Chokwe states were at the top of a local prestige gradient, while competing among themselves. To their east was the state of the Lunda, around the court of the Mwaant Yaav, its prestige still high, partly because the Chokwe had not united to establish a rival on the same scale. Between the Lunda and Lake Tanganyika the outstanding state of the nineteenth century was that of the Luba in the Luapula area, again top of a local league.

Further south, in the dryer country, the Lozi were the unrivalled giants in an area of small states and of stateless peoples, while the Bemba were the top people of their local league, including the Biisa and Lala. On a smaller scale, in the Fipa–Hehe highlands, both Fipa and Hehe, as well as the Nyakyusa between them, were at the top of localized prestige gradients. The Yao were the most powerful, and feared, group east and south of Lake Nyasa, with their place taken in the lower Zambezi valley by the Portuguese, and to the north by the Swahili, in the hinterland of Dar-es-Salaam.

West from here, and beyond the Gogo plains, the Nyamwezi were much imitated, their culture being absorbed by various groups on their borders. The Sukuma, however, towards Lake Victoria, were not in the Nyamwezi orbit but formed their own prestige system, and their states competed with each other.

The Sukuma–Nyamwezi Sub-region

The southern half of the East African Plateau, between Lake Tanganyika and the highlands of the Eastern Rift, is an enormous expanse of nearly level country, largely covered with dry *miombo* woodland. Population is sparse, and clearings in the woodland are few and far between. This area contrasts with the greener hills to the east and south, and also with the area towards Lake Victoria. Here, in the country of the Sukuma, the land-surface is rolling, with numerous granite tors, the population is much denser, and most of the area is under grassland or cultivation rather than woodland.

The Sukuma are divided into a number of small states, each with its own ruling family, although many of these are related to each other. As in the rest of Tanzania, the government withdrew official recognition from ruling families in 1963. Compared to most of the region Sukuma population is dense, and the cattle population is very large indeed. Away from the borders of their territory, where woodland persists, the area is free from tstetse flies, and hence from *nagana*, trypanosomiasis of cattle, a critical factor in the size of Sukuma herds. The absence of woodland over so much of the area results from a long history of relatively dense population, itself a result of rainfall less unreliable than further south. This is an effect of the nearness of Lake Victoria, and has made possible the build-up of population over many generations, as in other well watered areas of East Africa. Sukuma speak a language almost identical with that of the Nyamwezi, and could be regarded as the cattle-rich face of Nyamwezi, transitional to the well watered lake-shore zones of the two regions immediately to the north. However, they feel themselves to be very distinct from the Nyamwezi, and the Nyamwezi share this sense of their distinctness.

Most of the rest of the sub-region is occupied, if sparsely, by people who are either Nyamwezi or very similar to them. Apart from the

Sukuma, the only strikingly different peoples are those of the three little states of Isanzu, Iambi and Ilamba, which have been mentioned already. Situated on highlands on the eastern margin of Sukuma and Nyamwezi country, and above the swamps of the Wembere Valley, they are linked to their western neighbours by the presence of kings and the absence of clitoridectomy. Also, they have retained the matrilineal succession, descent and inheritance which were once general further west. Compared with each other, the three are so similar as to be three divisions of a single ethnic group. Below them on the north-east is the basin of Lake Eyasi, an area of dry woodland passing eastwards to the wet highlands of the Iraqw, members of a different cultural tradition and a different region. The Eyasi basin is the territory of the Hadza, a hunting-and-gathering group, mentioned earlier. They have some contact with the little states to the south-west of them, but are so unusual in their way of life, compared to other peoples of the area, that they are marginal to both regions.

The Nyamwezi themselves are divided, like the Sukuma, into a number of small states, the wealthiest by the period 1880–1900 being Unyany-embe, flourishing on the caravan trade between the coast and Lake Tanganyika. Their town of Tabora had become the most important centre in the whole of the southern plateau area by that time. Despite the absence of a single state incorporating all Nyamwezi, their role as traders and adventurers, their cloth and their guns gave them a consider-able reputation in the caravan era, and neighbouring ethnic groups who are now sometimes confused with the Nyamwezi by European writers seem to have imitated them at that time, and are still apparently doing so. On the north, near the Sukuma and Dzindza, are the Shumbwa, mentioned earlier, discernibly Interlacustrine people and growing bananas, but much "Nyamwezi-ized", and probably in the process of becoming another local variant of Nyamwezi. As a matter of fact, the father of the "Nyamwezi" Msiri, who founded his own kingdom in the Katanga area, came from one of the small states of Shumbwa.

West of the Shumbwa are the swamps along the Malagarasi River, inhabited by small Vinza fishing groups, culturally not unlike the Nyamwezi but so specialized in their way of life, spent largely in canoes, that, like the Hadza, they fall between regions. Beyond the swamps are peoples affected by the prestige of Rundi, and not of the Nyamwezi. These peoples, Ha, Vinza and Jiji, have been noted already in the context of the Interlacustrine region, and they form a transition zone between the regions in the dryer country south of the Rwanda–Rundi highlands. To the south of the Vinza and Jiji are the Tongwe and Bende, both apparently being absorbed by the Nyamwezi, as are the Holoholo, who live nearby. These are the descendants of recent immigrants into Bende country from across Lake Tanganyika, where the Holoholo live in dry woodland very similar to that east of the lake. Although near the Major States sub-region, they are actually themselves divided into small states, in a strip of country between Lake Tanganyika and the Hemba and Luba states to the west. South of the Holoholo are the Taabwa, and then the Rungu, in the highlands, near to the Fipa.

The southern borderlands of the Nyamwezi are occupied by the Konongo, to the west, and the Kimbu, both of them divided into numerous small kingdoms, and both of them apparently losing their cultural identity except as sub-divisions of the Nyamwezi. The Kimbu frequently form scattered colonies among the Nyamwezi, and also further east, for instance among the Sandawe. Here, however, they avoid the rolling hills where the Sandawe live, and are settled near the level *mbuga*. Even further south than Konongo and Kimbu, in a small area on the shores of Lake Rukwa, are the Bungu, clearly distinct, but again apparently in process of becoming yet another sub-group of Nyamwezi. The same appears to be happening to the Rungwa, further north-west.

Indeed Nyamwezi cultural features are even being borrowed by the western Gogo. Central and eastern Gogo are firmly part of the region where the Maasai have been the pinnacle of cultural excellence, and they live in country as dry as the Maasai Plains; but in the west there is more rainfall, *miombo* woodland, more tsetse flies and fewer cattle, all features strongly similar to Nyamwezi. More striking is the organization of the western Gogo. They are divided into small states, each with its own royal family, and some at least of these royal lines are descended from Nyamwezi immigrants. These western Gogo are thus in a transition zone between the two regions, affected themselves by Nyamwezi prestige but culturally akin to the other Gogo further east who are turned towards the Maasai ideal.

From the effect that Nyamwezi appear to be having on several neighbouring groups, it seems that the Nyamwezi cultural area is expanding to fill the whole of the habitat where they originated. In due time all the peoples of the *miombo* on the southern half of the East African Plateau would then be Nyamwezi. Their boundary would then lie up against the wetter country towards Lake Victoria and in the Rwanda–Rundi highlands, against Lake Tanganyika, and against the arc of highlands on the south and east. The gap in these highlands, occupied by the Gogo plains, would allow the Nyamwezi eastward as far as the dry country of central Gogo, towards the Maasai Plains.

It is clear from the account of the different peoples that this is a sub-region of small kingdoms. In the period before 1920 none of them had complicated administrations nor wealthy courts, except for Unyanyembe in Nyamwezi, grown rich on the caravan trade of several decades. The rulers had courts and, if the kingdom were large enough, provincial governors and village headmen, to gather taxes and preside over the settlement of disputes, as the king's local representatives. Beyond this, there was little social specialization apart from part-time smiths, priests and medical specialists. The period since 1890 has seen a number of people within the sub-region become Muslim or Christian, but earlier rituals are strong and widespread. God controls everything, and sacrifices are offered to the ancestors and, where necessary, to spirits of the bush.

Nyamwezi, Sukuma, and their neighbours in the sub-region have "secret societies", which still flourish. These organizations are groups of men who form a mutual welfare association, connected with hunting. In any one kingdom there is more than one society, and any one society's members are found in a number of states, so that membership unites people with loyalties to different states. The societies are secret, not in the sense that non-members are unaware that they exist, but in performing certain rituals which must not be revealed to non-members. Everyone who becomes a member has to undergo an initiation, which itself must not be revealed to people outside the society. Such societies are strongly similar to the Freemasons in Europe, and to similar organizations else-where, for instance the "secret societies" of China, but within East Africa they are found only among peoples of the Southern Savanna region.

Although these societies have survived the decades of European admini-stration, the situation of the rulers and their states has changed appre-ciably. Up to the period 1890–1900, when German administration began in the sub-region, states repeatedly split as rival members of the royal family claimed each their share of the kingdom. Also, princes of royal lines, and probably often aspiring commoners, set up new states in thinly inhabited country, establishing new villages and, where necessary, clear-ing the woodland, which still covers most of the sub-region. German administrators to some extent curbed the proliferation of little kingdoms by requiring kings to be agents of the government, and this process was intensified between 1919 and 1930, when British administrators sought to streamline the collection of taxes and the administration of judicial procedures. Setting up new states, and dividing old ones, now became impossible without official permission, and this was not granted readily because the kings, now called chiefs,[4] were part of the administrative hierarchy, and to recognize new kings was in itself a reshuffle in taxation and in other procedures.

With so many small kingdoms spread out over the considerable extent of the sub-region, there was room for a considerable number of prestige pyramids, before all the units were gathered together into a hierarchy, with European officials at the top. Before about 1900 the Sukuma formed their own league, the states of each area rivalling each other. As has been seen, in the rest of the sub-region Nyamwezi prestige was high, and imitating the Nyamwezi seems to have been usual among the groups neighbouring them. The Nyamwezi themselves, however, were not united into one state,[5] and each area had its own league-table of prestige. Even so, Unyanyembe was a giant among these states in the period 1850–1900.

The Fipa–Hehe Sub-region

South of the Konongo and Kimbu are the wet highlands which form an arc from the southern end of Lake Tanganyika to the northern end of Lake Nyasa, and then north-eastwards towards the coast. The spontaneous tree cover, where it has not been cleared, is typical of East African wet highland, but very large areas are now occupied with regenerating woodland, shrubby secondary growth and grassland. On the higher areas no species of tstetse fly is able to flourish, and, despite the low population of most of the sub-region, cattle are able to survive, and increase. This situation is in sharp contrast to that in the lower, dryer sub-region just to the north, where low population density, outside Sukuma, results in extensive woodland cover, and abundant tsetse flies. Away from the volcanic soils of Nyakyusa, and from the areas near Lake Nyasa, population has not built up despite the relatively reliable rainfall, a situation reminiscent of the highlands of Kenya west of the Rift Valley.

Strung along the western limb of the highlands are a number of ethnic groups, none of them very large, beginning with the Fipa and Pimbwe in the north-west. The Fipa speak the same language as the Rungu around the southern end of Lake Tanganyika. South-east from the Fipa are the Mambwe, Mwanga and Wanda; then follow the Nyiha and

Safwa, who adjoin the highly distinctive Nyakyusa at the head of Lake Nyasa.

These peoples of the western highlands show considerable cultural unity, of which the most dramatic example are the periodic witch-hunts. About every ten years, in one part of the area or another, a self-proclaimed specialist appears who asserts that he has both the power to detect witches and the medicines to counter their activities. Usually, news of his claims, and successes, travels swiftly from village to village, and from one ethnic group to the next. The witch-finder, and his followers, travel about the area, and accusations of witchcraft become suddenly very numerous. After a period of a few months, however, disillusionment sets in, and most people's interest wanes, until the next time. Witches are an unpleasant fact of life, known to all East African peoples, but in most areas ritualized cleansings are less frequent and less regular than here. Even so, there is no formalized procedure nor regular specialists associated with the witch-hunts, although there are memories of previous, unsuccessful, examples. Each hunt starts from scratch, with a different group of specialists from last time.

To the south-west of these highlands are the Bemba. Their country is dry miombo-covered plateau, with population even sparser than that of the highlands. The Biisa and Lala to the south share the same conditions. These three groups are all in the Minor States sub-region, and so are the Nsenga in the Luangwa trench.

The Tumbuka occupy the highlands on the north-west of the lake, much of their population clustered down along the shore, where they can fish. South of them are the Tonga, all clustered along the lake-shore. They are not closely related either historically or culturally with the Tonga already mentioned, who live further west in the region, nor to another group called Tonga, in south-eastern Africa. Their language is less closely related to that of the Tumbuka than to that of the Matengo and Ngoni east of the lake.[6] These lake-side Tonga are descended from, among other peoples, recent immigrants from Matengo country, who sailed across the lake from their own lake-shore villages, where they were presumably fishermen, as the modern lake-side Matengo still are. The Tonga are thus analogous to the Holoholo of Tanzania, who have migrated across Lake Tanganyika from their original territory on the western side.

South of the Tonga are the Nyanja, who form most of the population around the southern end of the lake and down the Shire valley. Their country is well watered and their population dense. Among them, and on their dryer western edge, there live groups who called themselves Ngoni, and who claim descent from Nguni immigrants of the mid-nineteenth century. Today, however, these Ngoni are culturally very similar to their neighbours. In addition to Nguni, other immigrants settled in the area, from the middle of the nineteenth century onward, and still speak their ancestral language. These are Yao, from east of the lake, who raided the Nyanja for slaves, and will recur later in this chapter.

As has been noted already, there is dense population all round the shore of Lake Nyasa, and a concentration around its southern end, while at the northern end, on wet highlands north of the Tumbuka hills, are the Nyakyusa. They grow bananas and coffee on fertile volcanic soils, and were the admiration of their immediate neighbours, the Kisi, Kinga and Safwa. They are remarkable too for their age-villages, abandoned only in recent decades. As boys and girls became adult they went to live in their own villages, away from those where they were born, and where their parents continued to live. At a determined time, so the Nyakyusa say, authority in each of the small states of Nyakyusa changed hands, the king in each case handing over to one of his sons, and at the same time the younger generation, roughly the new king's contemporaries, became the responsible elders, their parental generation retiring from active participation in affairs.

At the scale of the village this is an age-set system, rather like that of Maasai and other stateless groups further north. The orderly transfer of royal power from generation to generation, however, sounds more like an ideal than a practice, since presumably there were in fact struggles for office and untidy successions. Even the Nyakyusa are unlikely to have been that different from other peoples. It is significant, in any case, that they claim a practice so different from that of their neighbours. Since the Nyakyusa were at the top of their local prestige gradient, it is very likely that they were being unconsciously, but deliberately, different, rather as are the Maasai in sexual morality.

To the east of the Nyakyusa are the Kinga, in the hills, and the Kisi down on the lake-shore, and further south along the same shore are the Pangwa and Matengo. The communities of the lake-shore rely heavily on fishing, as well as on cultivating, while Nyanja fishermen from the south have colonized much of the Matengo shore. Above the narrow, and thickly peopled, lake-side, and stretching north-eastward towards the coast, is a mass of highland, drained by rivers of the Rufiji system. The peoples of these hills are very similar to each other, and they share a common recent history. East of the Matengo are the Ngoni, yet another group claiming ancestors from south-eastern Africa, although at the present time their language is not Nguni but related to Matengo. The identity of the immigrants of the mid-nineteenth century has been preserved in the name, but most of the ancestors of the modern Ngoni, as on the west of Lake Nyasa, are from much nearer at hand, and the local culture has predominated over any elements of Nguni origin. Neighbours to the Ngoni, to the north-east, and in dry lowlands, are the Ndendeuli. Among them descent is bilateral, as it is among the Lozi, and they presumably abandoned their earlier matrilineal descent because of the prestige-impact upon them of the "Nguni" invaders, but without adopting the patrilineal alternative. Like the Lozi again, they seem to have compromised. The Ndamba, further north, are also in dry lowlands, with the Pogolo and Mbunga nearby in similar habitats. Bena country lies south-west of Ndamba, in the wet hills, and the Hehe are to the north, with the Sango further west, but none of these three groups form dense concentrations of people. Rather are they spread over the hill-country, with no striking features separating the area occupied by one people from that of another.

Their common history is marked by the arrival of "Nguni" immigrants in the middle decades of the nineteenth century. When they first appeared they had already doubtless acquired a large number of recruits from areas through which they had travelled, and it is probable that at the time when they settled in the highlands they were culturally already more Southern Savanna than south-east African. Indeed, most of them probably had no ancestors who had ever lived in south-eastern Africa. The incursion of such an army into the highlands, however, probably upset the balance of power between the existing small states, and it is conspicuous that it is from the period of their settling that the Hehe emerge as the most formidable people of the area. Essentially, the Hehe state only then came into being for the first time, although the royal family who led them to such striking success probably ruled a small state in this area at an earlier period. It may not, however, have been called Hehe.

The arrival of the "Nguni", by defeating some established kings, and generating some refugees, gave these early Hehe rulers an opportunity to acquire followers, and become local champions. Whatever the factors or the process, by 1870 Hehe was established, the Ngoni state was contained, and the Hehe were able, in the course of the next twenty years, to make the Sango, Bena and their other neighbours their satellites. By this time, the Hehe, whatever their antecedents, were a new ethnic group, providing us with a warning not only that East African peoples are not always, if ever, of great antiquity, but also that new groups can appear in the space of a generation or two.

So successful were the Hehe by 1890 that the arrival of a German administrator in the following year was fiercely resented, presumably because German over-rule would cramp the style of the Hehe as military lords of their area. The defeat of the first German column in 1891 was followed, between 1894 and 1898, by a prolonged German attempt to subdue Hehe resistance, this time successful. There is an analogy here with the situation in the Rift Highlands east of Lake Victoria, where by 1890 the Nandi were enjoying a series of very successful raids on their neighbours. In that area it was the Nandi, and not their battered neighbours, who resented the early British administrators, and hence the Nandi rebellion of 1905.

The highlands continue, although not unbroken, into the hills of the Sagala and Vidunda and of the Kaguru, who are all three intimately linked, historically and culturally, to the peoples just to the east of them, on the coastal lowlands. The Vidunda and Kaguru have been mentioned already, because they retain matrilineal descent and inheritance, whereas most of the peoples of the sub-region, who once also showed these features, have now lost them. Another people of the area who have also retained these matrilineal features are the Ruguru, living on the steep, isolated hill-range which is called after them, the Luguru Hills.[7] To people familiar with the survival of earlier cultural features in hill-areas, such as the Welsh and Basque languages on the western edge of Europe, the Luguru Hills look an appropriate place for the spontaneous conservation of earlier customs, in this case of inheritance and descent. The Kaguru hill-country, however, looks much less appropriate, since it is gently rolling and fairly accessible. It looks as if factors other than terrain must be involved here, and distance seems to be critical. The Kaguru are further from the coast than are the Zaramo and Zigula, who have been more affected by the Swahili, while the whole area is too far north to feel the full impact of the "Nguni". The same positional factors apply to the Vidunda and to the Nguru, most of them on dry hills north-east of the Kaguru.[8]

The Ruguru, Kaguru and Nguru indeed are part of an area which has a complex discernible history. These three names, with a common stem—*guru*, and differentiated only by their prefixes, look remarkably like part of a process of self-differentiation, in which peoples who share a common traditional name are seeking, not necessarily consciously, to denote the modern differences which result from separation into three distinct habitats. The story is complicated further by their area's being the cultural hinterland of the Swahili, who have been much imitated, a theme to which we shall have to return.

Westwards too there are cultural connections. The Kaguru speak the same language as the Gogo, who live in a different habitat from the Kaguru, on the dry plains. In view of its affinities,[9] the language of the Gogo was probably brought in by immigrants from the hills to the east or south, while migrants from Gogo probably carried their language to the Kaguru. As we have seen already, the eastern and central Gogo are best classified with the Eastern Rift Coast peoples, since they lack royal lines and states, and are marked by a deference for the way of life exemplified by the Maasai, who are their neighbours on the north-east. At the same time, the western Gogo are culturally involved with the Kimbu and Nyamwezi, living as they do in small states with kings. Cultural factors have thus reached Gogo country from different directions, and there have certainly been migrants moving into the area from all sides. It will be necessary to return to this theme of immigration and cultural borrowing, in Chapter 10, when the emergence of distinct ethnic groups is examined.

South of the Gogo, and throughout the sub-region as far as Lake Tanganyika, the peoples of these wet highlands were divided into numerous small states. The Hehe and Ngoni were exceptional, in the period 1880–1900, for the size of their kingdoms, but some other ethnic groups also were united each into a single state. At that period the Sango, neighbours to the Hehe, formed a single kingdom, and so did the Bena. Further west, near Lake Tanganyika, the Fipa and the Pimbwe were each united kingdoms, at least in theory. For the small states administration did not need to be complicated, but Sango, Hehe and Bena rulers, as well as Ngoni, needed provincial governors as well as village headmen. The kingdoms were affected by the same processes as operated in the Sukuma–Nyamwezi sub-region to the north. States divided or were merged, according to the play of dynastic politics; and new states were established in empty, or nearly empty, areas by aspiring founders of dynasties. An important illustration of these processes was the establishment of a new state on the southern edge of the highlands by the Ngoni, and the response of the Hehe royal family, who either established a rival new state, or expanded a small kingdom which they were already ruling.

Social specialization was not intricate, and indeed still is not, despite the emergence of teachers and officials. There were part-time smiths, priests and medical specialists, as usual, and the sacrifices were addressed to the ancestors and, where necessary, to spirits of the bush, but God was, and is, supreme.

In the period 1880–1900, three peoples were the heads of prestige pyramids in different sections of the sub-region. In the far west, the Fipa were the most eminent of the groups of their immediate area, including the Pimbwe and Mambwe, but they were all overshadowed by the ceremonial splendour, and military outreach, of the Bemba. Around the head of Lake Nyasa the Nyakyusa were at the top of the local prestige gradient, which involved Safwa, Kinga and Kisi. To the north-east of these, military conflict and administrative organization were on a more ambitious scale. The Bena and the Sango were overshadowed by the remarkable rise of the Hehe, whose raids and prestige extended into the hills of the Sagala, below whom, on the plains of the coast, was the zone of maximum Swahili prestige.

The Southern Belt of Minor States Sub-region

This "Swahili" zone extends along the coastal lowlands from the foot of the Shambaa highlands to the valley of the Rufiji River. South of here the sub-region widens out, occupying the lowlands and plateau to the south-east of the Hehe–Bena highlands, and then south to the Zambezi valley, and west across Lake Nyasa to Bemba country, and beyond. Apart from the coastal lowlands, the area of the Minor States sub-region near to the East African Plateau is itself fairly level plateau-country, repeatedly drought-stricken and covered with *miombo* woodland. It is an ideal series of habitats for tsetse flies, cattle are very scarce, and over most of the area people are sparsely scattered. There is, however, a concentration of people around the southern end of Lake Nyasa, which has already been described, and dense population follows the shores of the lake on both sides up to the Nyakyusa highlands in the north.

In addition to the Lake Nyasa zone, there is a band of moderately well populated country along the coast from south of Zanzibar island to the mouth of the Zambezi, and also a concentration of people in the country of the Makonde, just inland. The soils of this coastal zone are not particularly fertile, although rainfall is greater than over most of the sub-region. However, one key to the relative concentration of people is probably several centuries of trade, with an increased demand for foodstuffs. In the course of these trading activities, fishing has provided a ready source of protein for the increasing population. Fish was not readily available again, before modern lorry-transport, until Lake Nyasa was reached, and the lake-shores are another zone of dense population.

On the whole, nevertheless, the sub-region is marked by very low densities of settlement, to such an extent that the Fipa–Hehe highlands, themselves not markedly thickly inhabited, stand out as a band of relatively well peopled territory between the lowlands to the south and the equally sparsely peopled area to the north of them, in the territories of the Kimbu, Konongo and southern Nyamwezi.

We have already noted that north-east of the Hehe, in the highlands, the Sagala and Kaguru have close cultural and historical links with the peoples of the coastal lowlands to the east of them. It was also necessary to mention these lowlands when discussing the group of peoples in the Nyika further north up the coast, and when discussing the Shambaa, in their highlands of the Transition sub-region of the Eastern Rift Coast. Between the Shambaa highlands and the Indian Ocean coast are the Bondei, closely linked to the Shambaa by historical events. North-east of them are the Digo and Duruma of the coastal group in the Nyika, traditionally stateless peoples; while on the seaward edge of the Digo live the Daisu (Segeju), much affected, as are the Bondei, by Swahili culture. South of the Bondei, and in very similar coastal scenery, are the Zigula, from whose country the present ruling family of the Shambaa arrived in the eighteenth century. Inland from the Zigula are the Nguru, much of their country in low hills, but reaching wet highlands in the west. Kaguru, Sagala and Vidunda all live in wet hills, and the Ruguru live on an outlier of highland in the coastal lowlands. By contrast, the Ng'wele, Zaramo and Kutu all live in the coastal lowlands. Zaramo and Kutu alike are bounded on the south by the Ruihi, occupying the lower valley of the Rufiji (i.e. Ruihi) River, where it crosses the coastal lowlands.

The peoples from the Zaramo northwards to the Shambaa, including the groups in the hills to the west, occupy an area with a remarkable meeting of cultures. Just west of the Shambaa hills are the Maasai Plains, which are bounded by the wetter country of the Nguru and Kaguru. More dry plains, inhabited this time by Gogo, bound the Kaguru hills on the west. Both Gogo and Maasai belong to the Eastern Rift Coast region, while the peoples of the Bondei–Zaramo lowlands, with their minor kings, and devoid of circumcision before they imitated the Swahili, are part of the Southern Savanna. The impact of the Swahili, however, has given these lowlands distinctive character, even though only a recent one, setting the peoples slightly apart from their neighbours to north, west and south.

One feature of the area has already been noted. The Kaguru, Nguru and Ruguru retain matrilineal inheritance and descent, while their neighbours have now lost them, through imitating the Swahili. In 1800, it appears, the whole area was marked by matrilineal features except for the Swahili city-states and their immediate hinterlands.

Already, when the peoples of the Nyika were being discussed, in their context of the Eastern Rift Coast region, it was necessary also to examine at some length the Swahili city-states along the coast, from the Soomaali area southward to the Zambezi. Moreover, the whole discussion of modern East African peoples necessarily takes place in the context of increased trade between the interior and the coast in the nineteenth century. It was apparently only from the middle of the century that the peoples nearest to Zanzibar became much affected by their Swahili neighbours. Before that the Swahili peoples on the mainland appear to have been confined to small enclaves or narrow strips along the coast. Inland, away from these Swahili zones, there was a sharp transition to the non-Swahili groups, for example the Digo and Zaramo.

The increasing importance of Zanzibar in the middle decades of the nineteenth century involved the peoples of the Bondei–Zaramo lowlands more and more in trade with the interior, since caravans from Zanzibar started through their zone of coastal lowland. The small kings of the area adopted the *kanzu*, the long nightshirt-like gown of cotton, favoured by Zanzibar merchants, and also the embroidered cap, from the same source. The nobility joined the kings in this process of adoption, and the fashions spread socially "downwards" as people outside the local elites joined in by imitating their rulers. At the same time the members of the elites began to profess Islam, and to speak Swahili as well as their own language; and again these practices spread to other members of the little kingdoms. Through trade the rulers obtained guns, and also new luxuries like beds and wooden chests, of Swahili origin. Their courts became copies of those of the city-state rulers along the coast, and the same was happening to the court of the Shambaa kings in the highlands above the Bondei.

In the interior also centres of Swahili culture were appearing, at Tabora, whose Nyamwezi elite adopted coastal fashions, and at Ujiji, on Lake Tanganyika. Off the main trunk-route, to the north, coastal traders established a camp, at the edge of Langi country, which became the town of Kondoa Irangi, so called to distinguish it from another such camp called Kondoa, in the hills of the Sagala. These interior centres, although locally important, did not have the widespread impact which occurred in the Bondei–Zaramo zone, where the process of penetration from coast to interior was carried a step further by German administrators. Situated on the coast opposite Zanzibar, this zone was visited early by Carl Peters, in the period 1884–90, and it was here that he signed the first treaties, whereby the little local kings placed themselves under German protection. It was from this zone too that German administrators drew the Swahili-speaking functionaries who were needed to fill local administrative posts in the interior, during the period 1890–1910, when effective control of wider areas was being attempted.

Since the zone is so distinctive, there is some case for recognizing it as a separate region, linked with the Swahili enclaves along the coast. Despite their distinctiveness organizationally, however, the city-states share much of their culture with the other peoples of the coast, and are indeed a local response to contact with traders from the Near East. In the Bondei–Zaramo zone the assimilation of some Swahili cultural elements is very recent indeed, and the links of the peoples to their southern neighbours are still transparent. To separate them as part of a special region would play down these important links. Even to establish a separate sub-region for them would underestimate their long-term cultural position, in an area where the Fipa–Hehe highlands meet the lowland Minor States. The Bondei–Zaramo zone is essentially a distinctive theatre of action, comparable to the Hehe sphere of influence in the nearby highlands, or to the Ganda sphere of influence on the northern Interlacustrine plateau. It is in fact the Swahili sphere of influence in the immediate hinterland of Zanzibar and Pemba.

At the northern extremity of the zone the Shambaa have received their dynasty from the Zigula lowlands, and by the period 1880–1900 their royal court was strongly affected by Swahili fashions, for instance in dress. Connections between the coastal lowlands and the Shambaa hills seem to be much older than the present dynasties, since both the Asu and the Shambaa languages appear to be more closely related to Zigula, Zaramo and Swahili than to Chaga.[10] From the distribution of the whole group of languages,[11] which also includes Hehe and Gogo, it is likely that they originated in the Bena–Hehe–Sango wet highlands, and spread from there to the coast. Wherever their origin, there is a strong likelihood that they spread from the coast to the Shambaa highlands and thence to Asu, implying migration from the Bondei area to Shambaa, and from Shambaa to Asu, as well doubtless as other migrations in quite different directions which have not left such clear traces.

At the opposite extremity of the zone, in the south, the dry country just north of the lower Rufiji valley is occupied by the Ndengereko, while the well watered river valley is the habitat of the Ruihi, Rufiji being the Swahili form of their name. Inland of the Ruihi are the Pogolo, in dry lowlands, but with a few permanent streams flowing down to the Rufiji; and further inland, still in lowlands, but right up against the Bena–Hehe highlands, are the Ndamba, sharing the same language as the Pogolo. Both these groups, with the similar Mbunga, have already been mentioned in the context of the Ngoni settlements, and the emergence of the Hehe state in the highlands.

Southwards from the Rufiji River, and its feeder-streams, is a vast expanse of dry country continuing east of Lake Nyasa down as far as the lower Zambezi valley. A feature of this area is the scattering of some of the language-groups, so that, instead of the majority of the people who speak one language being found within one area, there are a number of concentrations of people speaking, for example, Makua, and separated from each other by people who speak other languages, for example Yao. Scattering of population groups is by no means unusual in East Africa, although small-scale maps conceal the degree of interpenetration of different groups, especially in zones where more than one language is at the edge of its main territory. Also, the Kimbu, near the Nyamwezi, living in dry *miombo* country, very like that east of Lake Nyasa, are scattered into a number of concentrations, very much as are the Makua and the Yao. Such scattering results from the repeated migrations, often to escape from areas of drought and famine, which are an important factor in the redistribution of cultural elements in East Africa, and which are examined in Chapter 10.

South of the lower Rufiji valley most of what few people there are inland are Ngindo while Matumbi, Mwera and Machinga occupy the more populated coastal lowlands. Southwards again, on the coastal lowlands, and just inland on the plateau, the Makonde form a concentration of people unusually large for this area. Their strong sense of identity and separateness is remarkably paralleled by their tradition of carving masks and figurines in wood, a practice formerly widespread on the west coast of Africa, but on the east confined to the Makonde. At the present time this traditional carving has been expanded to produce ornamental objects specifically for foreign consumption, and the carvers have been organized by a few commercial companies, who have transformed the earlier activities into a profitable export trade.

The lower Ruvuma valley itself is the habitat of the Matambwe. It is a riverine strip, fairly well watered, and analogous to the Rufiji habitat further north. Just south of the lower valley, on the coastal plain, are the Maviha. However, most of the great expanse of territory from the middle and upper Ruvuma right down to the Zambezi valley in the south is occupied by scattered, and intermingled, groups of Makua, Yao and Lomwe. Roughly their main areas, and the probable zones of their respective origins, are: the Makua in the east; the Yao in the west, towards Lake Nyasa; and the Lomwe in the south towards the Zambezi. All three groups, however, live in a very similar country, and all have been involved in repeated famines, migrations, re-settlement in thinly peopled territory, and in the slave raiding and ivory hunting of the latter half of the nineteenth century. Placed as they were between the coast and the thickly peopled area just south of Lake Nyasa, they were well able to profit from coastal traders' need for slaves. In the process the inland people actually involved in the trade acquired the clothing, guns, and sometimes the Muslim confession, of the Swahili.

Some Yao are settled along the thickly populated eastern shore of Lake Nyasa, in the zone of fishing villages, and yet others live among the Nyanja group of peoples around the southern end of the lake, once the victims of Yao slave-raids. South of the lake, the Shire River flows into the Zambezi; and the Zambezi valley, another riverine corridor, forms the southern borderland of the region, on the east coast. The valley is inhabited by a number of small groups, all culturally similar to the Nyanja, and including the Sena who have given their name to a town founded by the Portuguese on the Zambezi.

In the previous section, it was mentioned that there are groups in the area west of Lake Nyasa who call themselves Ngoni, after some of their ancestors who migrated originally from south-eastern Africa. Those Ngoni who live among the Nyanja now speak Nyanja, and those who live among the Tumbuka now speak Tumbuka. During the period of British administration in the Nyasaland Protectorate, now Malawi, progressively fewer and fewer people bothered to claim to be Ngoni when required to return an ethnic label for successive censuses. This is presumably a sign that Ngoni prestige was dimmed by British over-rule, and that the memory of a splendid military past was fading. There are also a third group of Ngoni in this area west of the well watered and densely settled zone. These live sparsely scattered in dry woodland country, near the Nsenga, people spread up the Luangwa trench from near its confluence with the Zambezi. West of the Luangwa trench was the sphere of influence of the Bemba, which has already been considered.

The organization of the Bemba has also been briefly described. Even in the period 1880–1900, when they were raiding their neighbours extensively, the Bemba state was diffuse, its king paramount, but the authority of each of the, hereditary, provincial governors was effectively supreme in his own fief. Bemba looks like a Luba design struggling in adverse circumstances, but it must be added that the various Luba and Lunda states were also torn by divisive tendencies, which were often very successful. Much of the time, as throughout the larger states of the region, the villages were autonomous, their headmen able to act without deferring to any provincial governor or king.

East of the Bemba indeed the scale of organization was tiny. Some hereditary rulers "reigned" over solitary villages, as was commonly the case among the Makonde. Furthermore, as in other parts of the region, aspiring rulers set up new states based on a newly established village in a clearing in the woodland. Even those states which consisted of more than a few villages hardly needed provincial governors as an intermediate "layer" of officials between king and village headmen. Royal courts and tax-yields were small. There were, however, and still are, smiths, priests and medical practitioners. God is supreme, and the ancestors, and sometimes spirits of the bush, require sacrifices.

West of the Bemba, Biisa and Lala the little Lamba and Kaonde states were overshadowed in the period 1880–1900 by the might of the Luba and Lunda to the north of them. The Lala and Biisa were in the Bemba orbit of prestige, as were various groups north of the Bemba : Taabwa, Rungu, Fipa, Mambwe, and Mwanga. At the same period, further south, the lower Zambezi valley, from Nsenga country to the sea, was overshadowed by the Portuguese, black and white, of the area. To the north of them, between the lower Zambezi and the lower Rufiji, was the area through which Yao raiding-parties travelled between the coast and the slave-reservoirs near Lake Nyasa. The Yao were the high-prestige people of their area, recruiting members from the other scattered groups east of the lake, but were themselves impressed by the Swahili, whose guns and clothing they readily borrowed. Even further north, on the coastal lowlands opposite Zanzibar, was the area of most intense Swahili prestige, in the Bondei–Zaramo zone.

Having reviewed the distribution of ethnic groups and habitats, as well as the allocation of prestige among the different groups, it is now necessary to unravel the factors which have generated the complex mosaic of peoples. Before attempting this, however, we must examine more carefully some features of the societies which have so far been taken for granted. In the first place, it is important to discuss the differences between social organizations of widely differing scale, from Hadza hunting-bands to the great kingdoms of Rwanda and Rundi. In the second place, we need to look more carefully at the peoples' rites and their obligations to God and their ancestors.

7. Notes

1. The Lele are culturally transitional to the Wet Forest peoples, and, like them, have no kings.
2. Although the changes in descent and inheritance in the Sukuma–Nyamwezi and Fipa–Hehe sub-regions are here set in the nineteenth century, there is a distinct possibility of their having begun earlier, as a result of immigration from the Interlacustrine states.
3. The matrilineal Lozi were invaded by Sotho, patrilineal in descent and inheritance. The result here was an impasse; and the Lozi are now devoid of any lineal features, but are bilateral in both inheritance and descent. Among the Ndendeuli the "Nguni" invasion seems to have had a similar effect.
4. The term king was confined in Tanganyika, and most other territories in Africa under British administration, to the king of the United Kingdom.
5. The term Nyamwezi dates only from about 1800. Although it is accepted now by the Nyamwezi themselves to be the authentic name for themselves, it must have originated when they began to travel to the coast in the late eighteenth century. Swahili then began to call them

Wanyamwezi, the people of the moon, that is of the west. Probably, before this time, there was no one name for all the groups now called Nyamwezi.

6. M. Guthrie (1971). "Comparative Bantu", Vol. 2, p. 58.
7. R and L are interchangeable in their language. Swahili call them Luguru, and not Ruguru.
8. Vidunda, Kaguru, Ruguru and Nguru have matrilineal clans and matrilineal inheritance of land, but patrilineal inheritance of most movable goods. The patrilineal element in inheritance seems to have increased during the last one hundred and fifty years, and may well be increasing still.
9. Guthrie (1971), op. cit., pp. 48–51.
10. Ibid., p. 49.
11. Ibid., pp. 48–51.

8

Loyalties and Leaders

Bands, Settlements and States

It is clear from the accounts of the different peoples in preceding chapters that in 1890 there was a vast difference of scale between the smallest societies within East Africa and the largest. At one extremity were groups with only about fifty people, while at the other there were states with over a million people each. At the same time, most people in the area maintained themselves by farming, and only a very small number of groups were hunters-and-gatherers. What few hunter-gatherers there were, however, were always organized on a small scale, and never formed a state.

For the sake of clarity, it is useful to arrange the societies of around 1890 along a continuum, with those consisting of the smallest numbers of people at one end, and, at the other, those with the largest numbers. Such an arrangement looks like Fig. 8. The hunter-gatherer groups rarely or never had more than fifty people, and the very smallest farming

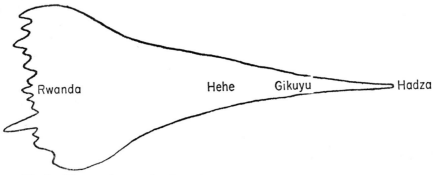

Fig. 8. The continuum of scale and social complexity in East African societies.

societies were sometimes as small as fifty people, but usually agrarian settlements were larger than this, running up to perhaps three hundred people in the larger examples. Over much of East Africa, for instance in the Eastern Rift Coast region, each settlement of farming peoples was autonomous, and the members had no loyalties to any authority higher than themselves, as a collectivity. However, most of the west and all of the south was occupied by peoples who had royal families and at least the rudiments of state organization. It is true that the smallest "kingdoms" or "states" consisted each of a single village or settlement, but usually a king governed, at least in theory, more than one settlement, and in some cases the state consisted of a very great number of settlements, all of whose members owed loyalty, well beyond their own settlement's borders, to a ruler whom many of them had never seen.

In this context the distinguishing feature of a "society", of whatever size, is that it is the largest unit of internal peace and of generalized moral obligation. People who belonged to a hunting-band or to a large kingdom, such as Rwanda, were not allowed to fight each other. Furthermore, there were other obligations which members of a single society expected from each other. They expected that people from their own society would not : kill them; steal from them; commit adultery against them; perform witchcraft against them; nor damage their reputation by slander or perjury. They also expected that if anyone did commit any of these offences they would be forced to pay a recompense or penalty appropriate to the offence. Moral obligations extended to a slight degree beyond each society, since frequently there were marriages between bands, settlements and even states, and such marriages bound the two groups of in-laws in different societies to respect each other's rights. Similarly, one had to respect the rights of kinsmen who had migrated to another society or who were descended from such migrants; and it was not uncommon for men to have personal friends in societies other than their own. Such friendships were often formed by trading contacts, and were very useful in maintaining trade-links with people who would certainly be suspicious of strangers, and might readily be hostile. Without specific ties of marriage, descent and friendship, or trade-partnership, there were no moral obligations between members of different societies. People from another band, settlement or state could not be trusted, and were often in fact dangerous enemies.

Even within the larger societies, most people's moral obligations did not extend effectively to all members of their society, although in theory the rulers expected these obligations to extend throughout the state. In hunting bands and in autonomous agrarian settlements theory and practice were closely, though not always perfectly, connected, but in the states the basic moral community was still the local settlement. Ganda or Rundi from one side of the kingdom felt little obligation towards fellow nationals on the other side, except sometimes in periods when their kingdom was being invaded by a rival state. On the other hand, members of the ruling class were more keenly aware of the unity of the whole society, and of the need for moral obligations to be fulfilled on a national scale. The fragmentation of the large states into a number of moral communities reflected their scale of organization, and the fact that they were made up of a variety of component sub-societies. Indeed, the large states had come into being by one state absorbing several others.

At this point it is essential to emphasize a distinction which has recurred throughout the chapters on the regions. Societies, that is moral communities, did not, and still do not, in most cases coincide with language areas. Around 1890 most East African societies were smaller than the groups of people who all spoke one language, or, to put it another way, most of the languages of East Africa were spoken by members of more than one society. For example, the Gikuyu language was spoken by members of a large number of autonomous settlements, all of whom recognized themselves to be Gikuyu, although they had no organizational unity or state. In the same way the Nyamwezi all spoke one language, but were members of a number of small states, each with its own king. Much simpler for a European, who is accustomed to relatively few languages, and to relatively large states, was the condition of the Ganda. Nearly all, if not all, the people who called themselves Ganda were members of a single state, and spoke one language. The Ganda, however, were exceptional in this respect.

This necessary distinction between society and language group highlights a confusion which frequently arises in accounts of East African peoples. Throughout the ethnographic and historical literature in English there is frequent use of the word "tribe". Furthermore, the English usage corresponds almost exactly with an older usage in Swahili, where the word in question is *kabila* (plural: *makabila*). *Kabila* means a group of people with a name for themselves as a group, such as Gikuyu or Nyamwezi, and who all speak a single language. Thus the Ganda, who number over one million, are a *kabila*, and so are the Hadza, who number several hundred. To a large extent, *kabila* corresponds with language group, but there are a few exceptions. Sukuma and Nyamwezi, for example, speak the same language, but have each a separate name for themselves, and are thus two *makabila* and not one. The important feature, which needs to be stressed, is that *kabila* and "tribe" do *not* refer to societies, as defined for the purposes of this account, except in rare instances, such as that of the Ganda.

The differences in scale between societies have been emphasized already. It is worth adding here that to a limited extent these differences correspond with differences in productivity also. The hunter-gatherers produce little per head compared to the agrarian societies, which are almost all larger than those of the hunter-gatherers. However, among the agrarian societies there is no neat correspondence between size and productivity. It is true that Rwanda and Rundi have high productivity, and were highly productive already before 1890. However, other states were markedly less productive at that date. The Hehe and the Bemba are examples. Admittedly, these were smaller states, in terms of population, than Rwanda or Rundi, but the contrast is made more striking by a consideration of the very high productivity, now and in the recent past, of the Gikuyu and the Luhya, both of them groups sub-divided into a large number of small societies, no larger than autonomous settlements.

By contrast, there is a closer correspondence between social specialization and the size of the society. Among hunter-gatherers there is little more specialization between adults than the universal division of tasks between the sexes. The people of the autonomous agrarian settlements, however, have, at the present time, smiths, medical specialists and priests, and they had them already in 1890. In even the smallest states specialization is carried one degree further in that there is a king, who is a full-time specialist in that he does not engage in cultivation or herding. There are also smiths, medical specialists and priests, but these are usually not full-time, any more than they are in the autonomous settlements. It was in the middle-sized and large states of the period 1890–1900 that social specialization was most marked. In Ganda, Rwanda, Rundi, the rest of the Interlacustrine states, and also elsewhere, for example in Nyamwezi and Hehe, there was a nobility who did not get their hands dirty, but engaged in various administrative tasks. In addition, the largest courts were able to employ full-time musicians and craftsmen.

There is circumstantial evidence, from different parts of the world, that societies cannot grow above the size of autonomous settlements unless a king appears in them. Once there is a king, however, the society may, but does not necessarily, increase in size. The factors which generate kings are therefore critically important in the history of societies, and they are considered later, in Chapter 10. Once there is a king, also, taxation appears, although it is unknown among hunting bands and autonomous settlements; and the processes of taxation become more elaborate the larger the society grows.

In order to complete the picture of social relations, it is necessary to add that societies are not isolated from each other, but rather people from different societies trade with each other, marry each other and fight each other. Furthermore, these links between societies generate differences of prestige between them, and also between different language groups. These gradients of prestige have figured prominently in the accounts of the different regions, and it is only necessary at this point to cite a few examples which have already been considered in more detail. In 1890 the Maasai, Ganda and Rwanda were all at the top of their respective local prestige pyramids, and to some extent they still are. On a smaller scale, and further south, the Hehe and Nyakyusa were the most admired peoples of their own respective areas.

The "league-tables" of relative prestige, however, change through time, and during the nineteenth century the Swahili from the coast became increasingly important in the estimate of peoples in the interior. Their prestige, however, was overshadowed by that of the Europeans, who gradually, after 1890, established administrative units and procedures on a scale unprecedented in East Africa. These new units, Kenya, Uganda and Tanzania, are the largest states that need to be considered in a continuum of societies which does not extend beyond East Africa. Before considering their special characteristics, however, it is necessary to examine briefly the earlier forms of societies, which have largely survived to the present time within the context of the new administrative units.

Hunting-and-Gathering Bands

The only hunting-and-gathering societies of modern East Africa are the bands of the Hadza, near Lake Eyasi, and of the Ogiek, in the wet forests of the Eastern Rift Highlands.[1] There are a larger number of hunting-and-gathering bands in the Wet Forest region, including, for example, those of the Mbuti in the Ituri Forest, but these pygmy groups are outside East Africa. Groups of hunters-and-gatherers also occur among the Maasai and the Soomaali, but these groups are not autonomous. They act as endogamous castes, sub-societies of wider societies; and their members speak either Maa or Soomaali, according to the society to which they belong. In effect they are the Maasai and Soomaali hunting specialists, set somewhat apart from the majority of members of their societies, who despise them for not being pastoralists, and also specifically for being hunters.

The only other hunters-and-gatherers within East Africa are the "Sanye", in the desert area east of the Tana River. Their social position is closely analogous to that of the Midgan, a hunting caste of the Soomaali, since the "Sanye" act as the hunting caste of the local Oromo, whose language they speak. However, the "Sanye" do also speak their own language, and may, in the nineteenth century or earlier, have formed autonomous bands like those of the Hadza today. On the other hand, their association with the Oromo is probably some centuries old, and they may well have drifted in and out of subservience to Oromo pastoralists, depending on the conditions of the period, and especially on the state of the rainfall and on their need for protection from attack. It is likely that other hunting-and-gathering groups also have changed their social status through time in much the same way. Pygmy groups in the Wet Forest probably have a history of such fluctuations.

The bands of the Hadza and Ogiek are small, consisting of about twenty people, but they are also very flexible, sometimes breaking up into still smaller groups for a period. This flexibility, and the ease with which an individual can leave one band and join another, makes it rather difficult to define the societies into which these two peoples are divided. Moral obligations extend to members of more than one band, and the effective societies are most conveniently defined as clusters made up each of a few bands. The total number of people in each society is thus about fifty.

Social specialization is minimal, as it is among all hunters-and-gatherers. The men hunt and the women gather; in practice, this means that about eighty per cent of the food is provided by the women, but that the high-prestige food is provided by the men. Certain men have reputations as good hunters, and their opinions on hunting are regarded attentively by the other men. Some men too have reputations for healing illness and for mediating in disputes, but their positions are very informal. Leaders and the professions of healing are present only in the most embryonic form. The absence of war-leaders in the present century might be attributed to the effects of European administration, but even

G

before 1890 there seems to have been little fighting among these peoples. Disputes between bands, or with neighbouring cultivating peoples, led to raids, and counter-raids, but on a very small scale.

Although until about three thousand years ago all East African peoples were hunter-and-gatherers, the Ogiek and Hadza are descended from ancestors who were cultivators. It is not clear, so long afterwards, why these cultivators took up hunting-and-gathering, but it is very likely, in the light of what has happened in some other parts of Africa,[2] that they resorted to this different way of life in order to survive during a famine.

Neither the Hadza nor the Ogiek have been markedly short of food, and their diet has been varied compared to that of their cultivating neighbours. Furthermore, the greater productivity of these neighbours does not attract the hunter-gatherers to take up farming. Indeed, no contemporary hunting-and-gathering group shows much enthusiasm for farming, and this raises the question of how it came about that most peoples in the world have in fact abandoned gathering for farming. In East Africa, and elsewhere, the critical factor has probably been the severe reduction in game-animals in areas into which cultivating colonists, from elsewhere, have migrated and then settled.[3] Such a solution, however, does not apply to the areas of the Near East where farming originated.

In this connection, the Hadza east of Lake Eyasi agreed with Tanzania government officials in 1965 that they would stop hunting-and-gathering as a livelihood, and take up farming. Since their food-resources were not depleted at that time, they were presumably overawed by the officals, who felt that hunters-and-gatherers are primitive, and out of place in a modern country. Whether, however, in the long term, these eastern Hadza will remain farmers we have yet to see.

Autonomous Settlements

Unlike hunting-and-gathering bands, autonomous agrarian settlements are abundant in East Africa, their autonomy only slightly affected by the intervention of governments. These settlements are spread throughout the Horn, the Eastern Rift Coast region and the Savanna Stateless belt. Also, apart from a relatively small number of hunting-and-gathering bands, the societies of the Wet Forest region are all autonomous settlements. In some areas these settlements are nucleated villages, as in the Wet Forest, as well as in the Horn, Lake Rudolf area and Maasai territory. Throughout most of the Eastern Rift Coast region, however, the houses of a settlement are scattered, and separated from each other by fields. Scattered houses are typical also of some parts of the Savanna Stateless region in East Africa, such as Lugbara, but in others, for instance Acholi, there are nucleated villages.

Although larger than hunting-and-gathering bands, the populations of these settlements are not large; they contain usually from about one hundred to about three hundred people. Social specialization is not very elaborate, although it is markedly more apparent than in the hunting-bands. In 1890, furthermore, most of the autonomous settlements of East Africa were characterized by the division of the adult male population into age-sets. Details of procedure varied from one group to another,[4] but the basic assumption was that all the men of an area initiated during the same period of years belonged throughout their lives to the same age-set. Men initiated before them belonged to a senior age-set, and men initiated after them to a junior set. Members of one age-set owed each other loyalty and, since age-sets included men from a number of neighbouring settlements, these loyalties provided a link between settlements which were often otherwise mutually hostile. Such age-set organization can be on a large scale. At the present time, for instance, all Maasai men belong to a system of age-sets which extends throughout Maasai territory.

Initiation for the peoples of the Eastern Rift Coast region and for the Oromo of the Horn always involved circumcision, but this was not part of the initiation to manhood status of most of the Savanna Stateless groups in or near East Africa. At the present time, all those peoples who practised circumcision in 1890 still do so, but the majority of them have discontinued the formal organization of the men into age-sets. Such organization, however, has been maintained vigorously by the pastoral peoples: Oromo of the Horn, Turkana, Sambur and Maasai.

The division of functions between individuals is not accentuated in the autonomous settlements but part-time specialists are usually present. Although much of the sacrificial ritual is performed by adult married men without special qualifications, most groups also have specialist priests, hereditary in certain descent-lines, who are responsible for the well-being of each community, and are required to perform sacrifices over and above those necessary for the benefit of individual households and groups of kinsmen. In addition to these specialist priests, there are medical functionaries who concentrate on the diagnosis and healing of illness. Diagnosis requires divination in most instances, frequently by means of reading the pattern of special collections of objects belonging to the diviner, and thrown on the ground before they are read. There are, however, also other means of divination. By divination the specialists sometimes discover that healing requires a sacrifice, by a kinsman, or sometimes by a specialist priest. Alternatively, illness caused by witchcraft requires counteracting medicines, another aspect of local specialist knowledge. Some ailments indeed are felt to respond to treatment by means of medicines alone, and these are compounded, largely from various plants, by medical specialists. Even in such socially undifferentiated societies the medical practitioners specialize among themselves, and refer some patients to other practitioners, or to the nearest hospital.

Smiths occur in most of the ethnic groups characterized by autonomous settlements, but not in most settlements; each smith usually serves a group of neighbouring communities, most of which are thus dependent on a smith in a settlement not their own. Since 1890 a major change has occurred in smithcraft in East Africa. At that time all the iron that was used was smelted in East Africa, peoples who practised smelting exporting the crude iron to their neighbours. However, with increasing trade, and the import of large quantities of iron and steel goods from Europe and elsewhere, smiths now rely on scrap-iron, especially old car springs, for their raw materials, and local smelting has faded out.

Disputes between members of the same settlement usually involve the mediation of men from the settlement who are known to be good at such negotiations. If these attempts at mediation fail the disputants can take their case to a local court, although such a course was not open to them before European administrators set up a system of courts. Disputes between members of different settlements can sometimes be settled with the aid of mediators acceptable to both parties, or else the contestants can take their case to court. Prior to European administration, however, disputes between individuals in different settlements usually involved the two settlements in fighting.

The killing of somebody by a man from another settlement led regularly to a feud between the settlements, and failure, or alleged failure, to hand over bridewealth in full, when a marriage took place between settlements, was another cause of feuding. Attempts to end feuds between settlements by negotiation often led to marriages between members of the different settlements, and such marriages could detonate fresh disputes over whether the bridewealth had been paid in full. In such conditions men successful in raids on other settlements acquired reputations which made them the likely leaders of later raids. Further success enhanced their reputations, but sooner or later they either failed badly or retired from fighting, and left the war-leader's role to the competition of younger men. Such war-leaders had no formal office nor officially recognized authority. There was more raiding between settlements than between hunting-bands, and raids for cattle continue at the present time in parts of East Africa, for example Maasai territory and the Pokot–Karimojong' area. However, it is misleading to call such raiding and counter-raiding war, since it is on too small a scale to fully justify the term.

States

On the other hand, the fighting between the larger states can be called war without any exaggeration or distortion. When Nyoro and Ganda were fighting each other during the nineteenth century, for example, the scale of operations must have been similar to that of wars, themselves admittedly small-scale, between the king of England and the king of France in the twelfth century. There were indeed further similarities between these two pairs of examples, as we shall see shortly.

Before the establishment of European administration there were states, and kings, throughout the Southern Savanna and Interlacustrine regions, with only a few stateless peoples in some areas on the margins of these regions. States also extended along the Nile–Congo watershed, at the edge of the Wet Forest. Further afield, on the other side of the Savanna Stateless peoples, were the kingdoms of the Ethiopian Highlands, which were part of the NANE, and not the African, Major Cultural Region. As pointed out earlier, some "states" were no bigger than one village, and could be classified with the autonomous settlements, but most consisted of at least a few villages, all owing allegiance to a single king. Most of the smallest states contained about a thousand people; and there were kingdoms of all sizes above this up to the scale of Rwanda and Rundi, with between one and two million people each. In the Ethiopian Highlands the largest kingdoms contained millions of people, and by 1890 Menelik of Shoa was in the process of subduing all the highland kingdoms to form provinces of a single empire.

In every kingdom larger than a single settlement there was at least a two-tier administration, with the king and his advisers, or court, at the top level, and with a lower "layer" of village headmen, each in charge of one settlement, and answerable to the king for the provision of taxes and services. Larger kingdoms, such as the Soga and Ziba states, and some of those of the Nyamwezi, had three-tier administrations, with district headmen below the king's court, but each with several village headmen answerable to him. The largest kingdoms, notably Rundi, Rwanda and Ganda, had four-tier administrations, with provincial governors forming a "layer" between the court and the district headmen.[5] A major function, if not the major function, of this hierarchy of officials was the gathering of taxes, which were collected in the first instance by the village headmen, and then relayed to the court either directly or by way of the intervening officials in the chain-of-command, depending on the size and complexity of the state in question.

In addition to officials, the important part-time specialists of the autonomous settlements flourished in the states. There were priests, medical specialists and smiths; and some of these three groups who were attached to the court could afford to be full-time rather than part-time. Patronage at the court in the larger states enabled some musicians and artisans also to practise full-time.

Taxes passed from hand to hand "up" the hierarchy of officials, each functionary who handled the produce (it was never money) taking a portion for himself in lieu of salary. The hierarchy of officials was maintained by these taxes, as was the court itself; and the perpetuation of the hierarchy depended not only on levies of livestock, iron goods and grain, but also on the labour of tax-payers, who owed some of their dues in the form of corvée. For instance, in Ganda, the foot-roads used by royal runners, carrying messages for the central government, were maintained by the tax-payers who lived near to the route. In one other respect also the central governments relied on dues from further "down" the hierarchy. There was no standing army in any of the states, and the kings depended for fighting men on the loyalty, or prudence, of the provincial governors, district heads and village headmen.

In return for their taxes in kind, their labour-service and their contingents of fighting men, the people of each kingdom looked to the king for protection from foreign attack and for the administration of justice. At each "level" of the hierarchy the officials presided over the settlement of disputes, constituting in themselves informal courts of law. Ideally at least, and often actually, litigants were able to appeal from a lower court to a higher, up to the king himself, sitting as a court of final appeal.

In the Interlacustrine region, and even in the Southern Savanna and Forest-edge regions, the king granted land, at least in theory, to his courtiers and provincial governors, who then granted parts of their royal grant to retainers and followers, and so on to the smallest farmers. In return the grantees were expected to behave loyally to their benefactors. Since in practice the land-tenure hierarchy was similar to, or identical with, the official hierarchy, loyalty to one's benefactor was about the same as maintaining the hierarchy of officials in working order. Despite the predictable protests of historians of Europe, it seems realistic to call the Interlactustrine administrative system feudal, by analogy with, for instance, twelfth century England and France. In the Southern Savanna and Forest-edge regions, land has been abundant at every stage, whereas by 1890 it was comparatively scarce in the Interlacustrine states. As a result feudal tenure has been more theoretical outside the Interlacustrine region. At the same time, even in densely populated Rundi and Rwanda there seems to have been no class of landless people, such as have been so important a feature in the social history of China, India and the Near East.

The smooth working which was inherent in the theory of the official hierarchy did not in fact occur, or at least not for more than a generation or two at a time. On the death of a king, fighting frequently broke out between possible successors from within the royal clan. Even successful candidates sometimes found themselves ruling a smaller territory than their predecessor because a rival had seceded with part of the former realm. At the same time, rivalry for glory between kings not infrequently resulted in one state annexing part or all of another, and so increasing in size.

Annexation, sometimes repeated a number of times, accounts for the great range of sizes between the different states which was noted earlier, and in the differing degrees of official hierarchization, dependent on the size of the state. However, it is worth emphasizing that even the largest states were fairly small by European standards, although not by the standards of Western Europe before Roman administration. Rwanda and Rundi together, for instance, are about the size of Belgium. One possible factor in this comparatively small scale of the states was the absence of writing, but this cannot have been critical since in South America the Inca dynasty ruled over an empire, which extended much of the way along the Andes, without writing. The Inca example equally refutes the absence of horses, camels or other fast riding-animals as the critical factor, since such domestic animals were equally lacking in South

America. At the same time, the lack of horses or camels must have made more difficult the task of a central government trying to curb the rebellious tendencies of distant provincial governors.

Whatever the factors preventing the greater size of East African states, and it may be that it simply takes more time, than they had had, for kings to become ambitious enough to build empires, they were not equipped in 1890 with bureaucracies, such as added a measure of durability to the states of China since *c.* 300 B.C. and to the states of Western Christendom between A.D. 1000 and A.D. 1500, where the clergy provided a very effective civil service.

The Contemporary States

Such a civil service was one of the conspicuously new features brought to East Africa by the European administrators, who also introduced ancillary technical departments, such as those dealing with health, farming, veterinary services, forestry and mining. Other important innovations were professional armies and police forces. All of these organizations existed in Belgium, Britain and Germany by 1890, and they were made possible, and sustained, in those countries by the wealth generated by the industrial revolution which had taken place there. Transported to East Africa, however, they had to be established in forms much less complex than in their countries of origin, because of the lack of an available tax-yield to support them in an elaborate version. At the same time, the administrators set about improving the tax-yield in order that such services and organizations could be sustained at all, and a similar task faces the contemporary local administrators.

Already some of the new organizations have had some striking effects. The health and veterinary departments, by largely eliminating epidemic diseases of people and of domestic livestock, have helped to detonate a rapid increase of the human and domestic animal populations. New crops, promoted by agriculture departments, are now part of the daily routines, and income-expectations, of small farmers, as in the case, for instance, of cotton among the Sukuma. More dramatic has been the role of the new armies, which in Burundi and Uganda have taken over the governments.

Of the five states of contemporary East Africa only the smallest, Burundi and Rwanda, have any traditions of long-established unity. The other three are recently established, devoid of any heroic past, and even their unity is tenuous. Compared to the largest of the earlier states, these three are huge. Uganda has about eight million people, Kenya also about eight million, and Tanzania about ten million. By contrast Rwanda has about three million, and Burundi somewhat fewer. All five now have the additional organizations, of European origin, which have already been mentioned, and they each have as head of state a president, an office of European origin also. There were no presidents in East Africa in 1890.

Rwanda and Burundi are essentially more complex versions of their earlier selves, but the other three have come into being by the incorporation into one organizational framework of a large number of, mostly small, societies. Where these earlier societies were autonomous settlements, they have been introduced to taxation and to law-courts, and in most areas their raiding among themselves has been effectively stopped. On the other hand, where these earlier societies were already states, taxes and law-courts were already familiar, and feuding between settlements was already forbidden. However, the ruling-classes of these earlier states found their supremacy undermined by the power of the new, overarching, governments, and the former sovereigns were no longer sovereign. For most of the people in the settlements which made up the states, however, the new conditions have been in many respects like the old. Even so, for some people, the more energetic, ambitious or restless, the new hierarchies offer opportunities not available either in the autonomous settlements or states of the past. It will be necessary to summarize the most important features of the new social patterns in Chapter 12.

8. Notes

1. As noted already, after 1900 the Ogiek began to cultivate a little and to keep livestock.
2. On the eastern borders of the Kalahari, during drought years, large numbers of Tswana rely heavily for food on what they can gather, thus partially adopting the way of life of their Bushmen neighbours.
3. Reduction in their resources, resulting from the rapidly increasing populations of their cultivating neighbours, Gikuyu, Nandi and Kipsigis,

presumably accounts for the Ogiek taking such an interest in crops and domestic animals after 1900.

4. Lucy Mair (1962). "Primitive Government", pp. 61–106, discusses some of the peoples with age-sets.

5. There are some detailed accounts of these "tiers" of officials in a number of East African states in : Audrey Richards (ed.) (1960). "East African Chiefs".

9

God, The Ancestors and The Spirits of The Bush

Divine Power and Human Frailty

So far we have been looking at the peoples of East Africa from the outside, examining the distribution of the different ethnic groups in relation to habitats and historical movements of peoples. Such an approach, however, is unfamiliar to the vast majority of East Africans, only a few of them, and those members of the literary elite, being interested in such a systematic outline of the dynamic pattern of peoples in the area. Although the systematic examination of the pattern is the main theme of this book, it is essential to redress the balance in the emphasis by paying attention to the viewpoints of East Africans themselves, and by examining their preoccupations and interests.

Not surprisingly, East Africans, like other people in all parts of the world, are overwhelmingly preoccupied with their own prosperity. They know that they require an adequate supply of food, that they need good health and that they also need children to carry themselves on into the next generation. At the same time, they are aware that such blessings, and they see them as blessings, are not available to them automatically, and that there is unending danger that something will go wrong : there is liable to be drought, famine or an epidemic disease. Furthermore, women, including one's own wife, are liable to be barren. There are dangers too in one's relations with other people. Strife within the community is always embarrassing, and sometimes positively dangerous. It can lead to false accusations and to murder, and, even if it does not, it will anger the dead ancestors. In the recent past also war and raids resulted in deaths and serious losses, for instance of cattle. There are still some areas where loss of lives and of cattle through raiding are part of everyday experience, but most people in contemporary East Africa are not immediately worried by such a prospect.

In addition to being preoccupied with prosperity and trouble, East Africans are aware that neither prosperity nor disaster occurs at random. They are caused by specific factors, some of which at least are identifiable by human beings, and for those troubles whose causes can be ascertained there are remedies which can, and ought to, be applied. The Universe appears to East Africans not as a chaos, a series of collisions of mutually unconnected events, but rather as a pattern, vast, complex, largely inscrutable to people, but orderly and, if one had the vision of God, comprehensible. This assumption of cosmic order is implicit, rather than explicit, in most East Africans, but it is very real, and underlies their responses to specific events in their daily experience. They are familiar with the normal regularities of recurrence, such as sunrise and sunset, the alternation of the wet and dry seasons, and take them for granted, without comment. However, they are aware, only too keenly aware, that not all wet seasons are adequate for the growing of good crops. Similarly, their very familiarity with the normal run of events makes them recognize immediately anything which is abnormal. There would be consternation throughout East Africa if one day the sun were to rise in the west.

The Universe then is ordered, but things still go wrong, and when they do so then something has happened to make them go wrong. However, ultimately, as all, or almost all, East Africans recognize, everything in the Universe is maintained by God. He made everything, and He keeps everything in order. In writing or speaking in English, it is unavoidable that a pronoun be male or female, but this is not true of most East African languages, and few East Africans would attribute a sex to God. "He" is neither male nor female, but rather "He" created people and other animals male and female, while being "Himself" above both maleness and femaleness, as Christians, Muslims and Jews well know, even when they speak languages which have no sexless pronouns. There is one other complication when referring to the knowledge of Divine Power among East African peoples, and this is that among the Ganda, of the pre-Christian period, authority and power appear to have stemmed ultimately from a number of gods, rather than uniquely from God.

At the present time, most Ganda profess to be either Christians or Muslims, and very few of them would like to be seen as associating with forces from the pagan past. However, in the period 1870–1900, most

Ganda acknowledged the power of a number of named major deities (*balubaale*, in Ganda), each with special control over some aspect of human prosperity or disaster. These gods were :

Musoke, controlling rain;
Nagawonyi, controlling drought;
Dungu, controlling hunting;
Kawumpuli, controlling bubonic plague;
Kawali, controlling smallpox;
Ndawula, controlling smallpox;
Kiwanuka, controlling lightning;
Musisi, controlling earthquakes;
Mukasa, controlling the fertility of women;
Kibuka, controlling success in war;
Nende, controlling success in war.[1]

Significantly, however, one of the gods was not associated with any specific current function. This was Katonda, who is said to have made people in the beginning. There is thus a great deal of force in the assertion of some modern Ganda who maintain that the pre-Christian Ganda acknowledged God as the unique source of ultimate power, the named *balubaale* being his manifestations or aspects. Such a view is also very probably correct in the light of normal East African acknowledgement of God's unique authority and power, and of the fact that the major named *balubaale*, apart from Katonda, are each specialized in an important function which other East Africans would see as a prerogative of God, for instance controlling rain. However, once we accept that the old Ganda view was centred on God, there are implications which go far beyond East Africa. For instance, were the gods of the ninth century Norse aspects of Odin? Were the gods of the pre-Christian Athenians and Spartans manifestations of Zeus? Indeed, are all so-called polytheistic systems of knowledge implicitly monistic and centred on God? Although the question is important, it cannot be answered in an East African context, and it need not concern us further here.

It is necessary, however, to add that, in addition to the major deities, there were known to be a great number of *balubaale*, most of them only important in one locality or a restricted area, and essentially the same as spirits of the bush.

Balubaale, great and small, readily possessed people, as do other spirits of the bush elsewhere. Ganda recognized too a second major category

of superhuman powers, the *mizimu*, spirits of dead ancestors, concerned
with the welfare and proper conduct towards them of their own descendants. It is possible, therefore, to summarize the earlier Ganda hierarchy
of superhuman powers as :

God

gods

spirits of the bush	ancestors

In this form, the Ganda were still recognizably different from the
other peoples of East Africa although less markedly so than they would
be if recognized as acknowledging a number of autonomous major
balubaale. The vast majority of East Africans recognized, and most of
them still recognize, a hierarchy which descends as follows :

God

spirits of the bush	ancestors

This hierarchy is known to peoples as scattered as the Yao, Fipa, Gogo,
Kamba, Nyoro and even, in a sense, the Soomaali, in the NANE Major
Cultural Region.

God is supreme. He created people, and all the Universe, and He
maintains it now. He controls the rain, sends lightning and makes women
and cattle fertile, to take a rather narrowly human-centred view of his
majesty and power. He is, however, strictly aloof, not in the sense that
He is inactive, since He is supremely active, but in the sense that people
are far removed from Him in their nature, and hesitate to move closer
to Someone so awe-inspiring. Although some Christians and Muslims
are bold enough to address their prayers directly to God, most East
Africans feel more comfortable praying in the first instance to their
ancestors.

Most people in East Africa indeed are confident that their prosperity
is controlled directly by their dead ancestors, and that it is proper and
effective to address prayers, sacrifices and other offerings to them. The
ancestors can be offended by their descendants, and they not infrequently
are, but they are ready to forgive offences if their living kin are properly
repentant.

Very different in these respects are the spirits of the bush, so called
because they are usually experienced by people away from settled areas,
in tracts of woodland or swamp. Repeatedly in writings on East Africa
these spirits are called "evil spirits", largely as a result of Christian

missionary literature. Since they usually do harm, for instance cause illness or death, they can properly be called evil, but they were not seen as
agents of the Devil, although increasingly East African Christians and
Muslims now recognize them as such. In a pre-Christian context, they
were marked by their unexpectedness of action, and their inscrutability,
rather than by their part in a grand design of Universe-wide deliberate
malice.

By contrast with most East Africans, there is a group of peoples who
have paid little attention to their ancestors or to the spirits of the bush.
These are the Maasai, Sambur, Turkana and Karimojong',[2] all of them
exclusive or would-be pastoralists occupying a belt of dry country from
the Lake Rudolf area southward. For them, God is the sole source and
channel for superhuman power, except that they recognize that sometimes
troubled people return from the dead to disturb the living. When this
happens, it is necessary to persuade or force the ghost to go away.
Troublesome ghosts indeed are widespread among East African communities, and not a speciality of the Maasai–Karimojong' group, and
there is an equally widespread desire to hasten them away from the
people still living.

Given these variations in the pattern of superhuman power, it is possible
to arrange the peoples of East Africa along a continuum with the Ganda
at one extremity and the Maasai–Karimojong' group at the other.
The vast majority of East African peoples are then bunched in the
middle, with the Fipa and Gikuyu, for example. This continuum is the
more convincing because the Rwanda and Rundi provide an intermediate
pattern between the Ganda and the main mass of peoples. In Rwanda
those who are not Christians acknowledge the power not only of God
but also of about thirty lesser beings (*maandwa*), gods, led by Ryaan-
goombe. The same name is used by the Rundi for the chief of these gods,
although they more usually call him Kiranga. Gods are repeatedly mani-
fested by possessing people, and the *maandwa* are thus not very different
from the *chwezi* of Nyoro and Tooro, who possess people, those who are
possessed forming a society of devotees, just as also happens in Rundi
and Rwanda (Fig. 9).

On the other side of the Ganda, the Soga recognize that some of the
beings called *misambwa* have names, as have the major *balubaale*, the
maandwa and the *chwezi*, while others are more obscure and anonymous
spirits of the bush, just as are found in most parts of East Africa. There
is another example of the same kind, but from the Southern Savanna

and not the Interlacustrine region. The Fipa recognize that there are spirits of the bush, an indeterminate number of them, but one among them is extremely important, being named Katai, and causing smallpox. Katai seems to be precisely analogous with the *balubaale* Kawali and Ndawula among the Ganda. All of this evidence from Rundi, Rwanda, Tooro, Nyoro, Soga and Fipa strengthens the view that the Ganda represent an extreme development of a general East African tendency towards plural manifestations of Divine Power. In the same way the Maasai and Karimojong' represent an extreme emphasis of the general East African knowledge that God *is* and that He *is* supremely.

That the strongest development of the tendency to plural manifestations is in the area from Rundi to Ganda is noteworthy because this is precisely

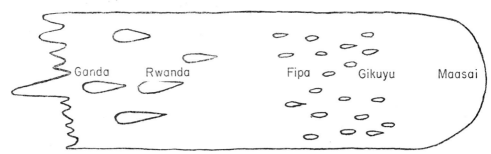

Fig. 9.   The continuum of cosmic complexity in East African societies.

the area where the largest and most complex East African societies have occurred. Furthermore, it is clear from other parts of the world that large and complex societies show a strong tendency to plural forms of Divine Power as complexly refracted. It is important to add, as a corrective, and Andean American. The tendency is not absolute, and it has been reversed by Christian and Muslim conversions, but as a tendency only it still exists; and the Interlacustrine peoples represent another example of a situation where those who live socially complex lives see Divine Power as completely refracted. It is important to add, as a corrective, that the socially much less complex Acholi, Jieng' and Naath, further north, also recognize complex refractions of Divine Power. One further feature is that the Ganda were the most complex of all in their plurality of *balubaale*, and it has been suggested already, in Chapter 6, that this complexity probably arises from an unconscious desire to be very different from neighbouring groups, itself derived from the Ganda sense of their own superiority to other peoples.

Turning to the Maasai and Karimojong' at the other end of the spectrum, there are no grounds for linking their cosmic simplicity to their social simplicity. Karimojong' and Turkana certainly are socially simple, but no simpler than the Otuho, who sacrifice to their ancestors; while the Maasai and Sambur are socially organized in a manner very similar to the earlier pattern of the Gikuyu and Nandi, both of whom treated their ancestors very seriously. The Maasai–Karimojong' group seem to be a parallel to the Ganda in that their cosmic simplicity reflects their unconscious desire to be different because superior. Certainly the peoples of the group do regard themselves as superior to their neighbours.

It needs to be emphasized that these social aspects of people's knowledge of Divine Power do not imply that this knowledge springs from a confused awareness of people's own feelings. Despite various attempts by different writers to reduce knowledge of God to a function of people's own workings, such knowledge remains logically and empirically irreducible. East Africans are on firm ground when they acknowledge that God is simply a fact.

Whatever then the precise details which they recognize in the Universe, all over East Africa groups of people find themselves in the presence of Divine Power, and most of them also recognize the power and authority of their ancestors. Not only are individuals fragile, but even villages are fragile, liable to be depopulated by smallpox, in the recent past, or to be scattered by drought or raiding. Prosperity depended, and depends still, upon Divine Power. Inadequate Power results in disaster, but so does too intimate an influx of that Power, as in a lightning-strike. There is a golden mean, which spells prosperity, only when the right balance is achieved between the local human community and Divine Power. Given that balance, people enjoy adequate food, good health, children, social harmony and victory over their enemies, but if that harmony is disturbed then there will be famine, disease, barrenness of women, herds and flocks, and also social discord and defeat. Each little community, and this is still true, is like a small boat tossed on a stormy sea, or like a clearing in a great forest, which it often literally is. The members of each community are surrounded by immense power which they cannot command (Fig. 10).

However, what they can do is to pray, sacrifice and make other offerings to God and to his manifestations, be they distinct gods or more shadowy spirits of the bush. They can also address their ancestors, who act as mediators between their descendants and Divine Power. As we have seen already, in Chapter 8, effective moral communities are small, two hundred people being a realistic estimate of median size, and these communities are the survival units. Moral obligations extend beyond their borders to only a limited number of people; and the essential rituals are performed by the people of a community in order to ensure their own, rather than general human, prosperity. Universal morality is recognized only by the devout Christians and Muslims, who are a minority in East Africa, as everywhere else.

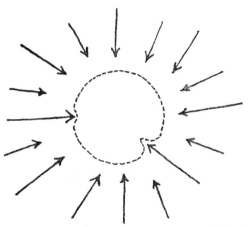

Fig. 10.   The moral community in its context of Divine Power.

People's awareness of the delicate balance between prosperity and disaster, of the ease with which good times turn to bad, and of the way in which people, by their own moral failings, bring down upon themselves the anger of God and their ancestors, finds expression in the system of symbols which is known throughout East Africa, although individual ethnic groups may not emphasize all parts of it alike. The system can best be demonstrated by reference to the accompanying diagram (Fig. 11). God is frequently represented by the sun. It is not that the sun is identical with God, for people know very well that the sun is created and not Creator. Nor is there a sun-god. The point of the imagery is that the sun expresses God's splendour and power better than does anything on earth. It is also far above people, just as God is immeasurably superior to people both physically and morally. Indeed the sky as a whole is also used as a symbol of God, who is seen as, and said to be "above"; but this does not imply that He is limited to a particular part of the Universe, since his power is everywhere active.

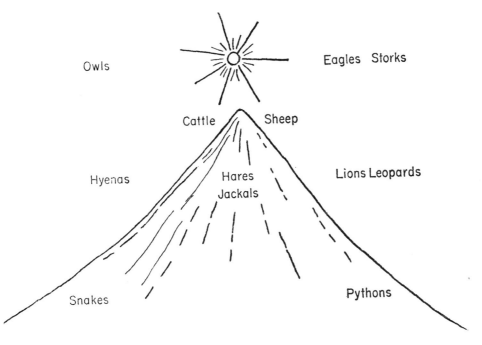

Fig. 11.   The pattern of symbols representing different aspects of Divine Power.

In the context of God's association with sun, sky and "above", it is appropriate that the tops of high mountains are also especially connected with Him. This is true, for example, of Kilimanjaro and Kenya in the eyes of the peoples who live near enough to see them. Again, there is no implication that God is limited to these summits, only that they are points where "below", where people live, meets "above", especially linked with God. Until Chaga men discovered that it was profitable to accompany Europeans as porters to the top of Kilimanjaro, it seems that East Africans usually avoided the tops of mountains, partly because there was no need to go there, but also because they are too awesome. Indeed Chaga still feel that local women ought not to go up the mountain.

In the same way as mountain-summits, high-flying birds are symbolic of God. This applies especially to eagles, vultures, storks and cranes, but Divine Power shows itself at three different levels, literally physical levels, in the Universe, a reminder that God acts everywhere. The symbols of his power at the level where people live are pre-eminently the large cats, lions and leopards, which are seen as majestic and authoritative. In the period 1890–1910 the kings of most, or all, East African states claimed a monopoly on the pelts of lions and leopards, and such pelts formed part of the royal insignia in many states. Other large and powerful mammals were also somewhat endued with the aura of divine majesty, especially elephants, whose tusks were also a royal monopoly, and one which the kings were increasingly eager to enforce as trading with the coast became more active during the nineteenth century.

The third, and lowest, physical level of the Universe was occupied by animals that the British would lump together as "creepy-crawlies". Most East African languages have a word which covers these creatures, the Swahili form being *madudu*. Divine Power expresses itself symbolically at this level through snakes, but there is a sharp distinction between pythons (*Python sebae*) and all other snakes. Whereas pythons are auspicious and majestic, other snakes are seen as malignant, terrifying and associated with witches. The same is true of chameleons, which fill the same role as the inauspicious snakes, while most of the peoples of the Eastern Rift Coast region identified fish with snakes until recently. Indeed the Maasai still do so.

This dual aspect of the lowest level's symbols is repeated at the other two levels. At the human or middle level, where the symbols are mammals, the inauspicious animals are hyenas, seen as wicked and loathsome, and intimately associated with witches. Their role in the highest level is filled by owls, more especially by the spotted eagle-owl (*Bubo africanus*). Like hyenas, owls are associated with the night, the time when witches are active and when decent people are in their houses. As in Europe, owls are birds of ill-omen, their calling near a house foreboding illness or death to those people or to their kinsmen. The dual pattern of these symbols emphasizes that Divine Power is ambivalent, causing both prosperity and disaster, weal and woe, but there is also the implication in these inauspicious animals of malice, which emanates from people who deliberately will to hurt other people. God himself is not accused of malice by most people.

The ambivalence of Divine Power is brought out, not only by the paired symbols just mentioned, but also by the occasional association of usually auspcious symbols with malice and wickedness. Among the Rimi, for example, lions are held in respect, but when lions kill people it is known that these apparent lions are people who have turned into lions, and they are hated and feared, much as if they were witches. Here the general symbol, lion, has both an auspicious and an inauspicious face. The same can be said of a parallel example among the peoples of the eastern Wet Forest, once famous for their societies of leopard-men, people who maintained that they could become leopards and thus kill anyone they chose.

Another indication of ambivalence is the Trickster, a familiar figure in symbolic systems all over the world. In East Africa the role of Trickster is played by hares for some peoples, jackals, for others, and by dikdiks (*Rhynchotragus kirki*), a species of small antelopes, for yet others. The main theme of stories about Trickster is that he is cheated and cheats back, but he is capable of both malice and quixotic generosity.

All these symbols express Divine Power, which is wholly other than human in its nature, definitely not part of the moral community, although maintaining it. There are, however, animals which bridge the gulf between Divine Power and people by their role as sacrifices. Cattle, sheep and goats are the classic sacrificial animals of East Africa. Although not human, they are domesticated and associated with people; and they are thus highly suitable intermediaries between the human community and the powers beyond it. Not all East African peoples, however, possess cattle, while in some areas chickens are important for sacrifices, for instance in many parts of the Southern Savanna and the Wet Forest. Also intermediate between people and Divine Power are the sites where sacrifices are regularly performed. Sometimes these are on mountains, appropriately in view of the significance of mountain-tops. More often they are under trees, and especially fig trees (*Ficus* spp.), which are huge, long-lived and covered with dark green leaves even at the height of the dry season, when most other trees are bare of leaves. These fig trees represent durability, strength and unfailing life, the hopes of all who sacrifice beneath them.

As has been noted already, East Africans are well aware of malice active against people in the desires and activities of witches, but they had no knowledge of the Devil, the mastermind of malice on a cosmic scale, until they came into contact with Muslims and Christians. At the present time the East African Muslims and Christians know not only of the Devil, but of the Day of Judgement, which was also absent from their earlier knowledge. Equally new to them is the glorious resurrection of the faithful dead, very different from the unexciting future faced by their dying ancestors, in the past.

Most of the peoples of the Ethiopian Highlands, with their strong cultural links to the Near East, are Christians or Muslims, and the Soomaali of the Horn are Muslims, and have been for centuries. Small concentrations of Muslims, also centuries old, occur on the coast, in and near the city-states, such as Mombasa. However, over most of East Africa Muslims are recent converts, and few families in the interior have been Muslim for more than four generations. On the coast itself the proportion of Muslims in the population has increased since 1850, but inland they are either thinly scattered or occur as local "islands" in an otherwise non-Muslim population. They are not numerous in the Eastern Rift Coast region, away from the coastal plain, but the Langi are a predominantly Muslim island near to the settlement of Kondoa, founded by coastal traders on a route into the interior. The same history accounts for the islands of Muslims around Tabora and Ujiji, both settlements on the important trunk-route from the coast to Lake Tanganyika. In the Inter-lacustrine region Muslims are most numerous in Ganda, where they are a large minority. At the same time, in many parts of East Africa the number of Muslims is increasing.

Professing Christians are numerous, but form only a small proportion of the population in many areas. In the Eastern Rift Coast region, al-though an important section of the populations in the Wet Highlands, they are a tiny minority in the Maasai area, as well as in the dry country of the Lake Rudolf area and towards the Soomaali in the Horn. A high proportion of people in the Interlacustrine region would say that they are Christian, but in the Southern Savanna Christians are usually a minority, albeit locally a large minority. At the same time Christians are divided, and very consciously divided, between Protestants and Roman Catholics. In some areas, the majority of Christians are Roman Catholics, in others most are Protestants, and in yet others the two groups are roughly equally represented.

Most people who become Muslims do not immediately change their behaviour very much, although with time increasing numbers of the men in an area where there are numerous Muslims attend the Friday prayers in the mosque. To become a Christian involves a more dramatic break with the past, notably in the abandonment of sacrifices to the ancestors. Converts are clearly aware, in both cases, of a change in rituals, but, as has been noted earlier, knowledge of the Devil, Final Judgement and Resurrection also becomes widespread. What most converts, of either kind, fail to perceive is that God is actually addressing Himself to people individually, and expects an individual response. They assume that God is aloof, exactly as their ancestors assumed, and so miss the point of God's self-revelation to the Jews.

However, in some areas very enthusiastic Christian revivals have taken place, the groups involved being in the Interlacustrine region, and east-ward from there across the wet area of south-western Kenya as far as the Gikuyu, who have been strongly affected. The revival Christians emphasize the personal tie to Jesus, the need to live like New Testament Christians, and the authority of the Bible. They are an important factor in Christian proselytizing in East Africa. Other signs of social and con-fessional change are also concentrated in the Interlacustrine and south-west Kenya zone. Independent churches, whose members stress their separateness from the missionary-bodies of their area, have been most numerous here, and especially on the north-east lake-shore, where break-away churches have been frequent occurrences in the last few decades among the Luo and Luhya. We are still in the early stages of Christian and Muslim history in East Africa.

Trouble, Rituals and Specialists

For most East Africans the presence of superhuman power becomes most urgent when something goes wrong. As has been mentioned earlier, drought, famine, an epidemic, a barren wife, social discord or military defeat all turn people's attention to the superhuman cause of these dis-turbing events. The usual immediate reaction to trouble is to discover by divination why such trouble has occurred. To do this one needs the services of a specialist diviner.

There are a number of different methods which are used by diviners to discover what is happening or has happened. Among the Maasai, for example, an *oiboni* is able to know the cause of events simply by consider-ing them. Such specialists are seers, in the strict sense, since they see the answer without any apparatus or special procedures. They have what the Scots would call "the second sight". Most diviners in East Africa, however, employ more elaborate methods, one which is widespread being the reading of the pattern of special objects. Each diviner who uses this method keeps his own collection of objects, often shells, pieces of bone or small stones. To obtain a diagnosis, he repeatedly throws these on the ground, and then "reads" the answer to the problem from the pattern which they make when they fall. By repeating the process he eventually confirms and amplifies his conclusion. Another widespread method is the "reading" of patterns which the diviner himself draws in the dust.

It is also possible to divine by methods which provide simply the answer "yes" or "no" to a question. The rubbing-board method involves pushing one sheet of wood over another, the answer being provided by the top board sticking at a certain point in the procedures. Alternatively, the diviner can hold straws or sticks of different lengths and ask a client to draw one, its length then answering the question which has been asked. Both of these methods are important in the Nile–Congo watershed area, the country of the Lugbara, Zande and their neighbours. Widespread is another form which gives simple answers. Usually called the poison-oracle, it consists of administering a poison to a chicken. This method is often used for establishing guilt; if the bird dies, the accused is guilty. Alternatively, the chicken can answer questions by the position in which it finally dies.

Searching for the superhuman causes of trouble yields three main kinds of results. One of these is that someone has committed an offence, and that this has angered God or the ancestors, usually both. The second type of answer is that someone has practised witchcraft on the sufferer, while the third type is that the motive is inscrutable, the cause being God, a god or a spirit of the bush. In such cases the causing agent has his reasons, but these are not known to people.

Although in discussing divination the specialist has been called a diviner, in practice most diviners are not confined to divination and diagnosis but are also medical practitioners. They are usually able either to provide cures for the condition identified, or else indicate an appropriate ritual which heals the trouble, or another medical practitioner who specializes in this kind of complaint.

Illnesses or other troubles caused by offences against the ancestors require a sacrifice to atone for the offence. The killing of the sacrificial animal involves the offering of its life, a major event, far more important than minor offerings, for instance of tobacco or flour, which may be made to ancestors on less grave occasions. It is generally understood that the ancestors' disapproval is justified, and not capricious, and that their attitude, and punishment, has the approval of God. Otherwise they would be ineffective. Among groups such as the Maasai and Karimojong', who pay little attention to their ancestors, such sacrifices are overtly directed to God. In most groups, faults which bring down upon the offender, or one of his kinsmen, the just wrath of the ancestors, and God, include not only improper treatment of other members of the community, but also the disobeying of specific prohibitions, such as those forbidding certain foods.

The diagnosis, however, may not reveal immorality and punishment, but rather that a witch, out of malice and jealousy, has attacked the sufferer. In such a case the medical specialist, or one of his colleagues, may be in a position to help the sufferer with medicines to strengthen him, and with others to hurt the witch. Witches are members of the community who act secretly to hurt other people by means of super-human power. The precise immediate source of this power (ultimately all power comes from God) is not regarded as an important issue by most East Africans, although Christians and Muslims see it as emanating from the Devil. When trouble is identified as the work of a witch it is important to expose him or her, again a task for a diviner. Prior to European administration witches were habitually killed, but very few are at the present time, because of widespread fear of official prosecutions for murder against the instigators of a witch-killing.

There are, however, some troubles which are caused by resentment and malice but do not emanate from witches. Their source is troubled ghosts, who have not passed successfully to the state of the dead ancestors, and who hover disconsolately on the borderland between the condition of the living and that of the dead. Such ghosts have to be laid, and here again specialists are involved, providing medicines against the trouble. For example, among the Fipa, a restless ghost is attacked with medicines, and the corpse of the ghost, once it has been identified, is burnt.

The third type of causes for trouble are inscrutable. Some of them, however, can be treated with appropriate rituals, while others cannot. Spirits of the bush not infrequently inflict illness on people, and here the cause can be diagnosed, although the motive cannot. Furthermore, these spirits are said to respond to sacrifices, and, if satisfied with the sacrifice offered, will heal the sufferer involved.

Closely allied to the afflictions caused by spirits of the bush is possession, since it is these spirits who are usually responsible. In the Interlacustrine region, there are regular societies of people who have been possessed, for instance those of the *maandwa* in Rwanda and of the *chwezi* in Nyoro. Earlier in this account *maandwa* and *chwezi* were categorized as gods, but in the East African context gods are essentially the most eminent and well-known of the spirits of the bush. Although conspicuous in the Interlactustrine region, possession is not confined to that area, but recurs throughout East Africa. Among the Sandawe and Kimbu an important spirit who guards the game-animals sometimes possesses people when they are travelling in wooded areas; and some Soomaali experience frequent possession.

There are, however, some troubles which do not respond to treatment, either by medicines or sacrifice. Some diseases prove to be fatal after every resource has been tried. In these conditions, and they occur frequently, people say that it is the will and the action of God. His reasons are not known to people, but they are doubtless right. In the last resort, all actions, all events, all causes and all power come from Him.

At the same time as people are searching for the main causes of trouble, and for ways of putting things right, they do not neglect any medicines which offer symptomatic relief. Such medicines, provided by specialists, can accompany the more basic cures already considered, or, in the cases which turn out not to be very serious, they constitute the whole treatment. These medicines are not only designed to cure illness in the narrow sense, but, more widely, to put things right. Thus there are medicines to cure barrenness in women and genital impotence in men, and there are others to attract a lover or retain a husband whose attachment to his wife is waning.

Although Europeans' knowledge of East African medicines is still very sparse, certain features of them are recognizably important. Most of them are derived from plants, and the roots are a favoured source. At the same time animal and mineral substances are not neglected or avoided. At least two major themes occur in the use of certain substances as medicines, or as parts of a compound medicine. On the one hand there are substances which have been found to work, and which repeatedly produce the desired effect. A very high proportion of plants contain medicinal compounds of some sort, and East African arrow-poisons, for example, used in hunting by many peoples of the area, are notably effective. On the other hand, there are substances which bear a symbolic resemblance to the malady they are supposed to cure or to the condition which is desired. Thus, herbs with red flowers may be used to heal wounds because the red colour is reminiscent of blood. Plants which are markedly hot, sharp or bitter to the taste are widely favoured because heat and pungency give an impression of power and effectiveness, just as British children feel that nasty medicine is bound to be the most effective medicine. Individual practitioners make their own discoveries and add to their own pharmacopeia. Charlatans, in the sense of people who deliberately mislead their clients, for the sake of personal gain, are rare in East Africa, outside Nairobi, Kampala and other large towns, where the crimes typical of complex societies flourish.

Although there are three main types of causation, from a human point of view, for those troubles which have superhuman sources, and although all ethnic groups in the area know about all three types, all groups do not attribute the same importance to each type. Witchcraft, for example, is not regarded by the Maasai as a source of trouble to be expected all the time. In contrast, some other groups detect the action of witches very frequently, and are often discussing the latest witchcraft evidence or suspicions. Two groups of this sort are the Mbowe and the Zigula, who are, in addition, both well known to their neighbours as people preoccupied with witchcraft. On the other hand, the punishments arising from the disapproval of the ancestors are very widely acknowledged, although not among the Maasai, Sambur, Turkana and Karimojong'.

It can be seen from this account of the causes of trouble that the main specialists, discussed in the previous chapter, are essentially concerned with the diagnosis and treatment of trouble, and not just of illness. Drought may also require their attention. Specialists are needed to administer medicines, to practise divination, to cope with possession and to carry out sacrifices.

In fact though most sacrifices are not performed by specialists. Usually, the sacrifices at times of illness or other individual trouble are conducted by a man who is a kinsman of the sufferer, and all adult men, with households of their own and children, are eligible as priests in this sense. Only the conscientious Christians would avoid the role altogether. Not all sacrifices are at times of trouble. Equally important are the sacrifices designed to maintain prosperity, performed either at regular times of the year or regularly on certain occasions. Sacrifices are normal at marriages and at funerals, and again are performed by kinsmen of the people most involved.

Seasonal sacrifices, on the other hand, normally do require the services of a specialist, and usually hereditary, priest. The beginning of the rains, or of the sowing-period, is an important time for sacrificing in order to pray for prosperity and a good crop in the coming season. Frequently too there are sacrifices after harvest, or at the time of first-fruits, in thanks to the superhuman powers for their continuing support.

In conditions, therefore, where outside observers see landscapes, wild animals and people adapted to their habitat, the local people see the prospect of well-being or trouble, and the need for proper attention to the ancestors, spirits of the bush and God.

9. Notes

1. Margaret Chave Fallers (1960). "The Eastern Lacustrine Bantu", p. 69.
2. The group also includes the other peoples very similar to the Turkana and Karimojong' : Jiye, Dudutho, Toposa and Nyang'atom.

10

The Processes of Cultural Change

The Increase in Complexity of Social Groups

Throughout the discussion of the individual ethnic groups in previous chapters there has been repeated references to the processes of cultural change. For instance, there have been occasions when it has been noted that a certain cultural element arrived from a certain direction, and it has been mentioned repeatedly that some of the migrants into a certain area came from another area nearby. At this stage it becomes necessary to look more systematically at these processes of change.

Already, in Chapter 1, the factors involved in these processes have been summarized as belonging to five complexes. These are (in a different order from that in Chapter 1):

1. the increase in social specialization within groups;
2. cultural features spreading to the boundaries of a habitat-area;
3. migration, generated by pressure on resources;
4. prestige gradients, generating imitation by lower status groups of higher status groups (but offset by people's desire to be different from the people of other ethnic groups);
5. the accumulation of factors, with the result that changes can occur even though one factor alone would not be sufficient to bring them about.

If we consider these complexes one at a time, changes in social specialization, and therefore social complexity, are implicit in much of the information on the ethnic groups which has already been reviewed. In East Africa there are some, but only a few, hunting-and-gathering peoples, now only some Hadza. There are also farming peoples, such as the Gikuyu and Kamba, who, in the period 1880–1920, were socially more complex than the hunters-and-gatherers, but still not very complex compared to some other peoples. In addition to farming peoples who practise hoe-cultivation, there are exclusive pastoralists, such as the Maasai, whose social specialization is no more complex than that of the small-scale cultivating peoples.

Some farming peoples, however, although organizationally on a scale as small as the Gikuyu or Kamba, were more specialized in one feature, since they had hereditary rulers, tiny versions of kings. An example of such a people are the Mbowe and another, from a different cultural region, are the Makonde. The importance of setting such societies, with very minor rulers, apart from otherwise very similar societies, who had no hereditary heads, has been noted already, because, once people have a king, they have the capacity to go on increasing in numbers, without dividing into several smaller societies. Capacity here does not imply necessity, since the "states" of the Mbowe and Makonde have remained tiny to the present day. However, peoples with no kings, whether gatherers or farmers, never produce large societies. Among such groups, the increase in size of a community leads eventually to the point where that community splits into two, or more, societies, each very like the parent-body. The presence of a king does not in itself prevent such fission or secession. Tooro, for instance, broke away from Nyoro; but once people have kings there exists for the first time the real possibility of growth without fission.

Any increase in size of the society, by whatever means, be it reproduction or conquest, can be accommodated by the king, who can appoint more ministers, more provincial governors and more village headmen. Various factors, such as the ambition of rival neighbours, may easily prevent the growth of the state, but the potential is there. However, even without rival states, cramping territorial growth, there are limits on the increase in size. The largest states anywhere, such as the Roman Empire and the empires of the major Chinese dynasties, for instance the Han and T'ang, have shown a remarkably uniform tendency to disintegrate, even though by that time they have lasted a few hundred years.

In East Africa, however, there is no need to consider the eventual disintegration of really large states, because no kingdoms in East Africa have begun to approach the size of the empires which are so especially prone to this fate. On a much smaller scale such distintegration also occurs, a good example being Burundi, which was apparently under moderate central control for about a generation before 1850, after which time the provincial governors ruled more or less as independent kings.

The emergence of kings, then, is a critical threshold in the history of any people, because, without them, increase in size is not possible; but, once they have appeared, then the largest of East African societies become possible. On a more ambitious scale than the Mbowe or Makonde "kings" are the rulers of the Nyamwezi, Sukuma and Ziba states; and on a larger scale still are the real giants of the East African Plateau before 1890: Rundi, Rwanda and Ganda. These three, however, are dwarfed by the three contemporary giants of the area, Kenya, Tanzania and Uganda, but these were established by European administrators, with very different cultural backgrounds from East Africans, and with the power of industrial countries in Europe behind them. They are therefore very different in origin from the hunting-bands, autonomous settlements and states of East Africa prior to 1890.

Until perhaps 1000 B.C. the whole of East Africa was inhabited by hunting-and-gathering peoples, with no cultivators at all; and such a state of affairs had continued for about two million years. Since all people were hunters-and-gatherers for about this time before any farming appeared, all the cultivators of modern East Africa, as well as elsewhere, must be descended from hunters-and-gatherers. This means that those peoples who are now cultivators must have adopted cultivation at some stage in their past. Furthermore, since hunters-and-gatherers never have kings, and since not all cultivating peoples have them, the emergence of kings must be a comparatively recent event in all those areas where kings are found. Kings must occur at some stage for the first time, and they only occur for the first time after people have adopted cultivation.

In East Africa, the archaeological evidence is still meagre, compared to Western Europe or the Near East, and dating the first farmers and the first kings is essentially guesswork, but it is certain that at some stage the first farmers appeared, that farming spread over a wider area from the early beginnings, and that at some stage kings appeared. In order to see the sort of sequence which occurred in East Africa it is worth considering very briefly the series of events in the Near East. Here the period of occupation by hunting-and-gathering groups is much shorter than in East Africa, from which in fact all people appear ultimately to have originated. Even so, there must have been hunters-and-gatherers in the Near East for over half a million years before the first traces of cultivation become discernible. By around 9000 B.C. there are clear signs that grasses, possibly still wild, were being carefully gathered, and by 7000 B.C. small farming communities were established in a number of different parts of the Near East.

At this stage there are no signs of the accumulated wealth in burials which presumably always indicates that the dead person was a ruler or a noble; but it must be remembered that most East African kings of the last hundred years would have left no archaeological trace of their social position. The origin of kings in the Near East, therefore, remains undatable, and probably always will remain so. However, it must have been after the beginning of farming, and before the first clear traces that there were kings in the area. By 4000 B.C. there are burials in Mesopotamia which show the accumulation of precious objects which presumably indicate a nobility, and probably, therefore, also kings. By 3000 B.C. both the Mesopotamians and the Egyptians had writing, and they have left records that there were indeed kings, in lower Mesopotamia ruling each an autonomous city-state, but in the lower Nile valley ruling over the first nation-state to appear since people began. That nation-state, Egypt, was formed by the fusion of two kingdoms, called by the local writers the Upper and the Lower Kingdoms, and these had themselves fairly certainly come into existence by absorbing each a number of small predecessor-kingdoms. The emergence of kings in the lower Nile valley, therefore, must predate, by at least a few generations, the emergence of the united kingdom of Egypt.

This excursus into the general sequence of events in the Near East is important and necessary partly because farming reached East Africa for the first time from the Near East, and it is highly probable that East Africans, or some of them, had heard of kings to the north of them, in the Near East, before any king had appeared in East Africa. Indeed, such news from further down the Nile may well have inspired the first East African would-be kings with the possibility of what they could attempt themselves. The excursus is, however, also necessary because East Africa followed the same general sequence, partially and at a later date, as did the Near East. It is possible that farming and kings appeared at about the same time in East Africa, but, as will be detailed in Chapter 11, it is much more likely that farming predated kings here as, probably again, in the Near East.

From what has been said earlier in this chapter it is clear that the conditions which bring about the emergence of kings for the first time, in any area, are of great importance. However, before examining what these conditions might be, it is well to begin with the more accessible process of social specialization which occurs, in some cases, but not all, once an hereditary ruler has been established. Archaeological evidence from East Africa is so far sparse, not because such evidence does not exist at all, but because very little excavating by archaeologists has yet been carried out. When we turn to specifically historical evidence, however, we find that, apart from the coastal city-states, and, in the interior, the last hundred years, it does not exist at all. There are some orally transmitted records, such as king-lists, but these are thin evidence compared to written chronicles, charters and the other familiar sources of historians. However, states do increase in complexity as they increase in size, as can be seen in some other parts of the world, and it is worth looking at an example from an area with written records.

In Western Europe, the kingdom of England came into existence between A.D. 900 and A.D. 1000. There was no question here of kings as such appearing for the first time, since there were certainly kings in the area for a millennium, back to the first century B.C., and pretty certainly for two thousand years before that. The process of England's emergence is clearly documented. In the course of the ninth century the kingdom of Wessex became the most powerful of all the English-speaking kingdoms. From the seventh century to the ninth there had been a number of these kingdoms distributed over the lowland, and more fertile, part of the British Isles. During these three centuries they vie with each other for prestige, but none of them absorbed all, or even most, of the others. In the course of the eighth century, Mercia, then top of the prestige pyramid, annexed Essex, Kent and Sussex, but in the first generation of the ninth century Wessex knocked Mercia from the top position, and took over Sussex, Kent and Essex from the Mercians.

The ninth century was a period of ferocious raiding by Danish and Norse Vikings throughout north-west Europe, and the English-speaking states were ravaged by repeated attacks. In the process, Wessex, and her eastern satellites, Sussex and Kent, were militarily very successful, while their northern neighbours were not only battered, but were taken over by Danish royal lines, replacing the dispossessed English lines. Having beaten the Danes off, however, Wessex now proceeded to defeat the new royal houses of the country north of the Thames, and by 960 they had turned most of the English-speaking area of Britain into an empire of Greater Wessex.

H

This process has been repeated a very great number of times, not only in Western Europe but in several other parts of the world. The growth of France, for example, although different in detail from events in England, is similar in that the state grew in size by swallowing neighbours who were once equals. Similar examples, in widely dispersed areas, can be produced from Mexico, the Ganges Valley and Korea. An expanding state, furthermore, is able, not only to take over other states, but, in some cases, to take over stateless peoples. In Europe, the Norwegians and Swedes have taken over the Lapps; and, in East Africa, Rwanda were still in 1890 apparently adding to their territory in the north by annexing the stateless peoples of the Rwanda–Chiga border-zone. At the same period, but on a larger scale, the British were converting the peoples of Kenya, most of whom were stateless, into a single administrative unit. This was not the same as the territorial aggrandizement of Britain, since the new territory was physically remote, and never officially regarded as British in the narrow sense. Even so, it is an example of peoples with states annexing peoples without them.

Once new territory has been acquired, it may be lost again through secession, or because of a period of general administrative disintegration. For example, the Chinese have never completely regained the Red River Delta after the Vietnamese declared their independence in A.D. 939, during the administrative disintegration which followed the T'ang Empire. If new territory is not lost then it becomes increasingly coloured by the culture of the annexing state. Because of the prestige which they acquire through their success and power. The people who have annexed territory are imitated by the inhabitants of the territory. This process of increasing cultural homogenization affects the nobility more than anybody else, because they are most immediately involved with the new elite which has absorbed them, or deliberately disdained them, but all people in the annexed territory are affected. An example on a large scale is the cultural, and administrative, expansion of China between 200 B.C. and A.D. 1200, a process which is still continuing indeed in the southern highland areas. On a smaller scale has been the incorporation of Bretons, Basques and Provencals into a fairly homogeneous France from A.D. 1300 to the present time. In East Africa, the cultural uniformity of the Ganda state presumably arises from the same process.

At the same time as cultural homogenization another process is occurring in those instances where the population continues to increase, whether by annexation or reproduction, and this is increasing complexity of social specialization. Already, in Chapter 8, we have seen that the smallest states in East Africa have priests, medical specialists and smiths, in addition to the king. The largest states in the period 1880–1900 were marked, furthermore, by more elaborate specialization of function. Kings were surrounded by a nobility, who included ministers of the crown and provincial governors. Also, the patronage which the courts could provide enabled some specialist craftsmen to practice their calling full-time rather than relying largely on cultivation for a livelihood. Analogies with events in other parts of the world make it most probable that all the larger East African states have their origins in small, only slightly specialized, predecessors.

Considering Western Europe again, between 1200 and 1800, England increased in population, wealth and social specialization. By 1800 the rapid industrialization of some areas of the country was introducing a degree of specialization vastly more intense than that of any East African state up to 1900. Between 1200 and 1800 too France underwent similar changes to those in England, and the same process was occurring throughout Western Europe in that period. The largest, and probably the most socially elaborate state, without any effect of industrialization, was China in about 1800, but in East Africa there is no need to consider such an enormous scale of activity. Rwanda, the largest native state of the period, had in 1900 a population of perhaps one and a half million people, whereas China's population was perhaps five hundred million.

The increasing scale and complexity of China in the period from 200 B.C. to A.D. 1900 is well documented in records collected by the Chinese themselves. Such increases are not recorded for East Africa. Nevertheless, in view of the similarities in the processes of specialization in other regions of the world, there can be little doubt that East African states reached their recent condition by such processes. Changes in scale and specialization, however, are not as critical as the first emergence in any area of a king.

Whereas the documented records of literate regions are informative with regard to social specialization, and to the processes of annexation, distintegration and secession, they tell us little or nothing about the origin of kings. In China, India, the Near East and Middle America, the earliest centres of literature, the first kings predate the first written records, probably in all cases by many generations. Hence, in those instances which have been recorded where a kingless people acquire a king for the first time, they do so in a context where kings are well established among neighbouring peoples.

In the Near East, there is one clearly discernible example. The generation of the people of Israel who lived around 1000 B.C. saw the emergence of the royal house of David, which was to rule in Jerusalem for about four hundred years. These hill peoples who called themselves the Children of Israel had been under pressure for some time from the Philistine city-states on the Levant coast. There had probably been a number of attempts to rally the hill groups into a united front against the Philistines, but it was David who, not only hammered the Philistines, but set up a lasting monarchy in an area where the people hitherto had been organized rather like the Gikuyu or Chiga. Even though, a generation after David's death, the new kingdom tore apart into two, the people of Israel never reverted to their earlier kingless and fragmented condition. Although in this instance they were responding to the felt need for unity against military domination, they did not have to look far for inspiration, since all their neighbours had kings.

In East Africa, the Bale and Ke accepted Aluur royalty as their kings, not because they were under any grave military threat, but because they wanted mediators and more effective rain-ritual. The key factor here, however, is the high prestige of the Aluur, in the estimate of the Bale and Ke, who saw them as a successful people, and hoped to acquire their success by importing some of their cultural features. This is an instance of cultural changes brought about by imitating peoples of high prestige.

There is another East African example, however, where such immediate borrowing has not occurred. The Mbowe, near Lake Manyara, have five tiny kingdoms, as well as one area with no kings. The word for king is *musungati*, which among the Langi, who speak the same language, means a wealthy man, a man with a large herd of cattle. The Langi have no rulers, their only hereditary figures being the priests of each locality, responsible for the rain-ritual. On the other hand, among the Mbowe the rain-ritual is performed by the kings, except in the kingless area. With this exception Langi and Mbowe are culturally extremely similar, and demonstrate the near-identity between the tiniest kingdoms and the communities of kingless peoples.

It is highly likely that the Mbowe have known for centuries of people with kings to the west of them, in the present Sukuma–Nyamwezi area, and possibly also in the Bondei–Zaramo zone near the coast; but the same applies to all the neighbours of the Mbowe, none of whom had kings. The Mbowe too were under pressure from the Maasai, but they were able to beat them off, and to retain some, at least, of their own cattle. Maasai raids did not lead inevitably to the emergence of kings, since the Langi and Gikuyu were also being raided at the same period, and they were kingless. From the name *musungati*, it is very likely that the emergence of these small Mbowe "states" was a local development, with little foreign pressure of prestige; and, from the analogy with the Langi, it is likely too that the modern royal clans are descended from eminent men of the past, perhaps more famed as mediators in disputes than as war-leaders. Somewhere along the line, however, they acquired the priestly attributes of sacrificing to God and to the ancestors in the rain-ritual.

A more impressive local development than that among the Mbowe was occurring between 1880 and 1920 among the Naath, just beyond the northern edge of the area discussed in this account. Leaders were appearing in different parts of Naath country who claimed to be possessed by a deity, or better by an aspect of Deity, and who also claimed success as war-leaders. They were similar in some ways to the *oibonok* among the Maasai further south, and they began to establish hereditary positions by passing on their authority to their sons. There were already hereditary priests among the Naath, but the new leaders did not usually come from priestly lines. They were partly a response to military pressure since the Naath, like their neighbours, had suffered from the raids of Arabic-speaking adventurers from the north during the nineteenth century. However, the kingdoms they seemed about to found were abortive, because the hostility which they showed to the British administrators led these to subdue their bids for local leadership, while at the same time protecting the Naath from external attack.

In East Africa, all peoples who have ever adopted kings may well have known of other groups who already had them; but this is probably equally true of most peoples who have adopted them, all over the world. It remains important, however, that many East African peoples knew about other peoples' kings, but adopted none of their own. There must, therefore, be more to adopting a king than knowing that kings exist.

Kings have one enormous attraction in their aloofness, "above" the other members of their society, and hence able to act as mediators in disputes. There are disputes in all societies, but not all East Africans felt inclined, like the Bale, to invite some foreign prince to come and be their judge. Gikuyu, Maasai and Chiga could do without such ruler-arbitrators.

In addition to their attraction as mediators or arbitrators, kings appeal to people's preoccupation with their own reality and identity. It is re-assuring to see something which reminds you of yourself, but is external to yourself, and is not only in your own feelings. Children are reassuring to their parents in this way; and kings are similarly reassuring to their subjects. Furthermore, kings have children, and so they are a living reminder of the whole group's reality, while at the same time spontan-eously maintaining their own continuity. There is thus no need for elec-tions or special selection-procedures; there is no break in continuity. This feature of royal clans, however, does not ensure that there is always a peaceful succession, as events in the Interlacustrine region have shown.

From the point of view of peoples who have kings, it is unthinkable to be without one, or at least to have no head of state of some kind. To such peoples the symbolic power of the king, as continuing self-emblem of the whole group, is compelling. Those peoples, however, who know about kings, and do not adopt them, must have equally compelling factors which drive them from accepting a monarch. In the Old Testament, Samuel points out to the people of Israel the disadvantages of having a king. The Israelites want a king of their own because the peoples round about them have kings, an example of prestige-and-imitation, but Samuel stresses that a king will tax them and conscript their young men into his army. Samuel's view is shared by all peoples who reject kings, and reject with them all state organization. Being part of a state involves taxation in various forms, and renders men less free, by the standards of stateless peoples.

People are therefore torn between the advantages and disadvantages of both states and statelessness. States make you more powerful in military terms, and more confident of yourselves as a group, but there is a price to be paid in the loss of some personal freedom. This choice was probably faced in this form by the Children of Israel during the whole of the period 1200–1000 B.C. Other peoples, however, never face the choice in this form, but adopt a king without any clear trappings of a state. The Mbowe seem to have adopted this minimal kingship. Once there is a king, how-ever, state formation can occur effortlessly, with no-one noticing that it is happening. Thus gifts to the king become gradually formalized into taxes, and other powers of the king grow slowly, or in emergencies rapidly. Possibly the first kings in most areas begin as the Mbowe began, and not as in Israel.

Imitation is one important factor which pushes people towards kings, as among the Bale; and military threat pushes them often in the same direction. In the case of Israel the people who were a military threat also provided the example of the organizational weapon needed to defeat them. Presumably individual ability enters into the process too. Some men are more likely to become the first king than are others, and if there are no forceful enough characters at the critical time then the kingdom may not emerge. Once the monarchy is established, however, the king may easily be a colourless character, since by this stage the established office and role will carry the individual incumbent.

In addition to the factors which trigger the adoption of a king there are background factors of productivity and wealth. Hunters-and-gatherers, as has been noted already, never have kings. They never build up the quantities of food necessary to support a ruling class, whose members do not work at food-production; but neither do they have minimal kings of the Mbowe kind. Such minimal kings require no great production of wealth above immediate needs for consumption, but the support of a state the size of Rwanda or Ganda requires a large number of officials, who are not engaged in producing food, and whose prestige would be injured if they dirtied their hands. Large states are therefore strengthened by dense population, since this involves a large production of potential taxes within a limited area, without long distances from the tax-source to the capital. Dense population, however, does not necessarily produce a state organization, since some of the densest populations in East Africa are those of the Chiga, Luhya, Luo and Gikuyu, all of them people without states or kings

The precise location of the first states in East Africa, and the period when they began, are both utterly obscure. It is possible that they arose through the imitation by local peoples of strangers of high prestige who arrived from further down the Nile valley, but any further consideration of them must wait until the next chapter.

Habitats as the Cradles of Ethnic Groups

The second complex of factors determining cultural change, and indeed also cultural stability, is that connecting people and cultural elements to specific habitats. During the detailed discussion of the distribution of ethnic groups in earlier chapters it was noted repeatedly that these groups frequently, although not always, coincided with a specific habitat. This can be seen clearly in the area occupied by the Teso, Karimojong',

Toposa and their neighbours, and also in the Iraqw–Langi–Rimi area further south, in Tanzania.

The connected processes which tend to make ethnic groups coincide with habitats can be likened to a sink, into which water is flowing from all sides. In this analogy the "sink" is a specific habitat, for example a high mountain, much of it covered with wet forest, in the midst of dry plains, a mountain such as Kilimanjaro. East Africa is made up of a mosaic of such habitat-units. The Interlacustrine region, for example, consists of the four habitats :

1. Rwanda–Rundi highlands;
2. Nyoro–Ankore wet zone;
3. The Dry Zone;
4. Ganda–Ziba wet zone.

It can be seen immediately that in this region there is more than one ethnic group to each habitat, and this must be examined in terms of another factor discussed in a later section. At the same time it is also clear that the Interlacustrine groups are arranged into a pattern which follows the habitats closely.

A more intimate connection between groups and habitats can be seen in parts of the Eastern Rift Coast region. Around Mount Kenya the wet highlands are occupied by Gikuyu, Embu and Meru, while the Maasai occupy the dry plains to the south, and formerly also the dry floor of the Rift Valley to the west. The lower hills stretching down towards the coastal lowlands, and intermediate in rainfall between the wet highlands and the dry plains, are the habitat of the Kamba.

A similar mosaic occurs further south in the centre of Tanzania. Here the Gogo occupy the dry plains between the highlands to the north and south. There are Maasai on the wider dry plains to the north-east, with the Burunge on a small dry plains area of their own. The Langi are centred on wet highlands; and the Iraqw and Gorowa are on another mass of wet highland. Between the Iraqw highlands and the Maasai Plains is the habitat of the Mbowe, moderately well watered, and at the foot of the scarp; while the Datoga, like the Burunge, have their own small dry plains-area, amidst higher ground.

From what has been said earlier about these peoples it can be seen that, within the habitat, they have adapted to the demands and limitations, but also the possibilities, inherent in it. Gikuyu and Iraqw have intensified their farming under the pressure of increasing population, settled on limited amounts of land. At the opposite extremity, Maasai and Datoga do not plant crops at all, but invest in cattle, goats and sheep, which can be moved to water in times of localized drought. Intermediate between these extremes are the Kamba and Gogo, cultivating but also investing heavily in livestock, and clearly affected, not just by prudence in their response to an unreliable habitat, but also by a strictly human factor, namely the high prestige of large cattle-herds. They are would-be pastoralists.

If the habitat is the "sink", then the water which flows into it, from all sides, are people, migrants moving from one habitat to another. People are repeatedly migrating in East Africa, usually in quite small numbers at any one time in any one direction. Their need to migrate will be examined more carefully later in this chapter, but famine is a major factor in moving them, and this repeated movement of peoples can be described as famine-swirl. Many of the migrants move from their original home area to another which is almost identical in culture, as when a Kamba moves to another part of Kamba country. Sometimes the move is to an area similar in general culture, but different in language, as when a Kimbu moves to Nyamwezi country. Sometimes the move involves a change of both language and livelihood, as when a Maasai moves to Gikuyu country or a Burunge to Langi country. In these cases the young children of the migrants, and any children born to them in the new area, will speak the language of that area, and not, or not necessarily, that of their parents.

There are other occasions when the immigrants will have elements of culture which are not already present in their new habitat. For instance, people who do not circumcize may arrive in an area with circumcision, as presumably happened on the eastern shore of Lake Victoria when the Luo-speaking immigrants appeared for the first time. A second example is the situation when people with a tradition of kings and states arrive in a habitat with people who have neither. In such situations the long-term outcome is determined by the power of the local people to absorb the newcomers to their practices or, alternatively, by the new practice making sufficient impact for the local group to adopt it themselves. Immigrants are not always wretched people; they may be impressive on the small scale of a local area, and their prestige may be high within the context of that area. For instance, this has probably always been true in East Africa of the people who first introduce iron smelting into an area.

It is very unlikely whether any group of immigrants, however large, and even when they are a conquering aristocracy, are ever able, in the East African context, to totally change the earlier culture. Here the habitat plays a crucial role, not directly but through the mode of livelihood, for instance intensive cultivation. Immigrants will either know a similar livelihood, and carry on with it once they arrive, or they will know a different livelihood, and then they will usually need to adapt to the new one, in order to survive. The recent immigrants rarely, if ever, outnumber the local people, so that, at any one period, most of the people of an area share a common livelihood and a common culture, which has come into being in that habitat. It is thus possible for immigrants to introduce new elements into that habitat, but not to change the whole culture, because the local people will retain most of their ways rather than change in the direction of the immigrants. The local habitat, with a resident population, and with a specific livelihood, thus has the effect of inertia on all changes, and is a kind of fixative in the flow of migrants.

From what has been said so far it follows that there have not been simple movements of culture from one area to another by the migration of specific groups of people. Wherever any migrants settle, their own culture will be modified, and often simply lost, because swamped by the culture of the local people. A clear example of this process is the present condition of the groups who call themselves Ngoni around Lake Nyasa. Only their name, and some traditions passed from mouth to mouth, record that some of their ancestors were migrants from south-eastern Africa. Culturally they are simply a part of their area. Immigrant nobility, like the Bito in Nyoro and the Sotho in Lozi, suffer the same modification. The only situations where cultures, as distinct from people, migrate are those where a cultural area, of whatever size, is growing at its margins, by neighbouring peoples' opting for the expanding culture. Examples of this seem to be occurring at the present time on the borders of the Jieng', Zande and Nyamwezi cultural areas.

If then anyone asks where a particular people come from, then the answer is that, in their present form, they originated in the habitat where they now live. It is true that if one asks this question of modern Americans or Australians, the answer is that they arrived from Europe, recently, in numbers so massive, relative to the local populations which were already there, that their immigrant culture totally swamped that of the earlier peoples, which survives in parts of the area side-by-side with that of the newcomers. This new culture is changing gradually away from its European originals, which have themselves changed, but in both North America and Australia the origins are still very clear. However, in East Africa migration on this massive modern scale has never occurred.

To the analogy of the sink can be added that of the cake. The ingredients of the cake in the analogy correspond to the cultural elements, and to the migrants, which move into a habitat, which is the baking-tin. "Cooking" consists of the adaptations to the habitat, and the adaptations of the local people, and of successive migrants, to each other. The finished "cake" is the local culture in its present form.

Where did the English come from? In the lowlands of Britain in A.D. 400 there were cultivating peoples who spoke a Celtic language related to modern Welsh. Migrants from the North European Plain settled in parts of the lowlands, and their Teutonic language totally replaced the Celtic language which was its predecessor. The livelihood, however, and much of the genetic content of the population, changed little; but Christian missionaries from Ireland and Italy greatly affected ritual, and even architecture. Later also, in the eleventh century, ecclesiastical reformers from French-speaking Europe introduced changes in administration, and again architecture. By this time new immigrants, the Danes, had brought little in the way of cultural change, but had had a great impact on organization, and the power-play of rival rulers had resulted in the emergence of a single kingdom, England, the cake in the analogy.

Returning to East Africa, we find, as usual, that the documentation is largely lacking until the nineteenth century. Even so, it is possible to reconstruct some of the events which lie behind a number of the modern peoples. On the plateau west of the Albert Nile, at some stage, Luo-speaking immigrants moved in among people rather like the modern Madi or Lugbara. Nowadays the people of that area speak Luo, and call themselves Aluur; they retain the minor kings of the immigrants, but their age-sets have been dropped, following the earlier usage of the local people. Similar Luo-speaking immigrants arrived on the eastern shore of Lake Victoria, not necessarily at the same time as near Lake Albert. The people beside Lake Victoria who now call themselves Luo speak the immigrants' language and, like the immigrants, do not circumcize, whereas the other peoples of the eastern lake-shore do circumcize, as did the peoples who were there when the first Luo-speaking immigrants arrived. However, the immigrants probably had minor kings, like those of the Aluur and Acholi, whereas the local people did not, and the local practice has prevailed.

A more complex example are the Maasai, their habitat the great expanse of dry plains occupying the centre of the Eastern Rift Coast region. Without attempting to piece together the sequence of cultural history in the area, age-sets, circumcision and clitoridectomy can be recognized as coming from the Horn or from the Ethiopian Highlands, while the knocking out of the lower median incisors derives from the eastern savanna. The presence of these elements implies migration, of at least a few people from the north-east, and from the north-west, possibly both groups via the Lake Rudolf depression. A relatively new element is the Maa language, spreading in from the Lake Rudolf area, probably carried by migrants during the seventeenth century. The other elements arrived much earlier, it seems, and the exclusive pastoralism of the plains is also old. A local adaptation to the habitat, the reliance on livestock rather than crops has great value for survival in an area of low rainfall reliability. At the same time, the high value of cattle spontaneously gives exclusive pastoralists high prestige in the eyes of all the peoples of the region. Had there been large states, such as Rundi or Ganda, in this area they would presumably, by their greater power, have dimmed the lustre of the Maasai, but no such states grew up here.

Below the Maasai, on the dry coastal lowlands, the Digo, Duruma and Rabai have received their age-sets (now faded out), circumcision and clitoridectomy ultimately from the Horn or the Ethiopian Highlands, although the route may not have been direct. Immigrants from the south have brought in matrilineal descent and inheritance, which has merged with patrilineal forms from elsewhere to produce bilineal procedures. However, the Bantu languages of this coastal zone, apart from the dialects of Swahili, probably derive from the area where Kamba and Gikuyu are now spoken.[1] Swahili, on the other hand, derives from the south,[2] like matrilineal descent and inheritance. Kilimanjaro is not far distant from the coast, and has undergone a similar cultural history but in the context of a very different habitat. The Chaga have the circumcision and clitoridectomy common to the region, and they used to have the age-sets also. Their language probably derives from the Gikuyu–Kamba area,[3] while immigrants from the south have brought kings and states. These probably spread from the coast to the Shambaa highlands, from there to the Asu highlands, and from there to Kilimanjaro.

Also bordering on the Maasai Plains are the Gogo, themselves also on dry plains. Since they are on the southern edge of their region, circumcision, clitoridectomy and age-sets must have come to them from further north, but their language has spread in from the south or east;[4] and, in the west, migrants from Kimbu and Nyamwezi have brought traditions of kings and states.

In the Interlacustrine region, kings, states and, later, castes probably spread into the Rwanda–Rundi highlands from the north-east or east, before a local differentiation of these traditions took place in the highlands themselves. The Bantu languages of Rundi and Rwanda, however, do not belong to the same group as do most of the languages of the region, but instead to a group most of whose members are in the wet forest of the Congo Basin.[5] Presumably migrants from the wet forest brought the language ancestral to Rwanda and Rundi up on to the highlands.

These examples demonstrate the importance of cultural mixing and adaptation *in situ*. There have been no discernible examples of a large body of migrants travelling long distances, and then setting up in a new area a complete reproduction of the cultural area from which they originated.

The Pressures Causing Migration

Since the complexes of factors causing cultural change operate simultaneously, and are often intimately connected, it is sometimes necessary to discuss more than one of them at a time, and migration has already been involved in the discussion of habitats and their associated ethnic groups. The causes of migration can be divided into five groups:

1. chronic overpopulation;
2. famine;
3. epidemic;
4. military disaster;
5. adventure.

Some parts of East Africa are exceptional, as we have seen, in having very dense populations. Outstanding in this respect are three areas: the south- and east-facing slopes on and near Mount Kenya; the north-eastern shore of Lake Victoria; and the Rwanda–Rundi highlands. In these areas, and in other smaller concentrations of population, as in Nyakyusa country, the pressure of people on land resources is high at the present time, and has presumably been high for some generations, even though the present populations probably represent an unprecedented peak. With a land-shortage over a considerable period, such areas have been unable to absorb immigrants readily in any numbers at a time; and the shortage of land has tended to push people out to other, less congested, areas.

In the twentieth century this can be clearly seen in the Rwanda–Rundi highlands. Large numbers of Rwanda are now settled in Ganda, as tenants and workers on the land, having migrated from Rwanda more or less permanently. Most of them have retained links with Rwanda, and it is likely that the modern administrative and political situations are less favourable to the absorption of these immigrants than were the conditions of the past. In the nineteenth century they would probably have just become Ganda. The Chiga also, just north of the Rwanda, are pressing heavily on their land, and many have moved down from the highlands during this century into some western areas of Ankore. Some of this resettlement has been sponsored and encouraged by the Uganda Government, which has, among other aid, provided lorries to help households move their belongings to the new areas.

Peoples in areas with pressure on their land resources have been conspicuously ready to enter schools and to take the new kinds of jobs established by Europeans. Since schooling and the new jobs often involve moving away from one's home area, the process is a new kind of migration. The key factor in this process is that the new jobs, as teachers, government officials, or employees in private companies, provide wages or salaries, which are more alluring to people whose opportunities at home are cramped by shortage of land than to others; but further factors enter in here also. These areas of dense population are all well watered, population having built up because of the relative reliability of the crop returns. One result has been that a high proportion of the early schools were sited in these areas precisely because they could thus serve large numbers of people in a relatively compact area. This has given groups like the Gikuyu and Chaga an advantage in obtaining jobs over people from dryer, more thinly populated areas, with few schools, such as Kamba or Gogo. One specialized example of wet-country people seizing new opportunities for employment is provided by the Ziba, large numbers of whose women are prostitutes in Dar-es-Salaam and in some other towns of Tanzania. In more general terms, other densely populated areas provide large numbers of prostitutes in the towns.

Since they are high-rainfall areas the densely populated habitats suffer relatively little from drought compared to other parts of East Africa, but droughts still occur; while outside the areas of high rainfall droughts are recurrent, and even frequent. Drought regularly leads to famine, and famine has been a repeated, and even normal, part of the history of most East African peoples. Famine can result from the eating of the standing crops by locusts, bush-crickets (Tettigoniidae), birds or other animals, but the most frequent cause of famine is drought, and this has presumably been true for hundreds of years. Famine in its turn detonates movements of population, and from these movements result the situations already described as being like sinks filling with water. It ought to be added that they are also emptying to some extent, since people move out as well as in.

One of the features of rainfall in tropical Africa, and indeed throughout the tropics, is that, ouside the regions of high rainfall, the amount which falls varies markedly not only from year to year but also from place to place in any one year. In many parts of East Africa it is possible to stand where you live, and to see it raining ten miles away, repeatedly through a whole wet season, although only a few showers have fallen on your own, withering, crops. In such circumstances it is not difficult for emigrants to decide which way to go. So regular is this feature that people expect it to happen, and Kamba even refer to "looking for rain", an expression for this kind of migration. Elsewhere, for example in the centre of Tanzania, recurrent droughts have led to famine-swirl, with people moving to areas inhabited by groups who do not speak their language, or at least to other parts of their original language-area. Rimi have moved about repeatedly in this way. Sometimes migrants move back to their original area, but not always.

In this process of famine-swirl, there has doubtless been a tendency for people to gravitate slowly towards the well-watered areas, but some of these are densely populated, and tending anyway to "export" people. During this century Burunge have moved into Langi country, probably because it is better watered than their own. In the same way, in the period 1870–1900, Maasai who had lost most of their cattle in severe epidemics and droughts settled in the Gikuyu highlands.

Epidemics have probably not had the same massive effect as famines. Where people do move because of an epidemic it is probably in most cases because so many people have died in one locality that the survivors settle as refugees in another area, since they no longer feel able to defend themselves from raids.[6] Epidemics have faded out since 1900, as a result of the increasing use of European medicines, but they must have been recurrent before that date. Smallpox was probably the most important epidemic disease, in terms of the numbers of deaths which it caused, but bubonic plague, and other highly dangerous infections, occurred, and they are still there, although not in epidemic proportions. Not only epidemics affecting people were involved, but also those which killed domestic animals, notably rinderpest and east coast fever. Although most groups could survive on their crops if they lost their livestock, the exclusive pastoralists, such as Maasai and Datoga, could be very hard hit by epidemics; and at such times large numbers of them had to settle as refugees among their cultivating neighbours.

Since the widespread use of European medicine, populations in most of East Africa have been increasing, but it seems likely that before 1900 recurrent epidemics pegged population sizes to well below present levels. In this respect, by keeping down the numbers of people in the most densely settled areas, epidemics must have reduced migration rather than increasing it.

Movements of people were sometimes affected by fighting. Some groups moved from areas where they were raided too frequently; and there were probably occasions when so many people in a settlement had been captured or killed that the survivors, as after an epidemic, felt it safer to move, and settle with other, less afflicted, people. Particularly dangerous in this way were the borderlands between large states in the Interlacustrine region, where territory changed hands repeatedly. In this context it is worth noting that some people moved, without being disturbed by fighting, because they did not like the government of the state of which they were currently members. Some movement of this kind occurred, for example, in Sukuma country.

The people who changed locality in the course of fighting, however, were not all refugees. Some of them were adventurers, engaged in raiding or trading, the two being closely connected, who settled in areas away from those where they were born. Some adventurers of this kind in the nineteenth century were men, of various different groups, who joined "Nguni" raiding-parties, and eventually came to rest wherever their party settled, or was scattered by defeat. In the same period, Swahili and Nyamwezi adventurers were moving over a wide area, some Nyamwezi settling on the Katanga plateau. Ambitious Nyamwezi and Swahili gathered followers from among any ethnic group in their area of activities, and the men who became the professional soldiers in these bands were called in Swahili *rugaruga*. The travel, trade and fighting of the nineteenth century resulted in a considerable redistribution of people, but without destroying the mosaic of ethnic groups, many of them linked to specific habitats.

Although migration has been a constant feature of East African peoples, and probably since long before the last century, the scale of any one of these migrations was small, not to be compared with European migration to North America between 1870 and 1900, or even with European migration to Australia in the same period. The largest groups of people who moved about in East Africa before 1900 were the armies of the largest states, Ganda, Rwanda and Rundi. Each of them contained thousands of men, but most migrants were in groups of tens or less. Even a well defined movement in one direction, such as the movement of Luo-speakers up the Nile valley, may well have involved only a few hundred people in all, and have consisted of a series of small groups dribbling in the same direction over a long period.

Prestige and Imitation: Identity and Differentiation

In discussing the distribution of the different ethnic groups, it was necessary at some points to refer to the imitation of people of one group by those of another. Such imitation might be the borrowing of a single element, such as guns, or it might involve such detailed imitation that the borrowing group eventually disappeared completely, and its members became simply whatever people they were imitating. In all cases the borrowers are impressed by the people they imitate, impressed either by their power or by their excellence, the two being intimately connected, since excellence has connotations of divine approval, and hence divine power.

A number of examples of prestige and imitation are on a large scale. In the Horn, since the fifteenth century, the Soomaali have spread at the expense of the Oromo, and seem to be poised to absorb the remaining Bararetta and Boorana groups. Soomaali communities, over a period of time, have beaten their Oromo neighbours in fights, and seized their water-holes and their best grazing. Although some Oromo have moved away as refugees, most of the people who were Oromo have descendants who are Soomaali, since the losers have imitated the winners.

In a similar way, on the savanna, Jieng' communities have repeatedly beaten their southern and western neighbours, who have become Jieng', and some are still, apparently, in the process of changing in that direction. Here the Jieng' have established no administrative hegemony over these southern and western peoples. These have simply recognized Jieng' success, and with it probably the implication that God favours the Jieng'. These small groups indeed seem to be disappearing since those of them who are not joining the Jieng' are becoming Zande. In these cases formal hegemony was established by the rulers of states, although the setting up of new Zande states in this zone was halted after 1900 by the Anglo–Egyptian administration. Again, however, the admiration for winners, who became in this instance a formalized upper class, swung over the losers to imitate them.

The situation was probably different in the Eastern Rift Coast region, where the Maasai were the pinnacle of excellence. At the present time there are no peoples who are beginning to imitate the Maasai for the first time, and none are increasing their imitation. As will be detailed in the next chapter, there is some serious doubt whether the Maasai were ever imitated as Zande, Jieng' and Soomaali have been. Indeed the Maasai in their present form probably did not exist prior to the eighteenth century, whereas the standards of excellence which they embody and typify are probably much older. In this region, although so many groups admired the Maasai, they did so as an ideal type of themselves. They were not being absorbed by the Maasai, and they were not all being beaten by them in raids. Gikuyu, Chaga, Mbowe and Langi could certainly beat off some, or even most, raids by Maasai. Otherwise they would have had no cattle by 1900, whereas in fact they were all fairly well endowed with herds. Indeed in the period 1880–1900 the Nandi were actually hammering the Wuasingishu Maasai of the hills near the Rift Valley, but without ceasing to admire the pure pastoralist ideal which the Maasai embodied.

Very different was the situation further south where the Nyamwezi cultural area seems to have been expanding not by conquest but by settlement, and by the earlier peoples in these sparsely populated woodlands then imitating immigrants notable for their wealth, through trade, and for their power, through guns. The Nyamwezi were themselves imitating the Swahili, whose prestige nearer the coast was leading the peoples of the Bondei–Zaramo zone to adopt Swahili ways.

Imitation on account of prestige was also occurring on a smaller scale. Not only were the Aluur providing kings for the Bale and Ke, but they were also probably absorbing them. Indeed the modern Aluur seem to have come into being by the transformation of people like the Bale, who imitated Luo-speaking immigrants.

It is noteworthy, however, that, although imitation through prestige was so widespread, there are still a very large number of ethnic groups in East Africa. Indeed groups which now see themselves as large units also recognize local named sub-divisions of themselves, as do the Nyamwezi and Jieng'. In some cases the demands of contemporary political manoeuvring have led to the adoption of new names to cover groups which did not earlier have a common name. Such are the Luhya in western Kenya, and the Kalenjin in the nearby highlands. Similar aggregation may well continue.

At the same time the great number of local named groups is an important, and to most European readers bewildering, fact in East Africa. They do not all coincide with a specific habitat, and they give the impression that most people just like being different from their neighbours. Such a conclusion is open to fierce objection on the grounds that it is too emotional or psychological, too "internal" to individuals to be open to thorough examination. Nevertheless, there is abundant evidence, from all over the world, that people are worried about their identity, both as individuals and as groups. Indeed, in the industrial societies of Europe and North America many people have become uncomfortably aware that not to belong to a small group is a diminishing of one's identity even as an individual. To be British or American is not enough, since these groups are too large to be comforting in everyday life. Hence arises the interest in communes and clubs, and the fierce persistence among Americans of ethnic self-consciousness, based on the country of origin of one's immigrant ancestors.

In areas where there are no counter-influences of military expansion or administrative centralization, ethnic groups proliferate, not only as sub-divisions of peoples who all speak a single language, but as groups each with a distinct language. A very marked example of the effects of such proliferation, over a long period, is New Guinea, which has a population of only about five million, but with probably a thousand different, and mutually unintelligible, languages. In New Guinea state-organization has hardly existed until after 1880.

A similar, but less extreme, proliferation of ethnic groups, and of languages, occurs in those areas of East Africa which have had no states, until European administrators arrived, or where the states remained very small. On the eastern savanna, the Moru, Avukaya, Logo and Lugbara are peoples very similar to each other, sharing the same habitat, and speaking languages which are closely related to each other. However, all these groups' members are conscious that the groups are distinct. The same awareness of ethnic distinction is found in western Kenya, in the wet highlands west of the Rift Valley. There the peoples who from 1960 onward began to call themselves collectively Kalenjin form a series extending along the highlands, all in the same habitat, and all speaking closely related languages. Indeed only two languages are spoken in this area, the Pokot speaking one, while the other is shared by the Markwet, Geyo, Tugen, Nandi and Kipsigis.

The situation is similar to the west, on the lake-shore below the highlands. Although the Luo are very distinctive, there is not much difference between the other groups spread through this habitat. In the north are the peoples of the Luhya group. Luhya, like Kalenjin, is a term which became general in the 1960–4 period to denote a grouping of peoples who, their politicians hoped, would vote together in elections. Strictly therefore the Luhya are the peoples of the group in Kenya, and they do not include very similar peoples across the border in Uganda. Saamia, Nyuli and Gisu are in Uganda; Kusu, Hanga and Logooli are in Kenya; and to the south are yet more peoples, very similar, but not grouped as Luhya: Gusii, Kuria, Nata and Zanaki.

Much further south the proliferation of ethnic groups recurs, but in an area with kingly traditions. In the wet highlands between Lake Tanganyika and Lake Nyasa are yet another series of peoples who resemble each other closely: Fipa, Pimbwe, Mambwe, Mwanga, Nyiha and Safwa. In this same Southern Savanna region, but in the dry areas east of Lake Nyasa, the peoples again resemble each other, but are conscious that they differ in identity. Thus Ngindo, Mwera, Maviha, Makua, Yao and Lomwe all insist that they are distinct from one another.

In all of these areas there have been no large states before the European administrators, and in some areas no states at all until the last few decades. In such circumstances, it seems, a tendency to proliferating ethnic diversity sets in. The process appears to be that there is a fundamental desire to be different from the people who are not members of one's own group. Any slight differences which do occur are emphasized, and unconscious, but deliberate, movement towards the separateness of this group leads first to a distinct name for these people, and ultimately to a separate language. Distance between settlements helps strengthen the sense of separateness, but much more fundamental is the fact that most people do not recognize a very large group to whom they have any moral obligations. Their moral community is small, as was discussed in Chapter 8.

One example of the conscious stress upon a distinguishing feature has occurred in Uganda since 1960. As the time of independence approached, in 1962, and in the years just after, the Gisu laid increased emphasis upon their circumcision ceremonies. Although circumcision is normal among the peoples of Kenya, in Uganda very few groups circumcize, and none of the larger peoples, who were prominent in the political situation, do so. The Gisu selected a feature in which they were very unusual, in their particular theatre of action, in order to highlight their identity, at a time when they felt it was threatened.

Unconscious emphasis upon distinguishing features probably accounts for some striking cultural aspects of peoples at the top of their local prestige gradients, as has been argued at various points already. The sexual morality of the Maasai, the abandonment of castes by the Ganda, and the former age-villages of the Nyakyusa all seem to result from these peoples' sense, conscious and unconscious, of superiority over their neighbours. In these instances we are dealing with a special kind of separateness.

Remarkably, there is a recognition of the human tendency to spontaneous ethnic diversity in the myths of many peoples. In widely scattered parts of the world there are accounts of all peoples once being a single language group, but this split up, for reasons which differ in different accounts, and so now peoples are all distinct from each other. The version best known to Europeans is that in the book of Genesis (Genesis 11 : 1–9), the destruction of the Tower of Babel.

The Accumulation of Factors

During the examination of the different complexes of factors, it has been necessary in some instances to discuss more than one factor of change at a time. For example, the role of habitat and livelihood has had to be considered in conjunction with migration. In most instances of cultural change in East Africa it is safe to assume that more than one factor has been operating, and in many cases one factor alone would not have been sufficient to effect the change. There are many occasions when it is the combined effects of two or more factors which push events over a sort of critical threshold.

In order to illustrate such a change, involving an interplay of factors, it is useful to return to the densely populated groups in wet highlands. One of the most numerous of these are the Gikuyu, on the eastern slopes of the Rift Highlands in Kenya. Their country has been densely peopled for generations, although the introduction of European medicine, by suppressing epidemic diseases, has sparked off a rapid increase both in total population and in density since 1900. Between that date and 1960 the total number of Gikuyu probably doubled. The reliable rainfall and the fertile soils of their habitat had enabled population to build up over a long period, but they had also turned Gikuyu country into an area which tended to expel people, through too great pressure on resources. Just how many people left this area in the centuries before 1900 is not known, nor is it possible to find out, but it is likely that settlers from here carried Bantu languages as far as the coast (Chapter 11).

By 1900 the Gikuyu were in a condition where many of them were ready to migrate, and also to learn new jobs if the opportunity offered. The arrival of European administrators and missionaries led to the establishment, between 1890 and 1920, of jobs which were unknown in Gikuyu communities hitherto. The founding of schools enabled Gikuyu to read and write, which fitted them for jobs as clerks in the administration and as teachers in the schools. At the same time the European farms which were set up in the Rift Highlands provided an opening for migrants, who settled there as labourers and tenants, even though the country was different from the habitat of the Gikuyu, and most of it not suitable for their style of farming. All this time, as more and more Gikuyu earned wages, and moved out of their country, they tried to retain land there, at least as a kind of pension for their old age.

Thus the Gikuyu were imitating immigrants of high prestige, the Europeans, while impelled by necessity to find alternative sources of wealth to their increasingly crowded land. In the course of these processes their social specialization was also increasing. A new class of clerks, teachers and officials was emerging, all of them with salaries, but interested in investing in land, and all the time the gulf between richest and poorest was widening. The salaried group were able to buy land, and the poorest often needed to sell theirs, and thus became tenants or share-croppers on the land of the salaried group. As a result of the new administrative pattern, combined with the pressures of population on land resources, the Gikuyu changed from a stateless, kingless, roughly egalitarian people to people with landlords, smallholders and landless labourers. They had acquired a class-system. Much the same process has gone on among the Chaga, where, however, there were kings and minor states already by the last century.

The rapid emergence of the new class-order was a profound shock to the majority of Gikuyu, who found themselves either landless, or with limited land, which they could increase only with difficulty, and which they were likely to lose altogether to the larger landowners, who could better survive times of shortage. The changed distribution of the land, and the new class-pattern which went with it, were the basic detonator of the oath-taking and killing which came to be labelled Mau Mau. In the period from 1950 to 1958 the active rebels were landless or had little land, and their resentment was turned against the Gikuyu landlords, the European farmers on the Rift Highlands, and possibly, if remotely, against the government which sought to protect these from the rebels.[7] Insofar as the rebels were seeking an outlet for resentment, they were successful up to a point; but if they had plans for redistributing the land, then they failed, and the new order of landlords and tenants remains.

During the twentieth century, the sense of identity of the Gikuyu has intensified, and the new jobs available have made ethnic ties an important form of "old boy network" in Kenya, as in other African countries. Indeed, with the approach of independence, in 1963, and from then on, the number of important jobs available increased, and Gikuyu found themselves well placed to fill them, because of their long educational history. Such opportunities, however, are largely for the members of the salaried group, rather than for the landless. The Gikuyu provide a remarkable instance of very rapid social specialization, and at the same time of the interplay of various factors in bringing about the changes.

If we compare the Gikuyu with their neighbours the Kamba and the Maasai, in the period since 1900, some striking differences are apparent. The Kamba have had a history marked by social change, but on a less dramatic scale. A salaried elite have emerged, but there is no great pressure on the land, and no landlord class. The dryness and unproductiveness of their land relative to that of the Gikuyu is critical in this slowing of social change. They have had no Mau Mau, although in 1938 they did per-suade the government, by a sit-down demonstration in the streets of Nairobi, to reverse the policy of reducing the numbers of their beloved cattle.

If Kamba country is dry, the Maasai Plains are dryer; the population too is sparser, and the opportunities for changes in production are mini-mal. In this context it is not surprising that, although some Maasai have been to university, and others have become large-scale farmers in a European style, the great majority have retained their earlier way of life even in detail. Factors which have greatly affected the Gikuyu, and which have partially affected the Kamba, have left most Maasai largely unmoved.

In this chapter the discussion of social changes and of the factors generating them has been systematic, and each process has been dealt with in turn. The processes have operated over a long period of time, but no attempt has been made to discuss the order in which major cultural changes have occurred, nor has the age, and cultural history, of the present regions been assessed. At this stage it is worth attempting the hazardous exercise of reconstructing the series of changes through time which have resulted in the modern cultural pattern of East Africa.

10. Notes

1. M. Guthrie (1971). "Comparative Bantu", Vol 2, gives the details of the E-group of Bantu languages on pp. 44–47.
2. Ibid., pp. 48–51, for the G-group of Bantu languages.
3. It belongs to Guthrie's E-group.
4. Probably from the (now) Kaguru–Hehe highlands. Ibid., pp. 48, 49.
5. Ibid., pp. 42–44. This is Guthrie's D-group.
6. They probably also felt impelled to move by the inauspicious nature of a place where they had suffered such disaster.
7. In this brief sketch no attempt has been made to assess the ways in which Gikuyu politicians of the period reacted to the oaths and killing. These politicians belonged to the landlord-class. The rebels were undergoing a crisis because their expectations were traditional, and they felt that most people ought to have land, whereas, in fact, most people did not have land. Young Gikuyu growing up now probably accept that most of them cannot have land.

11

A Reconstruction of Later East African Prehistory

The Later Hunter-Gatherers and the First Farmers, c. 5000–c. 0 B.C.

Because of the absence of written records, away from the coast, until the last hundred years, the cultural regions of East Africa have been examined here only in their modern aspect, and essentially in the period 1890–1940. Nevertheless, despite the lack of records, there must have been a complicated series of events leading up to the formation of the regions which are recognizable in the modern period. There is presumably an enormous amount of evidence on these events buried in the floors of numerous living sites scattered across East Africa, and in the course of time it is likely that archaeologists will be able to piece together the story of many of the important cultural changes which lie behind the modern pattern.

At the present time, however, the archaeological knowledge of East Africa is rudimentary compared with that of the Near East and Europe. Furthermore, the digging which has been done is mostly concerned with periods long before the last few thousand years, which are the critical period in the formation of the modern cultural regions. Some important details too will probably never emerge with certainty from the excavations of archaeologists. The spread of languages, or of whole language families, leaves no traces which survive for archaeologists to recover, unless the languages are written on some durable material. In East Africa no language except one was written until after 1850. Even Swahili, which has a longer literary history, has no reliable records which go back to A.D. 1000. A second feature of the story of human populations in the area which may escape future definition is the distribution of racial types at different periods. Despite repeated efforts by various physical anthropologists to recognize racial types from skulls alone, the types clearly apparent at the present time are based upon hair, skin and facial features, none of which are preserved for long periods after death, except in the unusual event of mummification, either by human intent or by special features of the local conditions. Mummification cannot be expected in East Africa.

Prehistory, in north-western Europe, fades out about two thousand years ago, when written records become numerous enough to permit the subsequent period to be called history. By contrast, in the Near East, history, or better the historical era, extends back about 5000 years. East Africa is at the opposite extremity. On the coast, written records extend back to perhaps the twelfth century, but in the interior such records date only from the middle of the nineteenth. Even the coastal records are scanty up to the nineteenth century, and it is hardly an exaggeration to say that in East Africa the historical era begins in the nineteenth century. Before that is all part of the prehistoric era.

In the absence of historical documents, and with only a few snippets of archaeological evidence yet known, the narrative of events in the few thousand years before the nineteenth century must be guesswork. Since almost every statement needs to be qualified by the words possibly or probably, or in some other way, the narrative will be given as if it were clearly known, but with the understanding that the whole chapter is guesswork, and needs to be treated as such. Nonetheless, it is guesswork within a firm framework. Farming methods spread into East Africa ultimately from the Near East, and this sets a limit on the date by which they can have first appeared. Iron smelting certainly and kings probably spread from the same ultimate source, and there are thus also limits on their earliest appearance in East Africa.

Another guide to the probable course of events has already been noticed in the previous chapter, and that is that elements of culture, including languages, can spread independently of each other, and thus there is no need to assume that cultures always spread from place to place in their entirety. Furthermore, physical types can spread independently of each other and of cultural elements. Hence a certain people may obtain circumcision from one direction, their language from another, and their physical type from a fusion between two or three, which have each arrived by migration from different directions. There is yet another guide to probable events in those movements of people which have left a trace in modern traditions or distributions. Thus if Luo-speaking groups drifted up the Nile valley in recent centuries, it is not unlikely that other peoples did so earlier. Certainly in the Near East, where surviving records are detailed, there were migrations on more than one occasion which followed the same routes. For instance, on different occasions peoples have migrated out of the deserts of Arabia into the Fertile Crescent. The Akkadian, Amorite and Arabic languages were all brought this way by different migrants.

For the sake of clarity, then, this narrative of events is written with a clearcut certainty which the available evidence does not support. It is, however, a very plausible version of the way farming, iron smelting and kings spread into East Africa, and of the way the present regions were formed. For confirmation or refutation of this account we must wait until the archaeologists have dug up more facts.

In 5000 B.C. the peoples of the Ethiopian Highlands and of the Horn were already caucasoid in physical type, as they still are. Caucasoid peoples also extended over the dry coast southwards to the Pangani River valley and to the Gogo plains, as they now are. The sparse population of the Lake Rudolf depression were caucasoid, and caucasoids had intermingled with negroids on the eastern part of the savanna. Westwards, along the savanna to West Africa, the peoples were negroid, as they were in the wet forests of the Interlacustrine plateau. There, however, caucasoid immigrants had moved in along the Dry Zone, coming from the north-east, and the populations of the plateau showed some people with a mixture of negroid and caucasoid characteristics. From the (now) Rwanda–Rundi highlands to the Atlantic Ocean, through the whole of the Wet Forest region, as it now is, were negroid populations, some of whom were pygmies. South of the wet forest, with its negroid peoples, and of the (now) Iraqw–Langi highlands, with their caucasoid peoples, was the dry woodland, not yet *miombo*, inhabited from coast to coast by bushmanoid peoples, as was the whole area southward to the extreme southern coast of Africa.

At what date these three major physical types had become distinct is obscure, but there had been humans on the East African Plateau for two million years, and possibly more. Indeed the genus of animals grouped as *Homo* had first appeared on the East African Plateau, before dispersing from there, at a much later date, to other parts of the world; and it was on the East African Plateau that hominids, of some genus, made

the first stone tools. Those two million years had been a period when all
the humans of East Africa were hunters-and-gatherers, spread extremely
sparsely over the area, and divided into communities of perhaps fifty
individuals each.

During that great expanse of time not only had the genus *Homo*
spread beyond East Africa, and beyond Africa altogether, but methods
of making stone implements had been refined, and a high degree of
specialization had appeared. Hence by 5000 B.C. each band had several
different types of implement, each used for different purposes; and the
peoples of sub-Saharan Africa had differentiated culturally to such a
degree that, on the basis of the surviving stone implements alone, they
can be divided into cultural regions. The bands of the Horn deserts used
tools belonging to the Wilton[1] industry, as did the peoples of the dryer
parts of the north-east of East Africa, in the area which is now the
Eastern Rift Coast region. The northern wet highlands of this region,
however, were peopled by bands using implements of the Kenya Capsian
tradition and of one of its specialized off-shoots, the Elmenteitan.

To the north-west, on the eastern part of the savanna, the traditions
were specialized Levalloisian. However, just to the south of the savanna,
in the wet forest areas of the Interlacustrine plateau, the peoples used
tools which were Sangoan, and these extended to the eastern shore of
Lake Victoria, then covered with lowland wet forest. Sangoan was also
the cultural tradition of the whole of the present Wet Forest region below
the East African Plateau. South of the wet forest, and of the extension
of this type of vegetation on the Interlacustrine plateau, the whole of
the transcontinental extent of the southern savanna dry woodland was
occupied by peoples with tools of Nachikufan culture. This cultural
region extended over the whole of the southern half of the East African
Plateau, and was bounded to the north by the Sangoan area around
Lake Victoria, and by the Wilton area to the east, which reached the
coast near the lower Galana valley.

It can be seen that the distributions of these specialized stone-industries
in some ways coincide with the cultural regions of modern East Africa,
although the dry areas of the Eastern Rift Coast region were then culturally continuous with the Horn, and the Interlacustrine with the Wet
Forest region. Furthermore, the eastern shore of Lake Victoria then
belonged westwards, with the Interlacustrine region, and not eastwards
with the Eastern Rift Highlands, while these highlands were culturally
set apart from the nearby dryer plateau areas with a distinctiveness which

is not apparent today. These hunter-gatherer cultures did, however, show a correspondence with vegetation distribution, as do the modern cultural regions. Furthermore, the physical types were distributed partly in accordance with vegetation patterns, with caucasoids in the dry north-east, and in the associated wet highlands, while negroids were in the wet forest, but also on the northern savanna. The southern savanna, however, was the habitat of bushmanoids, who also extended far to the south, beyond the southern dry woodland. Such a correspondence has since been obliterated by the movements of negroid migrants.

The southern savanna woodland was inhabited throughout by groups who spoke languages of the Khoisan family, and all the peoples to the south of them spoke Khoisan languages as well as being of bushmanoid physical type. On the northern border of the woodland, in the wet forest, the family or families of languages which were spoken have possibly disappeared without trace. If they have not, then they were related to the Moru–Mangbetu group, and to any larger grouping to which these languages belong, for instance perhaps a Shari–Nile family. The same uncertainty colours the view of the eastern part of the northern savanna, but ancestral forms of Moru–Mangbetu languages were present there. However, the great extent of the savanna was divided up between several independent language families, remnants of at least some of which have survived to perplex modern linguistic classifiers. Such remnants are "Tepes", Ik, and the languages of the Nuba Hills. Somewhere on the eastern part of the savanna were the ancestral forms of the Nilo–Maa languages, not yet widespread. Conspicuously absent, however, to a modern observer, was Zande, and there were no members of the Niger–Congo family this far east.

Most of the area of the present Eastern Rift Coast region was occupied by languages of the Iraqw family, but these did not extend into the deserts of the Horn. Even at that early date, the peoples of the Horn, and of the Ethiopian Highlands, spoke languages of the Afro–Asiatic family, also occurring in Arabia just across the Red Sea.

By about 4000 B.C. farming was spreading among the peoples of the Ethiopian Highlands, and was established in the middle Nile valley. Cattle, sheep, goats, wheat and bulrush-millet had spread to this area from lower down the Nile valley, with migrants who were moving upstream, in small numbers; and migrants from the middle valley were trickling up into the Ethiopian Highlands. The savanna away from the river, and dryer than the highlands, remained the territory of hunter-gatherers at this time, and these were only slowly involved in farming, as the new cultivating communities of the middle Nile valley generated their own migrants, who moved upstream in search of new alluvial soils. Meanwhile, no emigrants from the Ethiopian Highlands were able, even if they tried, to farm in the desert areas of the Horn and the Lake Rudolf depression. In this belt, the hunter-gatherers remained largely unaffected by events in the highlands.

However, between 4000 and 2000 B.C. the middle and upper Nile cultivators domesticated sorghum, a plant very well adapted to the savanna, and by 1000 B.C. farming communities were scattered along the savanna from the Atlantic Ocean to the foothills of the Ethiopian Highlands. Local migrants were still following the Nile upstream, and there were farmers on the East African Plateau towards Lakes Albert and Kyoga. Migrants settled too in the Dry Zone of the Interlacustrine plateau in the course of the next thousand years, but the wet forest areas deterred them, as they deterred all the other farmers right across the continent to the west coast.

Although farming migrants did not establish themselves in the Lake Rudolf depression, they did settle in the wet highlands of (now) Pokot, and migrants from there spread southwards along the Rift Highlands, cutting down the forest, and cultivating the clearings thus formed. The new farming communities' members spoke Iraqw-family languages, as had their hunting ancestors, since the newcomers were few, and most of the people had learnt farming from them rather than themselves being descended from the immigrants. On the dry plateau, and on the coast, there was no farming, and the hunting-and-gathering communities continued, and also spoke Iraqw-family languages, like the farmers in the hills above them.

This was the period of the Stone Bowl Culture in the Kenya Highlands; and during this time, from about 1000 to about 0 B.C., the highland farmers were in the practice of extracting their lower median incisor-teeth. The farmers of the middle Nile valley were doing the same, and hunter-gatherers there had done so already before 4000 B.C. The practice was spread throughout the eastern savanna, and had been adopted by the peoples of the Rift Highlands from the same groups of immigrants who had first practised farming in the highlands. In A.D. 1900 most of the peoples of the eastern savanna, and of the Eastern Rift Coast region, were still extracting these incisors, and a number still do so, after three thousand years or more.

The wet forest had deterred these early farmer-migrants, and their local imitators, and so had the deserts of the Horn and the dryer areas of the north-east of East Africa. Had the migrants reached the southern savanna woodland, they would have been able to clear it with no more difficulty than they had experienced on the northern savanna, with its similar vegetation. However, they did not reach it, but stopped short at the edge of the dry country immediately south of the Kenya Rift Highlands (Map 17).

The last millennium B.C., which was the first millennium of farming in East Africa, was a period of few changes in that area, beyond the introduction of farming itself, and even that affected only a fraction of the area. Physical types were still distributed in the last century B.C. much as they had been in 1000 B.C., and the language families had also changed little in their distribution. At the end of the pre-Christian era, there were small farming communities on the eastern savanna, in the Dry Zone, and along the Rift Highlands east of Lake Victoria. In the west, the wet forests of the Interlacustrine plateau were continuous with those of the Congo Basin, and hunting-gathering bands roamed throughout the area, with their Sangoan stone-industry still intact. Further south, the dry woodland was still a belt of Nachikufan stone-industry, the local hunter-gatherers speaking Khoisan languages (Map 17).

Beyond East Africa, however, changes were more marked. Already by 1000 B.C. there were small kingdoms in the middle Nile valley, and also in the Ethiopian Highlands, both groups of kingdoms drawing their inspiration ultimately from Egypt, which had periodically ruled part of the middle valley. Migrants from the middle Nile area continued to move upstream, and by the end of the last millennium B.C. small states, inspired now by the Nubian examples, were scattered up the main valley to the edge of the East African Plateau. By that date too the peoples of Nubia were using locally smelted iron. Iron smelting had spread widely in the Near East around 1000 B.C., but had only become generally used in Egypt during the ninth century B.C. and had thence spread to Nubia. The settlers moving slowly up the Nile, therefore, knew not only about kings, but about iron smelting.

The First Iron and the First Kings, *c.* 0—*c.* A.D. 1000

The first kingdom of East Africa appeared undramatically on the edge of the Nile valley where it forms a wide marshy trench below Lake

Albert. These early states were tiny, formed of a few settlements each, and ruled by kings who were slightly glorified hereditary headmen. Culturally the peoples of this stretch of valley differed hardly at all from the still kingless groups around them on the eastern savanna. Migrants also continued, not only to move about the eastern savanna, but also to penetrate the Dry Zone of the Interlacustrine plateau. In this way small kingdoms were formed in this zone, the forerunners of all later organizational specialization in the area which was to become the present Interlacustrine region. At the same period, however, the beginning of the Christian era, iron smelting was also spreading over the northern edge of the East African Plateau, and the increasing quantity of iron tools enabled the Dry Zone peoples to clear the neighbouring wet forest to an extent unprecedented in the earlier period of implements made exclusively of stone. Access to the soils of the wet forest, although these were not inexhaustibly fertile, nevertheless slightly improved the production of crops, and laid the foundations of the future prosperity of the Interlacustrine kingdoms.

At this stage, however, the Interlacustrine plateau was still part of the pattern of events on the eastern savanna and in the wet forest. It had as yet no separate cultural identity. On the eastern savanna itself, migrants continued to move about from one area to another, following already the dictates of famine, and the need to move on when soils were exhausted. Knowledge of both iron smelting and kings spread widely and rapidly along this belt, as farming had spread earlier. However, whereas iron smelting had immediate appeal in most areas, kings were adopted by only a few peoples, in better watered and more productive areas, especially those towards the edge of the wet forest.

The appearance of iron tools in numbers all along the savanna belt enabled peoples near the wet forest to clear areas just within it on an unprecedented scale, as was happening on the Interlacustrine plateau. At its northern edge the forest began to retreat, and was replaced by grassland, scrub and secondary woodland. The hunter-gatherers of the forest either joined the cultivating settlers or retreated southward into the still uncut forest, retaining their Sangoan stone-tools, as they had for millennia. In the interior of the forest the pygmies were still largely unaffected.

The changing vegetation along the northern edge of the wet forest effectively broadened the savanna southward, establishing a new wetter zone of cultivation. Migration within this zone resulted in the gradual spread eastward of Bantu languages from the edge of the Cameroon highlands. The groups who spoke these Bantu languages had iron tools, as had their neighbours, but no kings. Their migrations eastward were on a small scale, through thinly peopled territory, and no migration involved many settlers, nor did any group of settlers make large movements. Nevertheless, the search for new land when their current clearings were exhausted led in the long run to the arrival of Bantu languages on the East African Plateau during the early centuries A.D.

Settlers who spoke these languages were used to the wet zone at the edge of the forest itself, and they moved in the same general direction as Zande settlers have followed in recent centuries.[2] Their preference for the wet forest-edge zone brought the Bantu-speakers gradually along the Nile–Congo watershed, and into the Interlacustrine region, as it now is. Culturally they were little different from other peoples of the eastern savanna, and their languages did not spread in the dryer areas to the north of them. They did, however, become general in the cultivating areas of the Interlacustrine plateau. Hence, by about A.D. 500, kings, iron working and Bantu languages had reached the plateau, and were beginning to enter into the new culture which was differentiating there. In Chapter 6 it has already been pointed out that there is no evidence that the first states in the Interlacustrine region were established by Cushitic-speaking immigrants from the north-east of Africa, who entered an already Bantu-speaking area. Indeed Cushitic languages and north-east African caucasoids played no major part in the history of the region.

Even before the settlers speaking Bantu languages had first appeared on the Interlacustrine plateau, farming groups, armed with iron tools, had penetrated the wet forest on the west shore of Lake Victoria, and also the highlands of Rwanda–Rundi. Here again the hunter-gatherers either joined the new settlers, or left for uncut wet forest elsewhere. To the south of the highlands, and of the south-west lake-shore, was dry woodland, sparsely peopled by hunter-gatherers of Nachikufan culture, and unattractive to farmers used to the wet forest margin. When the Rwanda–Rundi highlanders looked for new areas of uncut forest, at the margin of the main forest-mass, they turned westward, down the slope from the East African Plateau, to the edge of the forest, where it borders the southern savanna (Map 18).

The movement of migrants on the Interlacustrine plateau, and into the Rwanda–Rundi highlands, diffused Bantu languages and eventually kings throughout the area, although not all the peoples of the highlands accepted kings, at this period or later. Furthermore, the diffusion of settlers, iron smelting, crops and livestock, kings and Bantu languages continued down the western slope of the plateau, and gradually westward along the southern edge of the wet forest, which retreated as the population of cultivators in the zone built up. By A.D. 500 there were small states at the mouth of the Congo River, on the Atlantic coast, as there were all the way round the rim of the wet forest back to the Interlacustrine plateau. Migration was also taking Bantu languages, cultivation and kings, as well as iron smelting, although not all together, or all at once, into the southern dry woodland. It was these movements of people which carried the savanna type of house from its place of origin on the northern savanna, where it was the home of the first cultivators, through the Interlacustrine area to the southern margin of the wet forest, and thence out into the southern savanna.

Further north, settlers were still moving at the eastern end of the savanna. The dry Lake Rudolf depression still deterred them, and was still at the time of Christ an area of hunter-gatherers; but the farmer-migrants continued to move into the wet highlands, as well as from there back to the savanna. By this means iron smelting spread down into the Eastern Rift Highlands, but it also reached the northern highlands from the eastern shore of Lake Victoria, whither migrants had brought it, from the Interlacustrine plateau. Kings, however, did not reach the highlands, and indeed were unimportant on the eastern savanna away from the Nile valley, and the edge of the wet forest, where better production favoured the growth of their states.

Down the wet highlands too, in the same general direction as the iron smelting, moved languages ancestral to the Nandi–Pokot group, although neither of the present languages of the group had yet appeared. The languages ancestral to them had originated in the eastern savanna area, where other languages of the Nilo–Maa family were differentiating out.

To the north-east, in the much larger highland mass of Ethiopia, the situation was very different. Iron smelting had followed farming into these highlands from Nubia; and the long established states had become generally iron-using after the seventh century B.C. In this respect, as in others, they belong to the history of the Near East; and from the fourth century A.D. onward the states of the Ethiopian Highlands have their history recorded, at least spasmodically, in writing. In the deserts of the Horn, however, there were no states or kings, and it was only in the early centuries A.D. that hunting-gathering ceased to be the only livelihood of the region. Increasing specialization in different forms of animal- and plant-husbandry in north-eastern Africa resulted not only in much more intensive cultivation in the highlands, where population was increasing, but also in the occupation of the dry foothills, neighbouring the Horn deserts, by groups who relied more heavily on cattle, sheep and goats for their livelihood than on planted crops. A rapid transformation was sparked off in this area by the introduction of camels from Arabia, where they had been domesticated from before 1000 B.C. Camels reached the Horn early in the Christian era, and the peoples of the dry foothills rapidly became exclusive pastoralists, wandering over the whole of the dry area, and absorbing culturally the hunter-gatherer groups.

Such specialization in livelihood also occurred at the same time in the Lake Rudolf depression, and by A.D. 500 the same differentiation between pastoralists and cultivators had come about on the East African Plateau, partly through the response of people there to local conditions, and partly through the example of migrants from the Horn and the country near Lake Rudolf. In the course of these changes in specialization the modern pattern of livelihood emerged in the Eastern Rift Coast region, which was now becoming distinctive within East Africa. In the wet highlands population was locally dense, on the volcanic soils, and farming became intensive. At the same time the dry floor of the Rift Valley and the great plateau area which is today the Maasai Plains became the habitat of exclusive pastoralists, who did not, however, speak Maa. In areas intermediate in dryness between the plains and the highlands the local peoples relied heavily on livestock, but cultivated to some extent, as has been the practice of the Gogo and Kamba in recent centuries. Already by A.D. 500 the exclusive pastoralists were the most admired peoples within the Eastern Rift Coast region, as it was now becoming. The emergence of cattle as symbols of strength, prosperity and divine favour gave a very high prestige to those groups who devoted all their efforts to tending cattle. Further north and north-east, however, the pastoralists of the Horn were not rated so highly by those Ethiopians who lived in increasingly powerful states, and so had a criterion of prestige which could overcome the special claims of exclusive pastoralism.

The hunter-gatherers of the dry plains in the Eastern Rift Coast region were culturally absorbed by the pastoralists, who drew immigrants from the wet highlands, as well as from the Lake Rudolf area and from the Horn. In the process the languages of the dry plains changed, those of the Iraqw group being replaced by Nilo–Maa languages. By A.D. 1000 the Nandi–Pokot group had differentiated out and was represented on the dry plains as well as covering the northern wet highlands.

Migration over an extended period was also introducing circumcision, clitoridectomy and age-sets from the Horn, and from the southern edge of the Ethiopian Highlands. These features had become established as part of the culture of that area in the early centuries A.D., spreading from the dry foothills to the desert as exclusive pastoralist groups extended their total area. Endogamous castes of hunters and smiths had also emerged in the foothills zone, as well as in the highlands, and such castes also became widespread in the Eastern Rift Coast region, as a result of immigration. From the highlands too migrants scattered westwards into the upper Nile valley, where peoples with kings lived scattered among groups who lacked them. Age-sets, and castes of smiths and hunters, became established in this part of the eastern savanna, and there may have been other elements derived from the Ethiopian Highlands, which have since disappeared in the upper Nile area.

During this millennium population was building up on the alluvial soils of the eastern shore of Lake Victoria, and some of the migrants from this zone moved up into the highlands just to the east. It was as a result of such migrations that in the last centuries before A.D. 1000 Bantu languages became established in the densely populated areas near Mount Kenya, and on the dryer country to the south-east. In the following centuries, and on into the next millennium, migrants from this Mount Kenya area, uprooted by drought and famine, and by general over-population, settled on the Taita Hills, on Kilimanjaro and along the Nyika belt near the coast.[3] With the migrants spread gradually, not only Bantu languages, but also the negroid physical type, hitherto unimportant in the dryer parts of north-eastern Africa, although increasing steadily since iron was introduced into the highlands, and first present in small numbers of people after 1000 B.C. The immigrants from the eastern savanna, like those from the eastern shore of Lake Victoria, were negroid. During the period A.D. 0–1000, therefore, the people of the Eastern Rift Coast region were becoming progressively "blacker" in appearance.

It is important to emphasize at every stage that migrations were occurring, in small numbers, in all directions at once, although some of these migrations have left no trace, while others have had an important cumulative effect on local cultural differences. Thus, while some migrants were moving from the eastern lake-shore to the highlands, and yet others from the middle Athi valley to the coast, some groups were moving from the coast to the Taita Hills, and yet others from the highlands to the lake-shore. It was through the combined effects of many such short-range migrations that during the first millennium A.D. important strains of bananas and yams, originally from Indonesia, spread from the coast inland to Kilimanjaro, for instance, and also to the Interlacustrine states.

Traders from Arabia, Iran and India had been visiting the East African coast since about 1000 B.C., but in the last centuries before A.D. 1000 there were established on the coast a number of villages, where the local peoples were strongly coloured culturally by the foreign traders. These cosmopolitan villages were the forerunners of the Swahili city-states of the modern period. By the time they were founded the voyagers from the Near East and India had been joined by Indonesian traders, from Sumatra, Java, Malaya and Borneo. Among the effects of their visits, and local colonization, was the adoption by the local peoples of the crops which the Indonesians brought with them and planted. Among these new crops, rice was locally adopted on the coast, but their bananas and yams became widely dispersed, spreading inland to the wet highlands, and over them to the kingdoms of the Interlacustrine plateau, where bananas became in places an important staple. Such contact between the Interlacustrine area and the coast, by way of trade between neighbouring groups along the way, was by this time very old. Before there was farming anywhere in East Africa, trading and movement between bands of hunter-gatherers carried obsidian from Eburru and Njorowa in the Rift Valley westwards as far as the Kampala area and eastwards to the coast near Mombasa.[4] In the case of bananas and yams, these were passed on, still before A.D. 1000, to the wet forest of the Congo Basin, which was by then sprinkled with cultivators, and where the Bantu languages, spreading from the northern border-zone, were covering an increasing area.

South of the wet forest, events on the southern savanna have already been indicated. Iron smelting and farming, as well as kings, were spreading along the zone where the wet forest met the southern savanna, and in this belt the wet forest retreated as the cultivating settlers cleared sections of it in order to plant their crops. The Khoisan-speaking hunter-gatherers of the savanna were involved in this process, some of them joining the new settlers in farming. At the same time some of the hunter-gatherers of the wet forest were also being forced into farming by the clearance of forest and the disappearance of many of their resources. Migrants around the edge of the wet forest were also carrying Bantu languages to new areas, where they gradually became established. More slowly Bantu languages were spreading southward through the wet forest from its northern margins. Iron tools made the forest less intimidating to cultivators than it had been in the era of stone tools, but the total numbers of cultivators remained very small, and large areas were inhabited by hunter-gatherers, some of them pygmies and others physically very similar to the peoples in the cultivating groups. By A.D. 500 Bantu-speaking farmer-migrants, pursuing their shifting cultivation through the forest, and without kings or states, had come into contact with the Bantu-speaking kingdoms along the southern edge of the forest.

Although not as attractive, in terms of crop returns, as the wetter zone along the forest-edge, the southern woodland was not difficult to clear, especially with iron tools. By A.D. 500 shifting cultivation had involved Bantu-speaking groups from the forest-edge in the clearance of parts of the woodland. As in other situations where cultivators move into areas hitherto occupied by hunter-gatherers, these either joined the cultivators, since their resources were now seriously depleted as a result of clearance, or else they moved away to areas not yet affected by the tree felling of the farmers. Gradually, because of the demands of shifting cultivation, settlers dispersed through the woodland, establishing new villages in clearings among the trees. By A.D. 1000 they had reached the Indian Ocean coast.

At the same time as these settlers were dispersing throughout the southern savanna, the states along the southern edge of the wet forest were increasing in size, and their culture was becoming increasingly distinctive. One feature which became general before A.D. 1000 was matrilineal descent and inheritance. Migrants from this zone, which was by now differentiated as the Major States sub-region, although in its early stages, spread out to other parts of the southern savanna, and increased the cultural unity throughout the region. At the same time, however, migration was, as usual, in all directions, and migrants from the dryer parts of the savanna were moving into the Major States sub-region.

By A.D. 1000 the modern regions were clearly distinguished from each other (Map 19). The Southern Savanna region, as just noted, was marked by features which have survived to the present time, notably by states and matrilineal descent and inheritance. In addition, the modern sub-regions were beginning to differentiate from each other. To the north the Wet Forest region was thinly peopled by cultivators, without kings, and also by hunter-gatherers. Indonesian bananas and yams had arrived, via the East African Plateau, from the coast.

By this date too the Interlacustrine region was not only distinct from surrounding regions but was differentiating internally. The Rwanda–Rundi highlands were already culturally distinct from the plateau to the east and north-east of them. Large areas were still inhabited by groups with no kings, but the small kingdoms which would later be swallowed to become parts of Rwanda and Rundi were already established. Migrant farmers from the Wet Forest region were repeatedly moving into these highlands, as well as into the Ruwenzori further north. There were castes in the highlands as well as on the plateau itself; and here there was a single sub-region around the west and north-west of Lake Victoria. The southern kingdoms, in the Ziba area, as we would now call it, were culturally very similar to those further north, in the modern Ganda–Nyoro area, where the Interlacustrine culture as a whole had first become distinctive.

Further north, the eastern savanna was settled by numerous small stateless peoples, but there were a few tiny kingdoms along the Nile valley, and in the basin, which was not yet all Jieng'–Naath country, the Luo-speaking groups were members of small kingdoms. In this eastern savanna area the Moru–Mangbetu languages were fairly widespread, but the most dynamic event was the continuing proliferation of the Nilo–Maa languages. Luo-speakers were spread through the great basin area, where the Jieng'–Naath group of Nilotic languages had also appeared, but had not yet extended their range very far. Other languages of the Nilo–Maa group were also spreading at this period, some up the Nile valley and others in the Lake Rudolf depression. Despite the changes, however, the Savanna Stateless peoples still resembled in culture the earliest farming groups of that area, as indeed their modern descendants still do.

By this time, in the Eastern Rift Coast region, the Nandi–Pokot group of languages was distinct within the Nilo–Maa complex; and the pattern of intensive cultivators, would-be pastoralists and exclusive pastoralists was long established. There were also some hunting-gathering groups, not survivors of the earlier hunter-gatherers, but people from cultivating and pastoralist groups who had adopted hunting-and-gathering during times of famine. Indeed by A.D. 1000 the region had already very many of its present features. The *tembe* type of house had come into use in the

Iraqw–Langi highlands, and had spread from there across the dry plains (now Gogo) to the southern highlands beyond (Map 19).

Just north of the region, in the Lake Rudolf depression, there were pastoralists, and also in the dry country of the Horn, most of the southern part being occupied by Oromo groups. The valleys of the few permanent rivers, however, were inhabited by cultivating peoples; and the lower Tana valley was already occupied by groups who were strongly negroid and who spoke Bantu languages. Into this area there had been repeated movements of people from the coastal lowlands just to the south, an area itself affected by migrants from the Mount Kenya and Athi valley areas.

The Emergence of the Modern Peoples, c. A.D. 1000–A.D. 1900

In the course of the fifteenth and sixteenth centuries large numbers of Oromo migrated from the Horn into the Ethiopian Highlands. Their later incursions are recorded in the chronicles of the highland states. Some of them settled peaceably, but others took over parts of the region by force, in the manner of a "Norman Conquest". Their language has survived over considerable areas to the present time, and their prestige is still high in some areas, for instance in the south-western highlands. However, the groups who now call themselves Oromo in the highlands are culturally very close to the other highland peoples, from whom they are largely descended; and the culture of the desert Oromo, which they brought with them when they first came, is now mingled with highland elements. Many of these highland Oromo profess to be Muslim and the number of Muslims in the highlands has been greatly increased by the indirect effects of the migrations between 1400 and 1600.

The movements of that period, however, involved not only Oromo but also the Soomaali groups in the northern part of the Horn. From the fifteenth century onward Soomaali pastoralists extended their range south-westward. They were Muslims, as they still are, and lacked the elaborate age-set organization of the Oromo. In the long run their military success, and their control of increasing areas of pasture, led to their absorption of the earlier Oromo inhabitants into groups which were culturally Soomaali. By 1850, Soomaali camel herds were grazing on the eastern flank of the Tana River, in contact with the Pokomo cultivators of the valley floor.

In the Eastern Rift Coast region the centuries after 1000 were a period when the general pattern of the area remained largely constant. The modern ethnic groups began to appear, by differentiation *in situ*, after 1500. Early in this millennium migrants from the Southern Savanna region's north-east coast were moving into the Nyika area, and emigrants from the Nyika were drifting southward in the opposite direction. It was this contact at the edge of cultural regions which generated the bilineal descent among the Digo, Duruma and Rabai. Similar local migrations introduced kings into the Chaga area on the slopes of Kilimanjaro. The settlers with kingly traditions came from the Asu, who had received immigrants from Shambaa, and these in their turn from the Bondei–Zaramo zone, as it can later be called. Migrants from Kilimanjaro later settled on the eastern wet slopes of Meru, establishing the local groups with kingly traditions and a Bantu language, who are today the Rwo people.

Further south, in the highlands of the Iraqw–Langi area, Bantu-speaking migrants were moving in from the west after the middle of the millennium. They originated in what is now Nyamwezi country, and they had kingly traditions, although they lost these among the local people of these highlands, who spoke Iraqw-family languages. In what are now Rimi, Langi and Mbowe country, the Bantu languages prevailed over those of the Iraqw group, the local people adopting the new forms in preference to their own. The prestige of the newcomers, it seems, sprang from their capacity at iron smelting. Hitherto the peoples of this area had known and used iron tools, but the nearest supply had been far to the west or north. At this same period Bantu-speaking settlers had also been moving into the Gogo plains, from the low hills to the east (now Kaguru–Sagala) and from the wet highlands just to the south.[5] Again it was Iraqw languages which lost ground, and the Burunge speak the only surviving Iraqw language in the area. Out of this series of migrations and fusions arose the Gogo.

By the time they had appeared, the language of the dry plains on their north-east was changing. Migrants, from the dry Lake Rudolf depression, with their herds and flocks, were moving southward during the seventeenth and eighteenth centuries. They spoke Maa, a language which was one product of the still differentiating Nilo–Maa complex on the eastern savanna, and in adjacent areas. The immigrants were sufficiently successful at raiding to impress the peoples of these dry plains near the highlands, and the local groups adopted Maa as their language. In this way the last ingredient was added to these people, who already had cattle, age-sets and other well established features, and they became the classic Maasai of the historical period. The cultivating Ongamo, on Kilimanjaro, and the pastoral Datoga, on their own area of plains in the highlands, retain the only languages which remain of the pre-Maasai era on the plains.

The need to survive during famines was still driving some groups to take up hunting-and-gathering, a necessity which had occurred locally ever since farming became general in the highlands. With changes in local conditions some hunting-gathering bands dispersed, and joined pastoralist or cultivating groups, while others formed for the first time. Consequently modern groups, the Hadza and Ogiek, have complicated histories, drawing their recruits over time from different communities, just as have the cultivators and the pastoralists.

With the increase in trade during the nineteenth century, the Gogo of some areas found themselves on the main trunk-route from the coast to Lake Tanganyika. As a result local war-leaders in the east and centre, whose territory lay on the route, were able to charge *hongo*, a form of transit tax, on the caravans. Further to the west, the hereditary minor rulers of the western Gogo did the same. Trade also involved the Kamba, further north, and many of them travelled to and from the coast, as the Nyamwezi were doing on the main trunk-route. The Gikuyu too were acquiring more expensive tastes by trading food to the caravans in return for cloth and guns.

By this time the Maasai were established at the apex of the prestige pyramid in the region. The spread of the Maa language southward from the Lake Rudolf area was part of the continuing proliferation of the Nilo–Maa group of languages. From the time of their origin, before 1000 B.C., in the basin of the upper Nile, these had spread to cover, by A.D. 1000, a wide area on the eastern savanna and much of the Eastern Rift Coast region. Other languages besides Maa differentiated out after A.D. 1000. Turkana and Karimojong' both spread to occupy their present areas west of Lake Rudolf in the eighteenth century, at the same time that Maa was extending southward over the dry plains.

The spread of these two languages in the dry country west of Lake Rudolf resulted in the present widely scattered distribution of the "Tepes", Upale and Ik languages, although these were already separated from each other by Nilo–Maa languages before A.D. 1000. At the present time they are confined severally to various hill-areas among or near the

Karimojong'. They are, however, the relicts of a language family[6] which in 1000 B.C. still occupied a compact and continuous, although limited, area at the extreme eastern end of the savanna; and they were then one of a series of independent language families strung along the savanna-belt.

Other old language families had also been affected by the Nilo–Maa group, and by other newly expanding language families. By A.D. 1000 the old-established language families were surviving only in marginal positions, as was the "Tepes" family, and especially in positions which were also hilly. Thus the western foothills of the Ethiopian Highlands already sheltered the ancestors of Tabi (Ingessana) and Gokwom (Koma); and on the Nuba Hills the various small relict language groups were clustered close together, as they still are.[7] The process which had reduced these older language families to such limited confines was the swirl of migrants over the savanna, leading to the dispersal of new elements of culture, including new languages. After A.D. 1000 the older language groups were confined even more closely by the effects of swirl. Even so they have survived not only in the areas just indicated but also further west in the Sahel zone, for instance in Darfur, another hilly area.

The Sahel zone[8] has been a favourable area for the survival of these linguistic relicts because it is marginal to two cultural regions, and indeed to two major cultural regions, the NANE and the African. The regions of the savanna were formed by diffusion and migration from bases well south of the desert-edge. Hence the Sahel zone is marginal to them, being affected both later and less by the new elements of culture than were the savanna areas further south.

From the opposite direction modern Saharan culture has been diffused from early bases on the desert-edges of the Atlas area, Tripolitania, Cyrenaica and the lower Nile valley. The key event in this extension of the elaborating Saharan culture was the adoption of camels on a large scale by Berber-speaking groups of Mediterranean Africa in the period A.D. 0–400. This was happening at the same time as Oromo and Soomaali were adopting them in the Horn. From the Sahara, as well as from the savanna, the Sahel zone is marginal, being remote from the centres of origin in the far north. The zone is therefore an area of cultural change at a relatively low intensity. It must be stressed that these relicts are strictly linguistic. The peoples who speak these survivors of older language families are in other respects very like other peoples of their general area. It is their languages which are remarkable. They are thus parallels to the

Basques in Europe. Furthermore, the same phenomenon, of relict languages, can also be discovered on the edge of the Southern Savanna region.

During this millennium the most extensive group of languages on the eastern savanna has been the Nilo–Maa, and by A.D. 1000 these had already played a major part in reducing other families to the status of relics. Large numbers of people had abandoned their own language to speak one of those from the Nilo–Maa group. After A.D. 1500 Bari and Otuho reached their present forms, but the most conspicuous language changes of the eastern savanna were those associated with the Nilotic section of the Nilo–Maa family.

In A.D. 1000 the great basin of the upper Nile, to the south of the Nuba Hills, was largely occupied by Luo-speaking groups, divided into a number of small kingdoms. However, in the Bahr-el-Ghazal and Bahr-el-Jebel swamp areas, the Jieng' branch of Nilotic had been distinct for perhaps a thousand years, and was slowly extending its area. Unlike the Luo-speakers, the peoples who spoke languages of the Jieng' branch had no kings. During the fourteenth century the kingdoms of the middle Nile valley, themselves moderately large and Near Eastern in culture, were savagely disturbed by the repeated raids of Arabic-speaking pastoral nomads. The tiny Luo-speaking states further south were also affected, and, under the pressure of the raids, large numbers of people emigrated up the Nile valley. These migrants travelled in greater numbers than had been usual in this eastern savanna area, and hence they made a considerable cultural impact when they settled on the northern edge of the East African Plateau, in numbers which increased with each successive group of migrants. From the fusion of these immigrants with the local people, during the fifteenth century, arose the Acholi and Aluur; and it was adventurers from the newly settled areas who, also in the fifteenth century, overran the kingdom of Nyoro, as we now call it.

The Luo language was thus established north of Lake Albert and the Victoria Nile. In the great basin area the Cholo (Shilluk) and Anywak remained as relics of the former extent of the Luo language while Jieng' and Naath extended their range greatly from the fifteenth century onward. Increasing numbers of Luo-speakers adopted Jieng' as their language, and this process of absorption seems to be continuing on the south-western margin of the Jieng', towards the Nile–Congo watershed.

At the same time that the Naath and Jieng' groups were expanding, Luo-speaking migrants from Acholi were moving eastward and south-eastward into the area north of Lake Kyoga, inhabited by would-be pastoralists speaking some language of the Nilo–Maa group. In the course of the seventeenth and eighteenth centuries Luo prevailed over the earlier language in this area, and the Lang'o emerged as a distinct group. Furthermore, migrants from this area trickled, during the eighteenth century, south-eastward into the well watered areas east of Lake Kyoga and near Lake Victoria. Locally, their language prevailed over Bantu forms already spoken in these areas. Out of the new fusion emerged the Adhola and Lake Victoria Luo. Migrants in this direction were not all Luo-speaking. Some of them spoke Teso, another Nilo–Maa language, established in the Lake Kyoga area before Luo. In one area Teso prevailed over the local Bantu forms, and the people of that area are the modern Tesyo.

Lake Kyoga is on the well watered southern edge of the savanna. Further west along the savanna belt, at the edge of the wet forest, where the forest was retreating under the impact of increasing cultivation, there were small states, which did not grow much in size after A.D. 1000. They were, however, affected by migrants from the west. Although people were moving in all directions, for instance both into the wet forest and out of it, there was after A.D. 1500 a gradual extension eastward of languages of the Niger–Congo family. These were not Bantu languages but their northern neighbours, whose eastern limit, both on the wet southern edge of the savanna and in the northern part of the wet forest, was north of the big bend of the Congo. The most easterly of these languages, Zande, spread from there right along the Nile–Congo watershed by the end of the eighteenth century. Zande was the language of a number of groups of adventurers, with traditions of kingship themselves, who carried out a series of small-scale "Norman Conquests" on the tiny states of the savanna-forest edge, and set themselves up as a new nobility in each.

During the nineteenth century Zande nobilities continued to proliferate in the watershed area. Peoples who had never had kings or nobility before were taken over by ambitious members of Zande royal clans who wanted kingdoms of their own. As has been noted earlier, further round the watershed, and at the same period, Aluur princes were establishing minor kingdoms among similar stateless peoples. In the area of Zande nobilities the Zande language was widely adopted by the non-Zande subjects, on account of the high prestige of the powerful new rulers. It seems likely that some ethnic groups of the watershed area are thus losing their identity, and becoming Zande.

At the same time as some migrant-adventurers were moving eastwards, other migrants from the savanna were continuing to penetrate the wet forest, as had been the situation on an increased scale since the arrival of iron tools, around the time of Christ. One effect of these migrations was that non-Bantu languages, originating on the savanna, occupy the north-eastern edge of the wet forest; and in this zone since 1000 the Bantu languages have lost ground. One of the invasive languages is Mangbetu, now apparently itself losing ground to Zande. Most peoples in the wet forest are stateless, but the Mangbetu resemble the Zande, being divided into a number of states, each with its own king. In their area immigrants from the savanna have had an effect not only on the language but on organization, and the kingly traditions of the Nile–Congo watershed have effectively penetrated the forest.

Migration within the forest continued in all directions, but with little effect on the distribution of cultural features because of the general homogeneity of the region. Away from the northern zone, Bantu languages, were now general, although diversified into different subgroups in different areas. Migrants were also moving into the forest from the Southern Savanna region. The Mongo, and neighbouring groups, in the area south of the big bend of the Congo, received numerous immigrants from the savanna peoples to the south. For a time, before the present century, matrilineal inheritance and descent occurred among some groups in this area, an affect of such immigration, but this has now faded out, and the peoples show the same patrilineal features as other wet forest groups. Furthermore, the languages of this area south of the big bend have not been perceptibly affected by languages from the Southern Savanna region. They all fit into the group prevalent in this part of the wet forest.[9]

In the generalized swirl of migration, some other cultural changes came about by the cumulative effect of local movements of people. Along the wet forest's eastern border, migrants were moving up on to the highlands which form the rim of the East African Plateau. One effect of these movements was the adoption by most of the groups in the Rwanda–Rundi highlands of languages originating in the eastern wet forest, in place of their earlier forms, which were related to Ganda and Nyoro. Migrants from the forest also strengthened the stateless tradition of the Chiga at the northern edge of these highlands, while emigrants from thickly populated Chiga country were spreading their language among the people of Ankore, where it is still spoken. An even stronger impact from the wet forest has occurred in the Ruwenzori Mountains, where the Konzo are in all respects culturally a people of the Wet Forest region, and not of the Interlacustrine. Further south, however, and in recent centuries, emigrants from Rundi have affected the languages spoken on the dry plateau in the country of the Ha, Vinza and Jiji, where the local people have adopted the form of the immigrants, which has now been diversified by local changes.

Events in the kingdoms of the Interlacustrine region during this millennium have already been summarized in Chapter 6. Competition between them led to local hegemonies and to annexations; but secessions were also frequent. Rundi, for example, broke away from Rwanda in the seventeenth century, and in the nineteenth Tooro from Nyoro. From the thirteenth to the seventeenth century the most powerful state of the northern half of the region was Nyoro, which occupied a position of supremacy in the local league-table. Its position was not disturbed when, in the fifteenth century, the Luo-speaking adventurers took over Nyoro, then called Kitara, and other states in the northern part of the region; but in the eighteenth century Ganda replaced Nyoro at the apex of the prestige pyramid, and social patterns throughout the north began to change.

Also, the scale of the largest states increased during the millennium. Nyoro increased in size and population until the eighteenth century, and there was a corresponding increase in social specialization. The subsequent growth of Ganda, to a size greater than Nyoro had ever reached, involved even more specialization, and a degree of governmental centralization greater than was achieved even in Rwanda and Rundi, the largest states, in terms of population size, to appear in the region.

An increase in the size of the states was also taking place in the Southern Savanna. There the largest states grew up in the relatively wet zone where the savanna adjoins the Wet Forest region. Although not all the states of this sub-region grew to any great size, south of the mouth of the Congo the kingdom which gave its name to the river gradually swallowed other states, to reach the scale recorded by the Portuguese navigators who first saw it in the second half of the fifteenth century. Further to the east, in the same sub-region, a number of Luba and Lunda states grew, at different periods, by competition and annexation.

The modern sub-regions had all become distinct from each other by A.D. 1000, and they continued to differentiate out during the present millennium. In the same period migrations, in all directions, continued,

and the sub-regions expanded further to fill the whole of the dry woodland belt. In the south-west migrants from the region came into contact
with Hottentots, and out of the meeting arose the Herero, very like
Hottentots in many respects, but markedly negroid, and speaking a
Bantu language. The would-be pastoralists of the area, such as the
Kwambi, also arose from the merging of Southern Savanna and Hottentot traditions.

The earlier culture of the southern savanna, before the spread of the
elements which contributed to the present version, was that of Khoisan-
speaking hunter-gatherers. Such groups were still widely distributed over
the middle Zambezi and the Kafue valley areas early in the millennium.
Fusion between the earlier culture and the new one gave rise to that of
the Ila, Tonga and Totela peoples. As has been noted earlier, the present
absence of kingly traditions in this middle Zambezi area seems to spring
from the strength of Bushman customs there. Many Tonga indeed still
look very bushmanoid, after centuries of interbreeding between negroids
and bushmanoids in the area.

Another relict of the earlier culture is the language of the Sandawe,
on the edge of the Iraqw–Langi highlands. Sandawe is a Khoisan language, like those of the Bushmen and Hottentots. Although these
languages were at one time the only languages of the southern savanna,
and of all southern Africa, Sandawe has survived as their only represen-
tative in the regions north of the Zambezi; and it is situated on the edge
of the Southern Savanna region, and near the northern limit ever reached
by Khoisan languages and by the bushmanoid physical type. Some
Sandawe show very clearly bushmanoid features, although all of them
have some negroid admixture, and most of the people are more negroid
in appearance than bushmanoid.

The area of the Iraqw–Langi highlands contains other relicts besides
the Sandawe language and some bushmanoid features. Apart from Ma'a,
in the Shambaa highlands, the surviving languages of the Iraqw family
are all in this area : Iraqw itself, Gorowa, Alagwa, Burunge and Hadza.
Another relict is Datoga, a Nilo–Maa language which was among the
precursors of Maa on the Maasai Plains. This cluster of relict-languages
lies on the border between two cultural regions, as do, for example, the
Nuba Hills further north. The languages have survived because of the
relatively weak pressure for change in the area, either from the culture
of the Southern Savanna region or from that of the Eastern Rift Coast.
Here too it is important to emphasize that it is the languages which are

relicts, not the peoples as a whole. Culturally the peoples of this area are part of the Eastern Rift Coast region except for some matrilineal features which originated in the Southern Savanna. Matrilineal descent and inheritance among the Langi, and the matrilineal element in the double descent of the Mbowe and Iraqw have moved into the area with migrants from the south.

A parallel situation further east has already been noted in this chapter. The Digo, Duruma and Rabai received the matrilineal element in their pattern of double descent from the Southern Savanna region, while the patrilineal element, together with their language, are of Eastern Rift Coast origin. In most of their cultural features these peoples belong to this region, but they live in an area where migrants from the two regions have met and mingled. The same is true of the Chaga on Kilimanjaro, who belong to the Eastern Rift Coast region in most of their features, but have acquired kings by way of immigrants from the Southern Savanna. This Kilimanjaro–Coast area, marginal to two cultural regions, also has two relict languages, Ma'a and Ongamo.

In recent centuries even matrilineal descent and inheritance have become relict features in East Africa. Iraqw, Mbowe and Langi, as well as Digo, Duruma and Rabai, are now surrounded by peoples with no matrilineal features; and the same is true of the Kaguru, Vidunda and Ruguru a little further south. The key factor in the disappearance of matrilineal features in this part of the Southern Savanna, and its borders, has been the prestige of the Swahili in the nineteenth century.[10] Their increasing importance in the interior was augmented by that of the Nyamwezi, who had themselves imitated the Swahili, in descent and inheritance as well as in dress and other features. The roles of the Nyamwezi, Swahili and, further south, the Yao in the trading and raiding of the interior during the last century have already been described in Chapter 7.

By 1900 the Southern Savanna region, and all the other regions in eastern Africa, had acquired the characteristics which have been recorded in the numerous written accounts of explorers, missionaries, administrators and anthropologists. The regions had come into being by way of a series of changes, and they have been changing in detail ever since they became distinctive. By 1900 a new era was beginning in East Africa, and the prestige of the Europeans was affecting all the regions in a variety of ways. What effect these new factors for change will have in the long run it is impossible to say at this very early stage.

11. Notes

1. The industries of stone tools in Africa seem to need considerably more precise classification and sub-division than has yet been attempted.
2. In the same way the Luo-speakers, from the fifteenth century onward, have drifted up the Nile valley, following a route which was old long before their time.
3. The evidence for a spread of Bantu languages from the Lake Victoria area to the coast is the unity of the languages in Guthrie's E-group. M. Guthrie (1971). "Comparative Bantu", Vol. 2, pp. 44–7. This group includes, among others, Nyoro, Ganda, Logooli, Gikuyu, Chaga and Giryama.
4. Sonia Cole (1964). "The Prehistory of East Africa", p. 158.
5. Again Guthrie's classification of Bantu languages provides evidence on the effect of local migrations. Rimi and Langi–Mbowe are related to Sukuma–Nyamwezi, in the F-group, while Gogo is with Hehe and Swahili, in the G-group.
   M. Guthrie, op. cit., pp. 47–51.
6. They may in fact belong to more than one family. A. N. Tucker and M. A. Bryan (1956). "Linguistic Analyses of the Non-Bantu Languages of North-Eastern Africa", p. 93. They feel that on the limited evidence available the languages seem to form a cohesive group.
7. Ibid., pp. 62–86.
8. Wrigley (1962) drew attention to the survival of a number of small independent language groups in this zone.
9. M. Guthrie, op. cit., pp. 39–42.
10. The process, however, possibly began earlier. See note 2, Chapter 7.

12

Continuing Changes

New Features

Whatever the obscurity of the prehistoric period in East Africa, there undoubtedly have been great changes since the first people appeared in that area. The modern cultural regions are partially defined by their crops and domestic livestock, as well as by artefacts made of iron, and they must therefore be no older than the adoption of farming and of iron implements by the peoples of these regions. The regions themselves, therefore, represent the end-products of important changes in the past. Indeed even before farming and iron tools, it is clear that the East African societies of hunters-and-gatherers were not strictly static, since their tool-types were repeatedly changing, albeit over long periods of time. Even though East Africans are aware that dramatic changes have taken place within living memory, it is still true that the greatest single change affecting people in East Africa was the introduction of farming.

The dramatic changes since 1890 have been mentioned, and assumed, repeatedly during this account. At this point they need to be summarized, and, where necessary, connected to each other. Even the term East Africa is new, dating only from the end of the nineteenth century; and it is used here to mean an area defined by five states, only two of which, Burundi and Rwanda, had any administrative unity before 1890. Furthermore, the governments of all five of the states are essentially European-introduced innovations established only during this century. The two aspects of formal government which have most affected East Africans are taxes and the substitution of law-court procedures or formal arbitration for the settlement of disputes by raiding.

All East African societies were to some extent internally peaceful, since small communities everywhere are marked by informal pressures and procedures for damping down disputes within the community. However, in 1890 East African societies differed widely among themselves in the number of minimum-size moral communities which were grouped together to form the societies. In the Savanna Stateless and Eastern Rift Coast regions the single local moral community was usually the whole society; and the same was true, on a slightly larger scale sometimes, in the Horn. However, in the Interlacustrine and Southern Savanna regions, such small societies existed side-by-side with states composed of several, or even a great number of, minimum-size communities, all recognizing the authority of a single king.

To the peoples of these states both taxation and a hierarchy of law-courts were familiar aspects of their daily living, as was the expectation that fighting between settlements or provinces would be suppressed by the government. On the other hand, the stateless peoples expected to have to fight for themselves, each settlement against others when necessary. They did not expect disputes between settlements to be readily ended by the decision of a judge or arbitrator; but, at the same time, they owed no-one any taxes, since they paid for no government services; and there was no-one to claim the precedence which required tribute. The new judicial and administrative order, introduced by German, Belgian and British officials, therefore marked a greater change for the stateless peoples than for those who already knew taxes and ranked courts.

Even for these members of established kingdoms, however, the new administrations introduced notable features, for example imprisonment as a punishment, but above all other innovations in importance were the new professional army and the police force. With such permanent means of imposing the authority of a government, the states stopped being essentially feudal; and the likelihood of prolonged civil wars or secessions was reduced, although not totally or permanently removed. It has been noted already that the importance of the regular armed forces has been indicated by the emergence of the respective heads of the army in Burundi and Uganda as heads of state; while in Uganda, at least between 1966 and 1971, the armed Special Force police became to some extent a rival to the army.

The European administrators introduced also technical services as part of the regular activity of the governments. Veterinary and agricultural departments dealt with increasing the yield of both livestock and crops, while the public works departments of the different territories provided, and maintained, roads and some other new facilities. General health also became a government responsibility, and the period 1890–1940 is marked by the dying down of epidemics, especially of smallpox, which had hitherto been a major factor in periodically reducing population, in all areas.

Quite apart from the effects of the agricultural and veterinary departments in reducing plant- and animal-diseases, and so increasing food supplies, the administrators were able, by large-scale storage and distribution of food, to reduce the effects of bad harvests, caused by drought or pests. The lessening impact of famine and epidemics led to an increase in population, the exact size of which it is not possible to gauge because of the hitherto unreliable census figures. There has, however, certainly been an increase, and the effects have been most felt in the areas which were already densely peopled in 1890, for instance the Chiga, Gikuyu and Nyakyusa territories. At the same time the pattern of population has apparently remained the same as it was in 1890, with a very marked concentration of many people in a few areas, while most of East Africa remains very thinly settled. Indeed the contrasts are becoming increasingly accentuated, precisely because population is expanding most rapidly in the already densely peopled areas.

These areas have also seen the greatest increases in total production and wealth, and the greatest investment in, and enthusiasm for, schooling. As stressed repeatedly throughout this discussion, the densest populations have built up on volcanic or alluvial soils under conditions of relatively high rainfall. Such areas have offered more opportunities for new crops than the average or very dry areas, and cash returns for the crops have been highest in the high density localities. Simultaneously, these places have been favoured by both governments and Christian missions for the foundation of hospitals and of schools. Furthermore, in addition to the sheer availability of schools, the increasing pressure of people on the land resources in the high density areas makes many young people, urged on by their parents, eager to acquire paper qualifications which will help them to obtain jobs with wages and salaries, and outside farming. Such ambitions are helped by the cash available from the sale of crops. The history of the Chaga and Gikuyu since 1890 are classic examples of these processes, which themselves derive from the increasing involvement of East African peoples in a widespread pattern of trade which extends far beyond East Africa. Hence coffee and cotton have become worthwhile crops for small farmers to grow, and Asian wholesalers and retailers have made a variety of goods, not all of them imported, available to the farmers, who now have the cash to buy them.

The Chaga and Gikuyu, however, illustrate some other features of the new conditions. Both of these peoples show in a high degree the increasing gap between the highest and the lowest social classes in East Africa. This gap has opened up more markedly in the prosperous, wet, densely peoples areas than it has elsewhere precisely because they are prosperous, and because of the combination of schooling, incentives, land shortage and opportunities which have already been mentioned. All over East Africa a white-collar, salary-earning elite has emerged with the new-style states, but the prosperous areas have contributed members to these elites out of all proportion to their numbers in the total population. Thus the Chaga occupy a remarkably high fraction of civil service posts in Tanzania, as do the Gikuyu in Kenya; and for this, and their success in other jobs, they are widely unpopular in their respective countries.

Increasing prosperity, at least in terms of money, and more widespread schooling have led to increasing expectations among young people, and hence to an increasing pressure on the limited number of wage- and salary-jobs. These relatively new ambitions do not sweeten the attitude of large numbers of frustrated aspirants towards the "successful" peoples, such as the Chaga. At the same time the shortage of regular-money jobs prompts people established in government departments, which are major employers, to ensure that any vacancies are filled by kinsmen, neighbours or at least people from the same ethnic group, a process known widely as "brotherization". It is also an important component in the process generally called "tribalism", decried by government spokesmen, but increasingly assumed to be normal. Prosperity and social complexity have generated tensions between ethnic groups which were not there in 1890. And in the process the prosperity of the Asians in commerce and the professions has attracted the same sort of jealousy and resentment which Chaga and Gikuyu have suffered. Expulsion of large numbers of Asians from Uganda in 1971–72 was an obvious move for a president seeking popular support.

The procedures of administration in all five countries are still those established by Belgian and British administrators, but these procedures are drifting towards new forms under the conditions building up since before administrative independence. Contemporary members of governments are under pressure from factions within the elite, and also faced with the need to keep the electorate not too discontent. The new rulers are not endowed with the olympian aloofness of their European predecessors, who were not engaged in a local struggle for power, and who enjoyed the prestige of being Europeans. The new elites' members, on the other hand, find themselves troubled by the classic insecurities of ruling classes, suspecting that other people in their class are after their jobs, seeking for allies to strengthen their own positions, and not at all sure what the silent majority, that is most of the people in their country, are feeling. The dilemmas of the elites can be most clearly seen in the towns, themselves the products of the increased commercial and administrative activities since 1890, and on an even larger scale since 1950. In the towns too are concentrated the majority of the new jobs, and there the gap between rich and poor is most evident. Although the old city-states of the coast provided urban conditions long before 1890, the scale of the urban habitat is now vastly greater than it has ever been before, and a high proportion of East African men have spent at least a short period of their lives in a town. Furthermore, the towns are the scene of the most intense political activity.

Factions have certainly emerged, although as yet in Tanzania, apart from Zanzibar and Pemba, they are very weak; but rival political parties have been officially, and severely, discouraged, with varying degrees of formal justification. It is therefore impossible to say what the power bases of rival parties might be if they were to exist for a generation or two. One possible prediction is that Muslims, Roman Catholics and Protestants could form the foundation for country-wide parties, because these are the only groupings which cut across the ethnic categories. However, there is no clear indication that this is happening. In Ganda, between 1880 and 1895, the denominations were used as faction-labels, and the practice persisted under the Protectorate Government; but in the period 1959–71 the denominational associations of the formal parties weakened, if anything, in most of Uganda. Christians and Muslims do, however, add further complexity to the increasingly complex states of East Africa, since the real enthusiasts among them are judging the conduct of the governments and elites by universal moral standards infinitely more demanding than the parochial morals which have been normal hitherto throughout the area. However, no East African government yet faces the moral scrutiny of a body comparable to the upper echelons of the clerical hierarchy in Western Europe during the twelfth and thirteenth centuries.

Becoming Christian or Muslim has had other effects also. Some rituals

have died out altogether; even the sacrifices to the ancestors have disappeared in strongly Christian areas. Other rituals have been streamlined, for example initiation ceremonies have frequently been reduced
to circumcision and clitoridectomy, with little or no formal elaboration.
Initiations which in 1890 took days or weeks in most areas now take
minutes. People are not only aware of the strength of the claims which
Muslims and Christians seem to be making: that their rituals are
better, that is more effective, than the older forms. They are also conscious of the power and the prestige of the Europeans, usually seen also
as being Christians. Anything which Europeans do not do is probably
not important and, since times are changing, such things can be abandoned. Music, dancing and the telling of stories have all suffered heavy
casualties as a direct result of this response to the Europeans; and no
amount of urging by Europeans that these features should be preserved
makes much headway against the new convictions. Hitherto the erosion
of these rather fragile features has been most severe in the prosperous,
densely peopled areas. It is now possible to travel through extensive tracts
of East Africa and hear no music, except that from the transistor radios.

Underlying Continuity

The same process of erosion affects features which are very important
in the differentiation of the cultural regions. Age-sets, for example, were
one of the distinctive features of the Eastern Rift Coast region, but they
have now faded out among most of the peoples there. The Maasai,
Baraguyu, Arusa, and Sambur have retained them, as have the Turkana,
Karimojong' and Oromo in neighbouring dry areas; but further to the
west many of the Savanna Stateless peoples are also no longer forming
them. Striking changes have also affected the Interlacustrine and Southern
Savanna regions, where the royal families have been overshadowed by
European administrators. Within East Africa indeed no royal family is
officially recognized by any of the governments.

A major distinction between cultural regions has been the presence
in some of them not only of royal families but also of state organizations,
whereas others consist of stateless societies. Such a contrast, which was
striking in 1900, no longer applies with any great force because of the
general application of taxes and the widespread recognition by local
people of the governments' power. It is true that the former state of affairs
still colours most people's attitude to authority in any area. Taxation

and orders from officials seem more normal, even perhaps more legitimate, to a Nyamwezi or a Ganda than they do to a Gogo or a Lugbara, but these attitudes themselves are presumably going to change as new generations of the recently stateless peoples assume that taxation is a fact of life, not just a recent coincidence. In the same way the peoples who have had royal families are still conscious that they each have one, even though the government chooses to ignore them. Again, however, new generations are not likely to take much interest in families which they themselves have never seen in office.

Another major difference between the regions was the presence or absence of circumcision and clitoridectomy. Although clitoridectomy has not spread appreciably, the distribution of circumcision has been affected to some extent by men becoming Muslims and being circumcized. Such professions of conversion to Islam, however, have left the present distribution very similar to that in 1890. All over East Africa men accustomed to circumcizing and women accustomed to excising the clitoris have retained these practices up to the present time. Clitoridectomy thus remains general in the Horn and the Eastern Rift Coast regions, where the men are also circumcized, as they are in the Wet Forest region. Circumcision, however, has not yet increased greatly in the Savanna Stateless, Interlacustrine and Southern Savanna regions.

Although these practices, affecting the genitals, and with their implications of reproduction and continuity of life, have proved to be very durable, the overall picture of changes in the twentieth century has been one of stripping down to essentials and of the fading of local colour. The initiation ceremonies are curtailed or discontinued, while the essential circumcision and clitoridectomy continue. Music and dancing are given up, but cultivation goes on, and is even intensified. At the present time the cultural regions of the period 1890–1940 seem to be disappearing.

It is much too early to divine what will take their place. Some of the politicians have ill-defined visions of nuclear power-stations, skyscrapers and even more vast international airports. However, so far none of the five countries have gone far on the way to becoming industrial. There is no steel industry, and all the republics are firmly agrarian.

The future pattern then is necessarily unknown, but it is worth introducing an analogy which should caution anyone from assuming that a new series of cultural regions will spring into being in the next few decades. During the second century A.D. the peoples of lowland Britain,

Gaul and the west bank of the Rhine were administered by Roman officials. To the north and east were other peoples not within the Roman imperial boundaries, but with some contact with the territories which were. Beyond the Mediterranean borders of Europe no-one had been literate until the period of Roman administration, and in A.D. 100 very few people were literate in northern Europe, and probably none east of the Rhine. However, in this expanse from the British Isles to the upper Volga were going to appear the cultural regions of Western and Eastern Christendom, in their northern forms. They would be marked: by cathedrals, in both the Romanesque and Russo–Byzantine traditions; by an elaborate literature; and by states far larger than those of the first century. Eventually, in the west of this area, factory industry began in the later eighteenth century.

Northern Europe, in the literate period, has been patterned into the cultural regions which are familiar from recent history: the British Isles, France, Central Europe, Scandinavia, East Central Europe, and the Russias. These, however, have replaced cultural regions, discernible only from archaeologists' evidence, which were in flourishing existence just before the time of the Roman Empire. A critical factor in the changing culture of northern Europe was contact with Mediterranean peoples, Roman officials, Italian missionaries, and, further east, Greek missionaries. What is important in the context of changes in modern East Africa is the time-scale involved. A distinctive West European culture had emerged by A.D. 1000, but Britain was a Roman provincial outpost as early as A.D. 43 and Augustine landed in Kent in A.D. 597. In north-western Europe a new pattern was a long time emerging. East Africa in 1890 was an agrarian iron-using area, but without literature, very similar in these respects to the northern Europe of the first century. By 1960 East Africans had experienced a few decades of contact with imperial administrators, with European traders (mostly indirectly, through Indians) and with missionaries. But how long will it be before a distinctive new culture appears?

Another analogy suggests something about the distribution of the new cultural regions, provided, that is, that people survive in East Africa the centuries which may be necessary before this happens. In the Near East there have been literate societies appreciably longer than anywhere else; and in the course of the five thousand years that literate societies have been there a major change of culture has taken place. The period from 3000 to 300 B.C. is marked by numerous and important changes, but throughout the period the Nile valley, the Levant and Mesopotamia retained their identity. In addition, Anatolia and the Iranian Plateau each remained distinctive throughout the period. Between 300 B.C. and A.D. 300 is a transition phase, when Hellenistic models are strongly imitated; and, positively or negatively, Hellenistic culture is a critical factor in the emergence of the new pattern, which is still visible. Sumerian, Akkadian, Canaanite, Egyptian and Hittite have all faded out as daily languages; and the area is dominated, in terms of language, by Arabic, Persian and Turkish. The pattern of the cultural regions, however, remains remarkably similar : the Iranian Plateau, Mesopotamia, Anatolia, the Levant and the Lower Nile Valley.

Behind this persistance of regional distribution, which outlives the distinctive regional cultures, are the vegetation regions, which here, as in East Africa, correspond closely with the cultural regions. Underlying the vegetation regions too are the rainfall amounts of the different parts of the Near East and, very important here, the critical role of ground water in the major river valleys. In the Near East then there is evidence that the vegetation distribution has been one of the factors in the new cultural regions, as in their predecessors. It is, therefore, probable that, whatever the distinctive features of the possible cultural regions of East Africa, the vegetation regions will continue to be one of the major factors in their differentiation, and critical in their distribution.

Speculating about the possible shape of an uncertain future, however, is only peripheral to the main theme which has run through this account of East African peoples. By 1890 there were in existence in East Africa two cultural regions and parts of three others. They owed their distinctiveness, not only to the habitats which the peoples occupied, but also to the contacts between the peoples, to their relative prestige and to specific cultural innovations and borrowings. As has been stressed already, the process by which the historic regions of the period 1890–1940 came into being can only be illuminated by archaeologists' future discoveries.

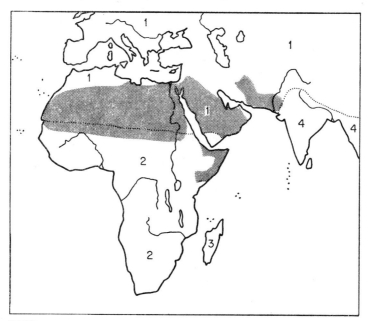

1

Afro-Asian Desert Belt

Transition from Western Eurasian to NANE Major Region

·········· Boundary between major cultural regions

2

Afro-Asian Desert Belt

·········· Boundary between faunal sub-regions

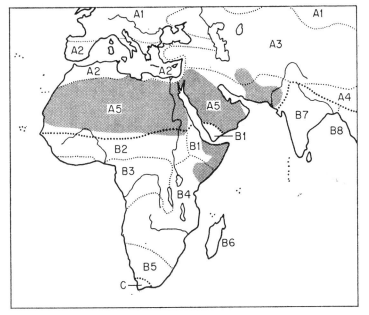

3

■ Afro-Asian Desert Belt ········ Boundary between floral kingdoms

········ Boundary between floral provinces

Map 1 The African Major Cultural Region and neighbouring major regions.
1. Western Eurasian; 2. North-African-Near-Eastern; 3. Sub-Saharan African;
4. Madagascar; 5. Indian; 6. South-East Asian; 7. Central Asian; 8. Siberian.

Map 2. Faunal sub-regions.
1. Palaearctic sub-region; 2. African sub-region (Ethiopian sub-region); 3. Madagascar sub-region; 4. Tropical Asian sub-region.

Map 3. Floral kingdoms and provinces. (Based partly on W. T. Neill, 1969.)
A. Boreal kingdom (not all shown):
    1. Euro-Siberian province; 2. Mediterranean province; 3. Central Asian province;
    4. Sino-Japanese province; 5. Afro-Asian desert province.
B. Palaeotropical kingdom (not all shown):
    1. North-East African province; 2. Savanna province; 3, Wet Forest province;
    4. Eastern African province; 5. South African province; 6. Madagascar province;
    7. Indian province; 8. Mainland South-East Asia province. (The African sub-
    kingdom consists of B1–5; Madagascar is a separate sub-kingdom; and B7–8
    form part of the Indo-Malaysian sub-kingdom.)
C. Cape kingdom.

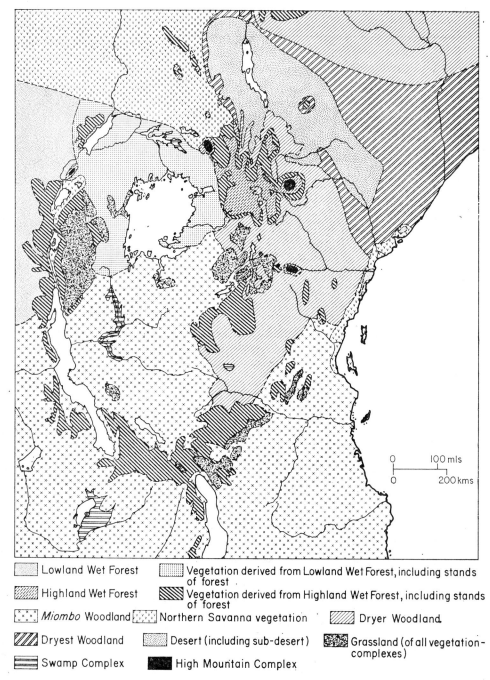

▦ Lowland Wet Forest	▦ Vegetation derived from Lowland Wet Forest, including stands of forest	
▨ Highland Wet Forest	▨ Vegetation derived from Highland Wet Forest, including stands of forest	
⊠ *Miombo* Woodland	⊠ Northern Savanna vegetation	▨ Dryer Woodland
▨ Dryest Woodland	▦ Desert (including sub-desert)	▦ Grassland (of all vegetation-complexes)
▤ Swamp Complex	▦ High Mountain Complex	

Map. 4 Vegetation-distribution at the present time. (Based partly on Lind and Morrison, 1974, and on Kingdon, 1971, their maps in turn relying on Trapnell and Langdale Brown, 1962.)

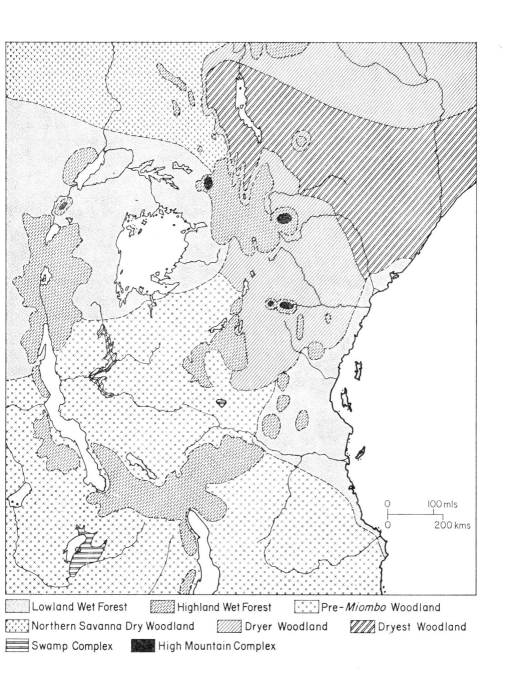

Lowland Wet Forest   Highland Wet Forest   Pre-*Miombo* Woodland
Northern Savanna Dry Woodland   Dryer Woodland   Dryest Woodland
Swamp Complex   High Mountain Complex

Map 5. Vegetation-distribution in *c* 1000 B.C.: a tentative reconstruction.

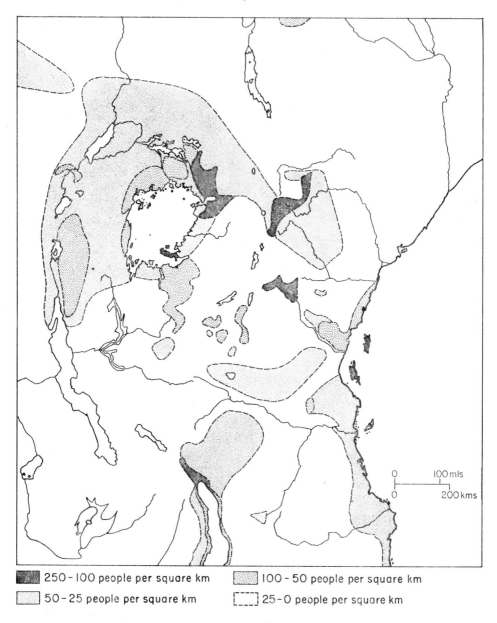

| 250 – 100 people per square km | 100 – 50 people per square km |
| 50 – 25 people per square km | 25 – 0 people per square km |

Map 6. Distribution of population. The map is diagrammatic and shows relative density in different areas. Figures are only approximate.

Map 7. (facing page) Cultural regions and sub-regions.

A. Ethiopian Highlands region, Southern Highlands sub-region. B. Horn of Africa region, Oromo-Soomaali sub-region. C. Eastern Rift Coast region: 1. Dry Plains; 2. Lake-shore; 3. Wet Highlands *a*) Western Cluster; *b*) Mount Kenya Cluster;

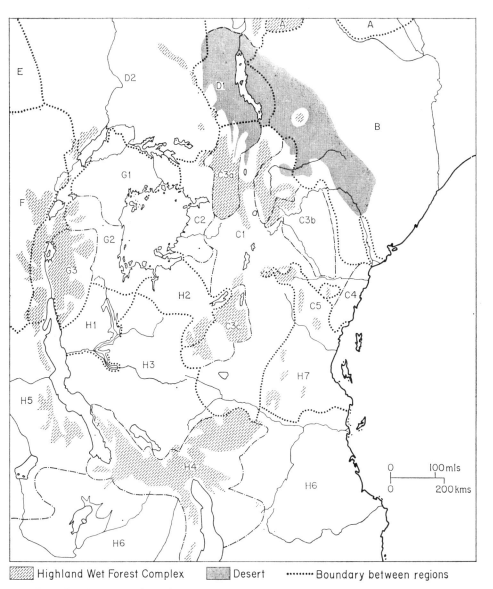

⬛️⬛️ Highland Wet Forest Complex   ⬛️ Desert   ⋯⋯⋯ Boundary between regions

—·— Boundary between sub-regions

c) Southern Cluster; 4. Coast; 5. Wet Highlands Transition. D. Savanna Stateless region: 1. Dry Transition; 2. Eastern Belt. E. Forest-edge region, Watershed States sub-region. F. Wet Forest region. G. Interlacustrine region: 1. Ganda– Nyoro; 2. Ziba–Ankore; 3. Rwanda–Rundi. H. Southern Savanna region: 1. Ha Transition, part of H3; 2. Sukuma Transition, part of H3; 3. Sukuma–Nyamwezi, without H1 and H2; 4. Fipa–Hehe; 5. Transition between Belt of Minor States and Belt of Major States; 6. Belt of Minor States; 7. Bondei–Zaramo Zone, part of H6.

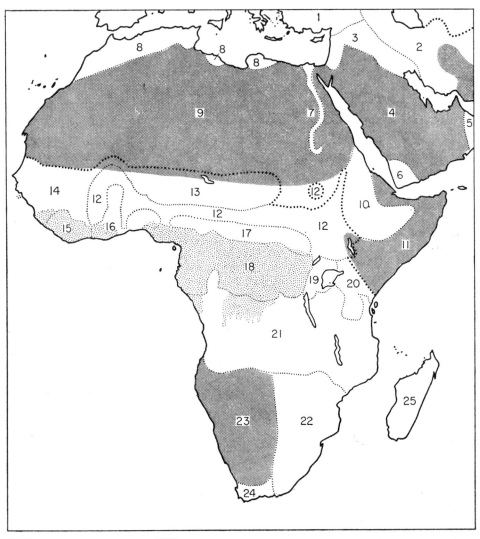

Lowland Wet Forest   Desert   ••••••• Boundary between major cultural regions

•••••• Boundary between cultural regions

Map 8. Cultural regions of Africa.

A. NANE Major Cultural Region:
    1. Anatolia;
    2. Iranian;
    3. Fertile Crescent;
    4–6. Arabia;
        4. Arabia Deserta;
        5. Oman;
        6. Yemen;
    7. Lower and Middle Nile Valley;
    8. Atlas–Cyrenaica;
    9. Sahara;
    10. Ethiopian Highlands;
    11. Horn of Africa.

B. Sub-Saharan African Major Cultural Region:
    12. Savanna stateless region;
    13. Lake Chad belt of states;
    14. Senegal–Niger states;
    15. Western Wet Forest;
    16. Coastal states;
    17. Forest-edge belt of states;
    18. Wet Forest;
    19. Interlacustrine;
    20. Eastern Rift Coast;
    21. Southern Savanna;
    22. South-eastern states;
    23. South-western;
    24. Area formerly part of 23, but now largely inhabited by other groups than Bushmen and Hottentots.

C. Madagascar Major Cultural Region:
    25. Madagascar.

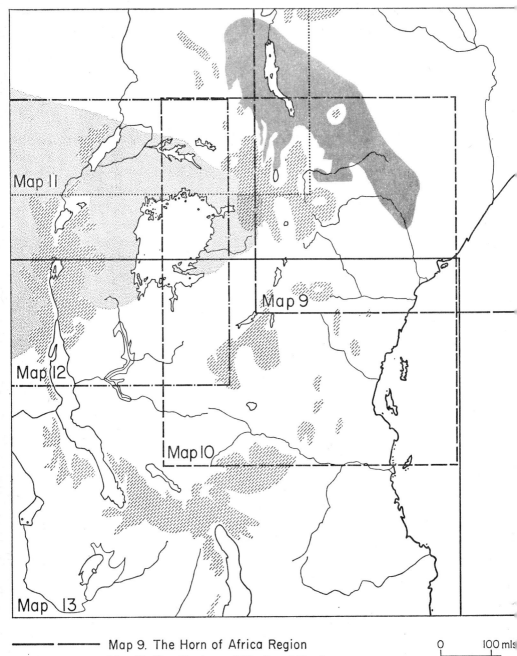

——— – ———	Map 9. The Horn of Africa Region	
—·— ·— ·—	Map 10. The Eastern Rift Coast Region	
··················	Map 11. The Savanna Stateless Region	
—·—·—·—·—	Map 12. The Interlacustrine Region	
———————	Map 13. The Southern Savanna Region	

0   100 mls

0   200 k

Key to maps 9–13. The facing page shows the key to maps 9–13 which appear on the following pages. The legend below applies to all maps 9–13.

Ethnic groups of East Africa.
These maps are intended to show only the area where most members of each group are concentrated. They are not detailed distribution-maps. For the sake of emphasis the Eastern Rift Valley, Mount Meru and Mount Kilimanjaro are exaggerated in size relative to other features on these five maps and also on 7 and 14. Map 4 gives a more proportionate impression.

Wet Forest region: 1. Zimba; 2. Lega; 3. Nyanga; 4. Konzo; 5. Amba and Konzo; 6. Bira of the forest; 7. Lese and Mamvu.

Transitional: 8. Bira of the plateau.

Watershed states (part of Forest-edge region): 9. Zande.

Savanna stateless region: Eastern Belt sub-region. 10. Mundu; 11. Avukaya; 12. Logo; 13. Bale and Ke (Lendu and Okebo); 14. Aluur; 14a. Nam (Jonam); 15. Lugbara; 16. Madi; 17. Bari group; 18. Anywak (Beri); 19. Otuho group; 20. Acholi; 21. Lang'o; 22. Luo (Jopaluo); 23. Lang'o Ikokolemu (Kumam); 24. Abuor (Labwor); 25. Teso; 26. Jiye; 27. Dudutho; 28. Upale (Nyangeya); 29. Ik (Teuso); 30. Diding'a and Larim (Long'arim); 31. Toposa; 34. Karimojong'; 35. "Tepes".

Dry Transition sub-region: 32. Nyang'atom; 33. Turkana; (34. Karimojong'–see above); (35. "Tepes"–see above); 36. Dasanech.

Transitional: 37. "Amar" and "Arbore".

Ethiopian Highlands region: 38. "Gowaze", "Gardulla" and "Gidole"; 39. "Bambala" and Konso; 40. Oromo, Arsi sub-group (Galla).

Horn Region: Oromo–Soomaali sub-region. 41. Oromo, Boorana sub-group (Galla); 42. Rendile; 43. Oromo, Bararetta sub-group (Galla); 44. "Sanye"; 45. Pastoral Soomaali; 46. Soomaali of Juba–Shebeli area.

Eastern Rift Coast Region: Coast sub-region. (Not all the peoples of the coastal groups are shown on the map): 47. Pokomo; 48. Giryama; 48a. Rabai; 49. Duruma; 50. Digo.

Wet Highlands Transition sub-region. 51. Davida and Sagala (both Taita); 52. Ma'a (Mbugu); 53. Shambaa; 54. Asu (Pare); 55. Chaga; 56. Ongamo (Ngasa); 57. Rwo (Meru) and Arusa.

Wet Highlands sub-region. Mount Kenya cluster: 58. Kamba; 59. Meru; 60. Embu; 61. Gikuyu.

Dry Plains sub-region: 62. Maasai; (62a. Cultivating Maasai–see after 167); 63. Sambur; 63a. Molo; 64. Tyamus (Njemps); 65. Sonjo; 79. Datoga (Taturu); 81. Gogo; 82. Burunge.

Wet Highlands sub-region. Western cluster: 66a. Pokot of the hills (Suk); 66b. Pokot of the plains (Suk); 67. Sabiny (Sebei) and Gony; 68. Markwet; 69. Geyo; 70. Tugen; 71. Nandi; 72. Kipsigis; 73. Ogiek (Ndorobo).

Southern cluster: 74. Iraqw (Mbulu); 75. Mbowe (Mbugwe); 76. Gorowa (Fiome) and Alagwa (Asi); 77. Langi; 78. Sandawe; (79. Datoga (Taturu) – see after 65); 80. Rimi (Nyaturu); (81. Gogo – see after 65); (82. Burunge – see after 65).

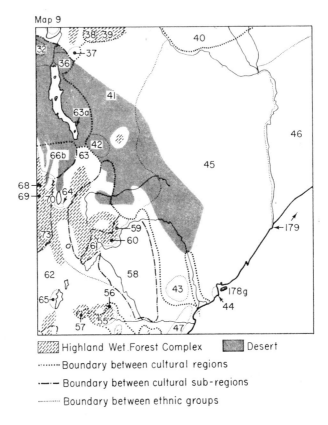

Map 9

Highlighted Wet.Forest Complex   Desert

········· Boundary between cultural regions

—·— Boundary between cultural sub-regions

·········· Boundary between ethnic groups

Lake-shore sub-region. (Not all the peoples at the southern end of this sub-region are shown on the map): 83. Luhya group; 84. Adhola (Jopadhola); 85. Tesyo; 86. Luo; 87. Gusii; 88. Kuria; 89. Nata; 90. Zanaki; 91. Jita.

Interlacustrine region. Ziba–Ankore sub-region: 92. Kerewe and Kara; 93. Dzindza; 94a. Ziba (Haya): 94b. Nyambo (Karagwe); 95. Ankore;

Transitional: 96. Chiga.

Interlacustrine region. Ganda–Nyoro sub-region: 97. Tooro; 98. Nyoro; 99. Ganda; 100. Soga.

Rwanda–Rundi sub-region: 101. Rwanda; 102. Rundi; 103. Hangaza; 104. Shubi.

Transitional: 105. Ha; 106. Hunde; 107. Haavu; 108. Nyabungu; 109. Fuliiro; 110. Bembe; 111. Jiji, with Ha; 112. Vinza; 113. Shumbwa; 114. Hadza (Tindiga or Kindiga); 115. Ilamba, Iambi and Isanzu; 116. (see below).

Southern Savanna region. Sukuma–Nyamwezi sub-region: 116. Sukuma; 117. Nyamwezi; 118. Tongwe; 119. Bende; 120. Konongo; 121. Rungwa; 122. Kimbu; 123. Bungu; 146. Eastern Holoholo.

Map 10

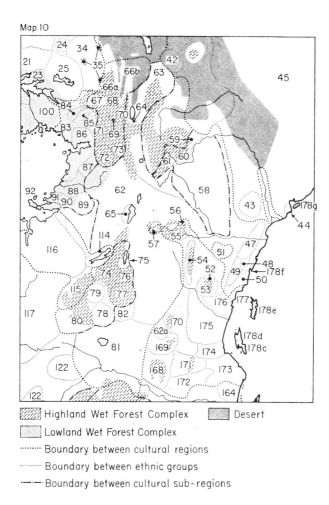

Fipa–Hehe sub-region: 124. Fipa; 125. Pimbwe; 126. Rungu; 127. Mambwe; 128. Mwanga; 128a. Iwa and Tambo; 129. Wanda; 130. Nyiha; 131. Safwa; 132. Nyakyusa; 133. Tumbuka; 134. Kisi; 135. Kinga; 136. Pangwa; 137. Ngoni; 138. Tonga; 139. Matengo; 140. Ngoni and Ndendeuli; 141. Bena; 142. Sango; 143. Hehe.

Transitional: 144, Hemba, Luba colonies, Bemba colonies, Yeke, and other groups; 145. Western Holoholo; (146. Eastern Holoholo — see after 123); 147. Taabwa.

Map II

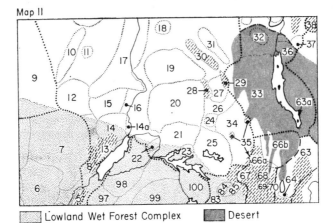

	Lowland Wet Forest Complex			Desert

Highland Wet Forest Complex

.... Boundary between cultural regions

—·— Boundary between cultural sub-regions

.... Boundary between ethnic groups

Map 12

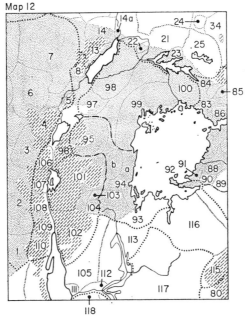

Highland Wet Forest Complex

Lowland Wet Forest Complex

.... Boundary between cultural regions

—·—· Boundary between cultural sub-regions

.... Boundary between ethnic groups

Map 13

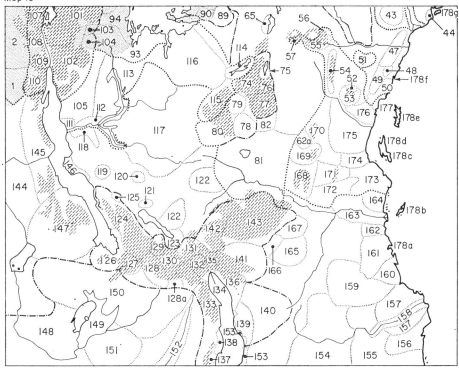

▨ Highland Wet Forest Complex

·—·— Boundary between cultural sub-regions

▨ Lowland Wet Forest Complex

········ Boundary between cultural regions

··········· Boundary between ethnic groups

Belt of Minor States sub-region: **148.** Lamba and Seba; **149.** Unga (Twa); **150.** Bemba; **151.** Biisa; **152.** Nsenga; **153.** Nyanja; **154.** Yao; **155.** Makua; **156.** Maviha; **157.** Makonde; **158.** Matambwe; **159.** Ngindo; **160.** Machinga; **161.** Mwera; **162.** Matumbi; **163.** Ruihi (Rufiji); **164.** Ndengereko; **165.** Pogolo; **166.** Ndamba; **167. Mbunga.**

Transitional: **62a.** Cultivating Maasai (Kwavi); **168.** Sagala and Vidunda; **169.** Kaguru; **170.** Nguru; **171.** Ruguru; **172.** Kutu; **173.** Zaramo; **174.** Ng'wele; **175.** Zigula; **176.** Bondei; **177.** Daisu (Segeju); **178.** Swahili; (not all the areas with a majority of Swahili are shown); **178a** Kilwa; **178b.** Mafia; **178c.** Hadimu dialect; **178d.** Tumbatu dialect; **178e.** Pemba dialect; **178f.** Mvita (Mombasa) dialect; **178g.** Amu (Lamu) dialect; **179. Tikuu.**

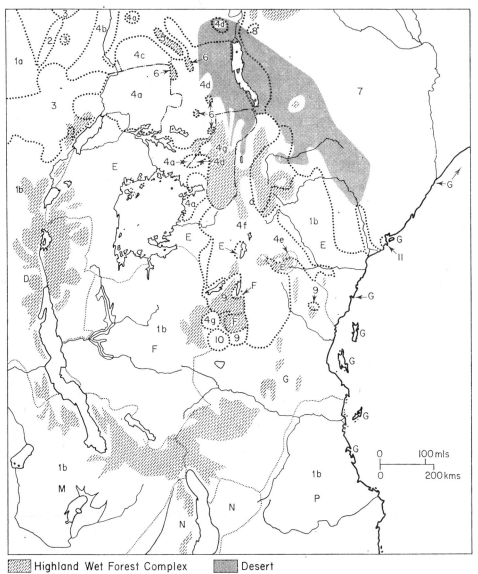

	Highland Wet Forest Complex		Desert

········ Boundary between language-families or major groups

—·—·— Boundary between subdivisions   ·········· Boundary between sub-subdivisions

Map 14. Language-families and their subdivisions in East Africa. (Based on Greenberg, 1963; Tucker and Bryan, 1956; M. Guthrie, 1971).

1. Niger—Congo family (see note on Map 15):
   a) Zande;
   b) Bantu languages;
      D. The D-group of Guthrie;
      E. The E-group;
      F. The F-group;
      G. The G-group;
      M. The M-group;
      N. The N-group;
      P. The P-group.

2. Sere-Mundu group (? family). On this map the language-area actually shown is that of Mundu.

3. Moru—Mangbetu group (? family).

4. Nilo—Maa group (? family):
   a) Nilotic group;
   b) Bari;
   c) Otuho;
   d) Teso—Turkana group;
   e) Ongamo;
   f) Maa;
   g) Nandi—Pokot group.

5. Diding'a group (? family).

6. Upale group (? family).

7. Afro-Asiatic family, Cushitic sub-family.

8. Are group (? family). On this map the language-area actually shown is that of "Amar".

9. Iraqw family.

10. Khoisan family. On this map the language-area actually shown is that of Sandawe.

11. "Sanye" (? family).

N.B. The subdivisions labelled a—g under 4 are not strictly comparable as units to those labelled similarly, a) and b), under 1; nor are they to the smaller units labelled D—P.

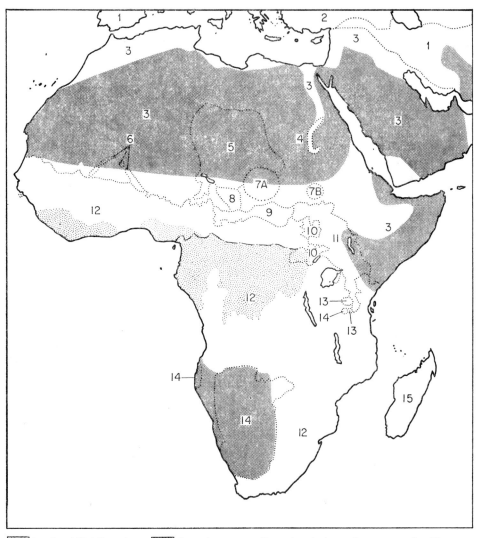

Lowland Wet Forest   Desert   ·········· Boundary between language —families or major
                                                                 groups
·—●· Northern limit of Bantu languages, within Niger-Congo area

Map 15. The Distribution of language-groups in Africa. (Adapted from Greenberg, 1963, partly by reference to Tucker and Bryan, 1956, 1966).

Note: Greenberg's Niger–Congo family is tentatively accepted. His Shari–Nile family largely consists of the groups here treated as mutually independent, and numbered 8, 9, 10 and 11.

His even larger Nilo–Saharan family includes these four, 5 and 6, as well as some other, small, groups. Not all the small language-groups with no clear affinities are shown.

7A and 7B are not language-groups but areas, Darfur and the Nuba Hills, of unusual linguistic complexity.

1. Indo-European family;

2. Altaic family;

3. Afro-Asiatic family;

4. Nubian ? family;

5. Kanuri ? family;

6. Song'ai ? family;

7a. Darfur;

7b. Nuba Hills;

8. Bongo–Barma ? family;

9. Banda–Gbaya ? family;

10. Moru–Mangbetu ? family;

11. Nilo–Maa ? family;

12. Niger–Congo family;

13. Iraqw family;

14. Khoisan family;

15. Malayo–Polynesian family.

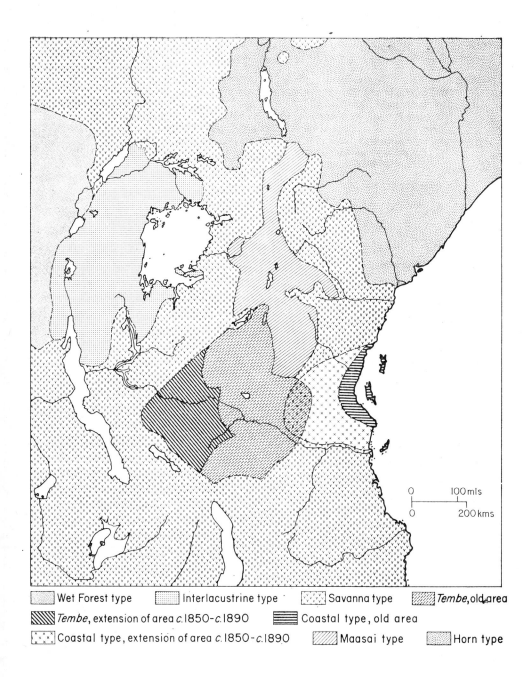

Wet Forest type	Interlacustrine type	Savanna type	*Tembe*, old area
Tembe, extension of area c.1850–c.1890	Coastal type, old area
Coastal type, extension of area c.1850–c.1890	Maasai type	Horn type

Map 16. The Distribution of house-type, in *c.* 1890 (Fig. 1).
There was an overlap of types in many areas. The coastal type has spread widely since 1890.

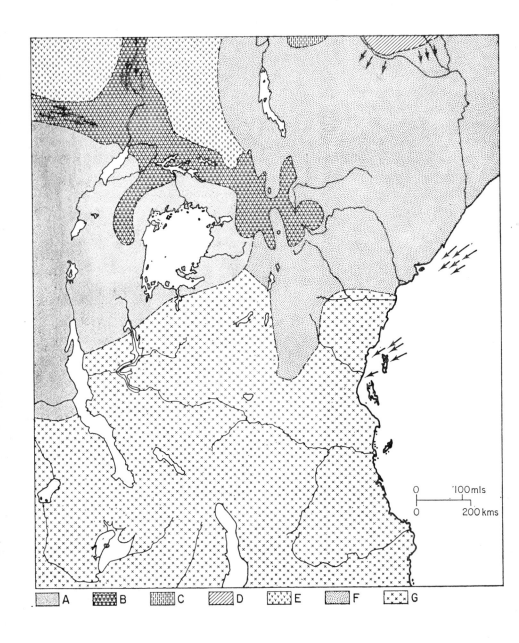

A ▦ B ▦ C ▨ D ▨ E ▦ F ▨ G

Map 17. East Africa in about the time of Christ.

Maps 17–19 are tentative reconstructions, based on slender evidence. The arrow-swarms on these three maps show not all the movements of people which were probably taking place at each period but rather those migrations which, over a long period, had significant cultural effects.

A: Hunters-and-gatherers, with stone industry of Sangoan type, living in lowland wet forest. Negroid predominantly.

B: Cultivators, some groups with iron smelting, some groups with kings, living in wetter parts of Savanna, and in Dry Zone and Eastern Rift Highlands. Negroid predominantly, except in Eastern Rift Highlands, where caucasoid.

C: Cultivators, with iron smelting, living in highland wet forest. Cushitic languages. Caucasoid.

D: Cultivators, with strong dependence on livestock rearing, and with iron smelting, in dry woodland. Cushitic languages. Caucasoid.

E: Hunters-and-gatherers, with stone industry of Levalloisian type, in dry woodland of savanna. Negroid predominantly.

F: Hunters-and-gatherers, with stone industry of Wilton type, in dry and very dry woodland. Caucasoid.

G: Hunters-and-gatherers, with stone industry of Nachikufan type, in pre-*miombo* dry woodland and highland wet forest. Khoisan languages. Bushmanoid.

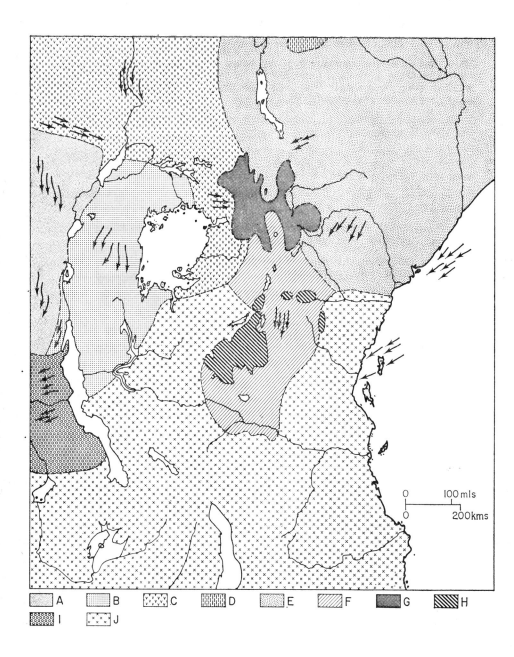

| | A | | B | | C | | D | | E | | F | | G | | H |
| | I | | J |

Scale: 0 — 100 mls / 0 — 200 kms

Map 18. East Africa in *c.* A.D. 500.

A: Hunters-and-gatherers, with stone industry of Sangoan type, and cultivators, with iron smelting, speaking Bantu languages, all in lowland wet forest.

B: Cultivators, most with kings, most iron smelting, many speaking Bantu languages, clearing lowland and highland wet forest.

C: Cultivators, some with kings, most iron smelting, some speaking Nilo–Maa languages, in dry woodland and lowland wet forest.

D: Cultivators, with iron smelting, in highland wet forest.

E: Pastoralists, with a little cultivation, and with iron smelting, in very dry woodland. Cushitic languages.

F: Pastoralists, with a little cultivation, without iron smelting, in dry woodland. Iraqw–family languages. Predominantly caucasoid.

G: Cultivators, with iron smelting, in highland wet forest. Nilo–Maa languages spreading. Negroid element increasing.

H: Cultivators without iron smelting, in highland wet forest. Iraqw–family languages. Predominantly caucasoid.

I: Cultivators, with kings and iron smelting, in pre-*miombo* dry woodland. Bantu languages. Predominantly negroid.

J: Hunters-and-gatherers, with stone industry of Nachikufan type, most in pre-*miombo* dry woodland, being absorbed by previous group.

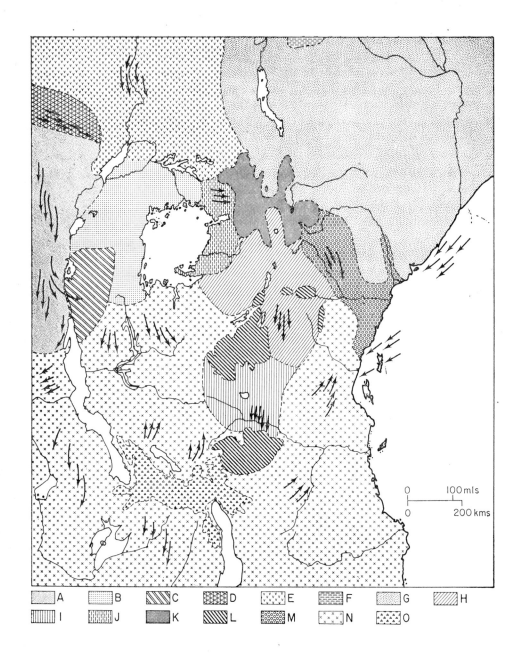

A	B	C	D
E	F	G	H
I	J	K	L
M	N	O	

0   100 mls

0   200 kms

Map 19. East Africa in *c.* A.D. 1000.

A: Cultivators and hunters-and-gatherers, with iron smelting (cultivators) and polished stone tools, in lowland wet forest. Many speaking Bantu languages.

B: Cultivators, with kings and iron smelting. Some lowland wet forest remaining. Bantu languages.

C: Cultivators, with kings and iron-smelting. Some highland wet forest remaining. Bantu languages.

D: Cultivators, with kings and iron smelting, in dry woodland nearest to lowland wet forest. Moru–Mangbetu languages.

E: Cultivators, some with kings, most with iron smelting, in dry woodland. Nilo–Maa languages widespread.

F: Cultivators, with iron smelting. Some highland wet forest remaining.

G: Pastoralists, with little cultivation, but with iron smelting, in very dry woodland.

H: Pastoralists, with a little cultivation, and with iron smelting, in dry woodland. Nilo–Maa language(s). Negroid element increasing.

I: Pastoralists, with a little cultivation, but without iron smelting, in dry woodland. Iraqw–family language(s). Still predominantly caucasoid.

J: Cultivators, with iron smelting. Some lowland wet forest remaining. Bantu language(s).

K: Cultivators, with iron smelting. Some highland wet forest remaining. Nilo–Maa languages widespread, Bantu languages spreading. Predominantly negroid.

L: Cultivators, without iron smelting. Some highland wet forest remaining. Iraqw–family languages. Still predominantly caucasoid. *Tembe* form of house, except in north-eastern outliers.

M: Cultivators, with iron smelting, in dry woodland. Bantu language(s) spreading. Negroid element increasing.

N: Cultivators, with kings and iron smelting. Dry woodland beginning to become *miombo.* Bantu languages. Predominantly negroid, but bushmanoid features still common.

O: Cultivators, highland wet forest version of previous group.

Bibliography

This is not a bibliography of the peoples of East Africa. It is designed to indicate sources from which information has been obtained, and which provide further details on many issues mentioned only briefly in this book.

The Ethnographic Survey of Africa
(all published in London)

North-Eastern Africa

I. M. Lewis (1955). "Peoples of the Horn of Africa: Somali, Afar and Saho".

G. W. B. Huntingford (1955). "The Galla of Ethiopia; the Kingdoms of Kafa and Janjero".

Ernesta Cerulli (1956). "Peoples of South-West Ethiopia and its Borderland".

East Central Africa

Mary Tew (1950). "Peoples of the Lake Nyasa Region".

W. Whiteley (1951). "Bemba and Related Peoples of Northern Rhodesia" (including: J. Slaski: Peoples of the Luapula Valley).

A. H. J. Prins (1952). "The Coastal Tribes of the North-Eastern Bantu: Pokomo, Nyika and Teita".

Audrey J. Butt (1952). "The Nilotes of the Sudan and Uganda".

J. Middleton and Greet Kershaw (1965). "The Kikuyu and Kamba of Kenya".

G. W. B. Huntingford (1953). "The Northern Nilo–Hamites".

Pamela Gulliver and P. H. Gulliver (1953). "The Central Nilo–Hamites".

G. W. B. Huntingford (1953). "The Southern Nilo–Hamites".

P. T. W. Baxter and Audrey Butt (1953). "The Azande and Related Peoples of the Anglo–Egyptian Sudan and Belgian Congo".

Jean S. La Fontaine (1960). "The Gisu of Uganda".
Margaret Chave Fallers (1960). "The Eastern Lacustrine Bantu (Ganda, Soga)".
A. H. J. Prins (1961). "The Swahili-Speaking Peoples of Zanzibar and the East African Coast".
Brian K. Taylor (1962). "The Western Lacustrine Bantu (Nyoro, Toro and others)".
A. A. Trouwborst, M. d'Hertefelt and J. H. Scherer (1962). "Les Anciens Royaumes de la Zone Interlacustre Méridionale".
Roy G. Willis (1966). "The Fipa and Related Peoples of South-West Tanzania and North-East Zambia".
T. O. Beidelman (1967). "The Matrilineal Peoples of Eastern Tanzania (Zaramo, Luguru, Kaguru, Ngulu, and others)".
R. G. Abrahams (1967). "The Peoples of Greater Unyamwezi, Tanzania (Nyamwezi, Sukuma, Sumbwa, Kimbu, Konongo)".

Other Titles, Horn and Eastern Rift Coast Regions
M. W. H. Beech (1911). "The Suk" (i.e. Pokot). Oxford.
P. G. Bostock (1950). "The Taita". London.
A. M. Champion (1967). "The Agiryama of Kenya" (J. Middleton, ed.). London.
O. Dempwolff (1916). "Die Sandawe". Hamburg.
C. Dundas (1924). "Kilima-Njaro and its Peoples". London.
R. F. Gray (1963). "The Sonjo of Tanganyika". London.
P. H. Gulliver (1963). "Social Control in an African Society" (Arusa). London.
A. C. Hollis (1905). "The Masai". Oxford.
A. C. Hollis (1909). "The Nandi". Oxford.
G. W. B. Huntingford (1953). "The Nandi of Kenya". London.
J. Kenyatta (1938). "Facing Mount Kenya" (Gikuyu). London.
G. J. Klima (1970). "The Barabaig" (a sub-group of Datoga). New York.
H. E. Lambert (1956). "Kikuyu Social and Political Institutions". London.
I. M. Lewis (1961). "Pastoral Democracy" (Soomaali). London.
G. Lindblom (1916). "The Akamba". Uppsala.
C. Meinhof (1912). "Die Sprachen der Hamiten". Hamburg.
M. Merker (1904). "Die Masai". Berlin.
D. J. Parkin (1972). "Palms, Wine and Witnesses" (Giryama). San Francisco.
J. G. Peristiany (1939). "The Social Institutions of the Kipsigis". London.
A. H. J. Prins (1953). "East African Age-Class Systems". Groningen.
O. Reche (1914). "Zur Ethnographie des abflusslosen Gebietes Deutsch-Ostafrikas". Hamburg.
P. Rigby (1969). "Cattle and Kinship among the Gogo". Ithaca.

J. Roscoe (1924). "The Bagesu and Other Tribes of the Uganda Protectorate". Cambridge.

P. Spencer (1965). "The Samburu". London.

P. Spencer (1973). "Nomads in Alliance" (Sambur and Rendile). London.

G. Wagner (1949, 1956). "The Bantu of North Kavirondo" (Luhya). 2 volumes. London.

Other Titles, the Savanna Stateless Region

Jean C. Buxton (1963). "Chiefs and Strangers" (Mundari, part of Bari group). Oxford.

J. H. Driberg (1923). "The Lango". London.

N. Dyson-Hudson (1966). "Karimojong Politics". Oxford.

E. E. Evans-Pritchard (1956). "Nuer Religion". Oxford.

F. K. Girling (1960). "The Acholi of Uganda". London.

P. H. Gulliver (1955). "The Family Herds" (Jiye and Turkana). London.

J. C. D. Lawrence (1957). "The Iteso". London.

R. G. Lienhardt (1961). "Divinity and Experience" (Jieng'). Oxford.

J. Middleton (1960). "Lugbara Religion". London.

J. Middleton (1965). "The Lugbara of Uganda". New York.

L. F. Nalder (ed.) (1937). "A Tribal Survey of Mongalla Province". London.

C. G. Seligman and B. Z. Seligman (1932). "Pagan Tribes of the Nilotic Sudan". London.

A. W. Southall (1953). "Alur Society". Cambridge.

Other Titles, the Interlacustrine Region

J. H. M. Beattie (1960). "Bunyoro". New York.

J. H. M. Beattie (1971). "The Nyoro State". Oxford.

H. Cory and M. M. Hartnoll (1945). "Customary Law of the Haya Tribe". London.

M. M. Edel (1957). "The Chiga of Western Uganda". New York.

L. A. Fallers (1956). "Bantu Bureaucracy" (Soga). Cambridge.

L. A. Fallers (ed.) (1964). "The King's Men" (Ganda). London.

R. Lemarchand (1970). "Rwanda and Burundi". London.

J. J. Maquet (1961). "The Premise of Inequality in Ruanda". London. (Maquet's view of the early history is conventional, but improbable, as argued in Chapter 6. Also he over-estimates the rigidity of Rwanda social stratification in the period of the kings.)

Lucy P. Mair (1934). "An African People in the Twentieth Century" (Ganda). London.

H. Meyer (1916). "Die Barundi". Leipzig.

J. Roscoe (1911). "The Baganda". London.

J. Roscoe (1923). "The Bakitara or Banyoro". Cambridge.

J. Roscoe (1923). "The Banyankole". Cambridge.

J. Roscoe (1924). "The Bagesu and Other Tribes of the Uganda Protectorate". Cambridge.

A. W. Southall and P. C. W. Gutkind (1957). "Townsmen in the Making" (Kampala). Kampala.

Other Titles, the Southern Savanna Region

R. G. Abrahams (1967). "The Political Organisation of Unyamwezi". Cambridge.

T. O. Beidelman (1971). "The Kaguru". New York.

W. Blohm (1931–33). "Die Nyamwezi". 3 volumes. Hamburg.

F. Bösch (1930). "Les Banyamwezi". Münster.

G. G. Brown and A. M. B. Hutt (1935). "Anthropology in Action" (Hehe). London.

H. Cory (1953). "Sukuma Law and Custom". London.

A. T. Culwick and G. M. Culwick (1935). "Ubena of the Rivers". London.

P. H. Gulliver (1971). "Neighbours and Networks" (Ndendeuli). Berkeley, California.

E. Kootz-Kretschmer (1926–29). "Die Safwa". 3 volumes. Berlin.

J. A. K. Leslie (1963). "A Survey of Dar es Salaam". London.

D. W. Malcolm (1953). "Sukumaland". London.

J. C. Mitchell (1956). "The Yao Village". Manchester.

E. Nigmann (1908). "Die Wehehe". Berlin.

Audrey I. Richards (1939). "Land, Labour and Diet in Northern Rhodesia" (Bemba). London.

A. Shorter (1972). "Chiefship in Western Tanzania" (Kimbu). Oxford.

J. M. Vansina (1966). "Kingdoms of the Savanna". Madison, Wisconsin.

Monica Wilson (1951). "Good Company" (Nyakyusa). London.

Monica Wilson (1957). "Rituals of Kinship among the Nyakyusa". London.

E. V. Winans (1962). "Shambala". London.

General

J. R. Baker (1974). "Race". London.

H. Baumann and D. Westermann (1948). "Les Peuples et les Civilisations de l'Afrique". Paris.

F. Boas (1900). "Primitive Art". New York.

J. P. Chapin (1932). "The Birds of the Belgian Congo". Vol. 1. New York.

Sonia Cole (1964). "The Prehistory of East Africa". London.

M. T. Dawe (1906). "Report on a Botanical Mission Through the Forest Districts of Buddu and the Western and Nile Provinces of the Uganda Protectorate". London.

J. Duffy (1959). "Portuguese Africa". Cambridge, Massachusetts.

J. D. Fage (1958). "An Atlas of African History". London.

J. E. Goldthorpe and F. B. Wilson (1960). "Tribal Maps of East Africa and Zanzibar". Kampala.

J. H. Greenberg (1963). "Languages of Africa". The Hague.

P. H. Gulliver (1959). A Tribal Map of Tanganyika, *Tanganyika Notes and Records*, volume 52.

P. H. Gulliver (ed.) (1969). "Tradition and Transition in East Africa". London.

M. Guthrie (1967–71). "Comparative Bantu". 4 volumes. Farnborough, Hants.

"History of East Africa". Oxford.
(1963). Volume 1. Edited by R. Oliver and G. Mathew.
(1965). Volume 2. Edited by V. Harlow, E. M. Chilver, with Alison Smith.
(1976). Volume 3. Edited by D. A. Low and Alison Smith.

N. Q. King (1970). "Religions of Africa". New York.

N. Q. King (1971). "Christian and Muslim in Africa". New York.

J. Kingdon (1971–   ) : "East African Mammals". 3 volumes. London and New York.

A. L. Kroeber (1939). "Cultural and Natural Areas of Native North America". Berkeley, California.

R. M. Lawton (1963). Palaeoecological and ecological studies in the Northern Province of Northern Rhodesia, *Kirkia*, **3**, 46–77.

R. M. Lawton (1972). A vegetation survey of Northern Zambia, *Palaeoecology of Africa, the surrounding islands and Antarctica*, **6**, 253–6.

E. M. Lind and M. E. S. Morrison (1974). "East African Vegetation". London.

Lucy P. Mair (1962). "Primitive Government". Harmondsworth, Middlesex.

J. S. Mbiti (1969). "African Religions and Philosophy". London.

J. Middleton and E. H. Winter (eds.) (1963). "Witchcraft and Sorcery in East Africa". London.

G. P. Murdock (1959). "Africa : its Peoples and their Culture History". New York. (Murdock's book must be read with caution since his view of the prehistory of Africa south of the Sahara is ill-supported by evidence and very dubious. Also, he is wrong on some detailed facts.)

W. T. Neill (1969). "The Geography of Life". New York.

J. W. Purseglove (1968). "Tropical Crops : Dicotyledons". London.

J. W. Purseglove (1972). "Tropical Crops : Monocotyledons". London.

Audrey I. Richards (ed.) (1960). "East African Chiefs". London.

"Tanzania in Maps" (edited by L. Berry) (1971). London.

C. G. Trapnell and I. Langdale Brown (1962). The Natural Vegetation of

East Africa, in "The Natural Resources of East Africa". (E. W. Russell, ed.). Nairobi.

A. N. Tucker and M. A. Bryan (1956). "The Non-Bantu Languages of North-Eastern Africa". London.

A. N. Tucker and M. A. Bryan (1966). "Linguistic Analyses of the Non-Bantu Languages of North-Eastern Africa". London.

F. B. Welbourn (1961). "East African Rebels". Oxford and Nairobi.

F. B. Welbourn and B. A. Ogot (1966). "A Place to Feel at Home". London.

C. Wrigley (1962). Linguistic Clues to African History, *The Journal of African History*, **III**.

Index of Ethnic Groups

General Index